El Español Bien Hablado

Leaving Certificate Oral Spanish

Bernadette Cosgrove

FOLENS

Editor
Hilary Coughlan

Design and Layout
Gary Dermody

Cover
Liz Murphy

© 1999 Bernadette Cosgrove

ISBN 1841 313 092

Folens Publishers,
Hibernian Industrial Estate,
Greenhills Road,
Tallaght,
Dublin 24.

Produced in Ireland by Folens Publishers.

Acknowledgements

The author would like to thank the following:

- Susana Bayó and Inma Montes for their advice and help with the text.
- Norberto Rivero Sanz, Fontxo Aberasturi, Teresa Jarrín and Laura Casanellas Luri, the native Spanish speakers who took part in the studio recordings.
- Mary Kettle of Trend Recording Studios.
- My editor Hilary Coughlan, Gary Dermody, Liz Murphy, and all the staff at Folens Publishers, especially Anna O'Donovan (Managing Editor) and John O'Connor (Managing Director).

For
Mrs Maureen Salters

Contents

Introduction

The purpose of *El Español Bien Hablado* is to prepare students for the Leaving Certificate Oral Examination in Spanish. The oral examination lasts for 15 minutes. 25% of the total marks are allocated to Higher Level students and 20% to Ordinary Level students. All students are awarded marks out of 100 for their oral examination and the adjustment for the different levels is made by the Examination Branch.

The oral examination comprises two parts:
General Conversation (70 marks) and **Role-play** (30 marks). The topics covered in general conversation are based on the syllabus content. In this part of the oral examination students also have the option of discussing a literary work. For the role-play there are ten different situations made available by the Department of Education, in advance of the oral examination, from which each school selects five. The examiner chooses **one** for each candidate. The student is allowed one minute preparation time to look over the selected role-play before continuing with the examination.

Following the format of the examination, *El Español Bien Hablado* is divided into two parts.

Part 1 – General Conversation

This covers 20 topics for the general conversation. Each topic is divided into four sections.

First section   –   Here students are given questions with a variety of different answers to each topic. A wide range of relevant vocabulary is included.

Second section –   The material in this section is recorded on tape in the form of two dialogues.

Third section   –   Students are given the opportunity to ask and answer the 10 questions in this section. This could form a useful classroom activity, encouraging students to practise aloud their responses to each topic.

Fourth section –   Students and teachers are given the opportunity to test the material included on each topic.

Part 2 – Role-play

The 10 role-plays included in Part 2 are those issued by the Department of Education for examination in 1999. Although the role-play situations will change in future years the basic content will remain very similar. Through regular practice of these role-plays, students should become confident in dealing with most situations and be able to adapt the language to deal with new ones.

On the day of the examination the candidate is given a card on which the instructions for the role-play are presented. In Part 2 of *El Español Bien Hablado* this card is reproduced in black print on the first page of each role-play situation. The examiner's instructions have been inserted on the same page in colour. The second page gives examples of how the candidate and examiner might act out the situation. The phrases in heavy type are translated and appear at the bottom of the page. Students should learn these phrases in order to be able to carry out the role-play situation with confidence.

A tape accompanies *El Español Bien Hablado*. The second section of each of the 20 topics for the general conversation has been recorded and also the 10 completed role-plays. Students will benefit greatly from listening to these dialogues and acting them out with other members of the class.
The material in this course is directed towards students to whom peninsular Spanish is most familiar. There are some significant differences between peninsular Spanish and the Spanish of Latin America, both in terms of vocabulary and pronunciation, but these differences have not been addressed here.

PART 1: General Conversation

ADVICE FOR THE GENERAL CONVERSATION

This part of the Oral Examination is to provide you with an opportunity to show the examiner how much you can say in Spanish. Approach the conversation confidently and enjoy it! After all, you are being given these 10 –12 minutes to talk about yourself and the things that are important to you.

The examiner will use the familiar form of address, **tú**, when asking questions.

Greet the examiner pleasantly when you arrive in the room with **Buenos días, señor/a** *or* **señorita**.

You will then be asked to sign your name. Do so saying something like **Claro que sí** *or* **Por supuesto**. Use every opportunity to show the examiner that you are confident in the language and want to communicate from the very moment you enter the room.

The examiner will then deal with many of the topics in this book. If you have prepared yourself thoroughly you will be able to speak with confidence on any of the chosen areas. Candidates will be assessed on their fluency and accuracy in speaking the language. Throughout this part of the Oral try to remember the following guidelines.

1. KEEP THE CONVERSATION GOING

Try to give an expanded answer to all questions. Short **Sí** or **No** answers have no place in your oral examination. Every question should be taken as an opportunity to talk at reasonable length.

Even the simple question **¿Tienes hermanos?** gives possibilities for a comprehensive answer:
Sí. Tengo dos hermanos. Mi hermano menor se llama Peter y es muy travieso. Mi hermano mayor, Philip, trabaja en una oficina en el centro de la ciudad. Me llevo muy bien con los dos.
In this response you have shown the examiner your ability to use correct, simple Spanish and your intention to communicate effectively.

> • Prepare yourself well in advance for each topic.
> • Learn your date of birth.
> • Know how to discuss the pastimes which appeal to you.
> • Hesitancy is not acceptable in these areas if you have prepared yourself properly.

2. MAKE SURE YOU KNOW THE RELEVANT VOCABULARY FOR EVERYDAY TOPICS

In order to exploit any topic fully you must be confident that you know the necessary vocabulary. *El Español Bien Hablado* provides you with a wide range of vocabulary on every topic, with translations of the more unusual words. In the last section of each topic you have the opportunity to test yourself on the key vocabulary and keep a written record of it.

3. IF YOU DON'T UNDERSTAND A QUESTION ASK THE EXAMINER TO REPEAT IT

The examiner might ask you a question which you don't understand. Don't panic! Ask for the question to be repeated:

Perdone, señor/señora/señorita. No entiendo esa pregunta. ¿Quiere usted repetirla por favor?

If there is a word in the question which is causing you a problem you could say:

Lo siento. Pero la palabra . . . no sé qué quiere decir.

Similarly, if you cannot remember the word for something in Spanish ask the examiner:

¿Cómo se dice ... en español?

This is very much part of what happens in our conversations. However, don't overdo it!

4. DON'T LEARN OFF LARGE AMOUNTS BY HEART

While it is the intention of this book to prepare you to speak on all the topics correctly and with confidence, you must avoid quoting large sections of Spanish by heart. Try to sound natural and introduce conversational forms which you have learned in the course of study for your Leaving Certificate Spanish Examination:

Bueno. Vamos a ver . . .
Ah, sí.
Me parece que . . .
Sí, es verdad.

5. A GOOD KNOWLEDGE OF BASIC GRAMMATICAL STRUCTURES IS VERY IMPORTANT

Students will be penalised for gross inaccuracies in the following areas.

> - verbal forms and use of tenses
> - agreement of adjectives
> - article and noun
> - pronouns

VERBAL FORMS AND USE OF TENSES

A thorough knowledge of correct verb forms is necessary in order to perform well and achieve the best results. You need plenty of practice in using regular and irregular verbs in all tenses. You must also be confident in the formation of radical-changing and reflexive verbs.

Present Tense	**Preterite**
j**ue**go *BUT* j**u**gamos	jugué
emp**ie**zo *BUT* emp**e**zamos	empecé
d**ue**rmo	dormí and d**u**rmió

Remember to use the correct reflexive pronoun with reflexive verbs:
me ducho/**nos** levantamos/mis hermanos **se** acuestan

Also, confusion often occurs between:

ser	*AND*	**estar**
es/son	*AND*	**hay**
gustar	*AND*	**querer**
pedir	*AND*	**preguntar**
poder	*AND*	**saber**
hacer	*AND*	**tener** *WITH* **calor, frío** etc.
dejar	*AND*	**salir**

Students often incorrectly introduce a preposition with these verbs:

escuchar	–	to listen **TO**
mirar	–	to look **AT**
buscar	–	to look **FOR**
pedir	–	to ask **FOR**
pagar	–	to pay **FOR**

Remember the following verbs require **NO** preposition before the infinitive:

quiero **ir**	*I want to go*
podemos compr**ar**	*we can buy*
me gusta estudi**ar**	*I like studying*
suelo jug**ar**	*I usually play*

The examiner will be assessing your knowledge of verbs and ability to deal with different tenses and you must take special care to ensure that you have the correct verbal ending to agree with the subject. This is particularly the case in the PRETERITE TENSE where there is frequent confusion between the third and first person of verb forms.

estudi**ó**/comi**ó** = **_he/she/you_** *studied or ate*
AND estudi**é**/com**í** = **_I_** *studied OR ate*

dij**o** = **_he/she/you_** *said*
AND dij**e** = **_I_** *said*

estuv**o** = **_he/she/it_** *was,* **_you_** *were*
AND estuv**e** = **_I_** *was*

Listen carefully to the TENSE the examiner uses when asking a question.

Is it a PRESENT TENSE?
¿Adónde **vas** los viernes por la noche?
ANSWER – **Voy/Salgo/Me quedo/Trabajo**

Do you hear the PAST TENSE?
¿Adónde **fuiste** el viernes pasado?
ANSWER – **Fui/Salí/Me quedé/Trabajé**

Perhaps you are being asked about where you **will** go.

¿Adónde **irás** durante las vacaciones?

ANSWER – **Iré/Saldré/Me quedaré/Trabajaré**

> Note the tense pattern with **desde hace** + time (for + time)
> AND **hace** + time **que**

Mi padre **trabaja** *(has been working)* con esta empresa **desde hace** cinco años.
    (PRESENT TENSE)

OR **Hace** cinco años **que** mi padre **trabaja** con esta empresa.

In the PRESENT TENSE be careful not to confuse **es/son** *(it is/they are)* with **hay** *(there is/are)*, and in the IMPERFECT tense **era/eran** *(they were)* with **había** (there were).

You should learn to use the SUBJUNCTIVE TENSE where appropriate:

Mis padres **quieren que** estudi**e** más.

Es una lástima que no pon**gan** programas deportivos todas las noches.

ADJECTIVES

Mistakes frequently occur between **mejor** *(better/best)* AND **mayor** *(older)*:

Mi hermana **mayor** *(my older sister)* BUT La **mejor** película *(the best film)*.

Learn the difference between **bueno** (ADJECTIVE) AND **bien** (ADVERB):

La clase es muy **buena** BUT Juego muy **bien** al tenis.
      (ADJECTIVE)   (ADVERB)

Other adjectives which require special attention are those which shorten in certain situations:

un buen libro   el primer día   ningún periódico   cien casas

> Remember to change the adjective to agree with the feminine and plural nouns:
> mis herman**as** pequeñ**as**
> seiscient**as** chic**as**
> **sus** estudio**s** (*her studies/his studies/their studies*)

ARTICLE AND GENDER OF NOUNS

The Chief Examiner's Report on the performance of students in the Leaving Certificate Oral Examination in Spanish highlights the fact that students make frequent errors in the gender of many everyday nouns. These are accompanied by the incorrect form of the article and/or adjective. The correct form of some of these are as follows:

el café	much**a** hambre	**el** tema	**la** mano
la calle	much**o** calor	**el** sistema	**la** radio
la carne	much**os** días	**un** problema serio	
la ciudad es ruidos**a**	**todos** los días	programa**s** deportiv**os**	

Take special care to use these correctly in your oral examination.

PRONOUNS

Try to use pronouns in your answers rather than repeating the noun of the question.

¿Dónde haces **los deberes**?	**Los** hago en mi dormitorio.
¿Quién **te** compró **la bicicleta**?	Mis padres **me la** compraron.
¿**Os** dan muchos deberes cada noche?	Sí, **nos** dan mucho que hacer.

PRONUNCIATION

One great advantage of Spanish is that the written language is a very close representation of the spoken language. Each syllable is pronounced as it appears in the written form e.g. a/yun/ta/mien/to.

You must, however, be aware of certain important differences in pronunciation and make every effort in your preparation for the oral examination to deal with these correctly. Vowel sounds tend to be sharper and shorter e.g. **inteligente** – the **i** is like the **ee** in the English word **seen**.
Your cheeks should be stretching towards the two walls on either side of you!
Consonant sounds to be careful with are:

h	–	it is always silent e.g. **hombre** is pronounced as **ombre**.
g	–	before an **a** , **o** or **u** is a hard sound e.g. **garaje**, as in the English **g**arden.
g	–	before **e** or **i** it is pronounced like the **ch** in the Scottish word lo**ch** e.g. **gente**.
j	–	always pronounced as **ch** of loch e.g. jardín.
q	–	found only in the groups **que** and **qui** is pronounced **k** like the sound of **c**at in English e.g. **quedo** sounds like **k**edo.
c	–	before **a**, **o** or **u** also it sounds like the **k** in **c**at e.g. **c**antar, **c**ostar, **c**umbre.
c	–	before **e** or **i** has the English **th** or **s** sound e.g. **centro** is pronounced as **th**entro in peninsular Spanish.
c+u	–	sounds like **qu**estion e.g. **cuando**, **cuero**.
rr	–	try to practise three trills for words containing **rr** e.g. pe**rr**o, fe**rr**oca**rr**il.

You **should** sound different when you speak Spanish! Practise all the above sounds regularly.

RULES REGARDING STRESS

- If a word ends with a **vowel**, **n** or **s**, the stress naturally falls on the second last syllable e.g. impor**ta**nte, tra**ba**jan, **li**bros.

- If a word ends in any other consonant the stress falls on the last syllable e.g. traba**jar**, ciu**dad**.

- If a word does not follow either of the above two categories an accent must be written on the accentuated vowel e.g. **sá**bado, a**zú**car, **jó**venes.

- You must remember to stress the PRETERITE and the FUTURE forms correctly e.g. traba**jé**, com**ió**, cumpli**ré**, compra**rán** but **di**je, **tu**vo.

By taking on board all that has been suggested you should enter your oral examination well prepared and confident.

Primera Sección

1. ¿Cómo te llamas?

Me llamo . . .

2. ¿Cuántos años tienes?

Tengo dieciocho años.
      diecinueve

3. ¿Cuándo es tu cumpleaños?

Mi cumpleaños es **el**

primero/once	**de**	enero.
dos/doce		febrero.
tres/trece		marzo.
cuatro/catorce		abril.
cinco/quince		mayo
seis/dieciséis		junio.
siete/diecisiete		julio.
ocho/dieciocho		agosto.
nueve/diecinueve		septiembre.
diez/veinte		octubre.
veintiuno		noviembre.
treinta y uno		diciembre.

4. ¿Cuándo cumplirás los dieciocho años?
   FUTURE

Los cumpliré dentro de poco.
          el mes que viene.
          la semana que viene.

5. ¿Cuándo tendrás dieciocho años?
   FUTURE

Pronto **tendré** dieciocho años. Los tendré en el mes de julio.

6. ¿Falta mucho para tu cumpleaños?

No. Falta muy poco para mi cumpleaños. Sólo faltan tres semanas.

7. ¿Cuándo cumpliste diecisiete años?
   PAST

Cumplí diecisiete años la semana pasada.
              el mes pasado.
              hace dos meses *(ago)*.

Acabo de cumplir dieciocho años.
(*I have just turned*)

8. ¿En qué año naciste?
   PAST

Nací en el año mil novecientos ochenta y uno.

9. **¿Eres el mayor/la mayor**
   de tu familia?

   Sí. Soy **el mayor/la mayor** *(eldest)*.
   No. Soy **el menor/la menor** *(oldest)*.

10. **¿Qué te regalaron tus padres**
    para tu cumpleaños?

    El año pasado mis padres

    | me regalaron | una máquina fotográfica. |
    | dieron | un reloj de pulsera. |
    | PAST | un **anillo de oro** *(gold ring)*. |
    | | una bicicleta. |
    | | un ordenador. |
    | | una guitarra eléctrica. |

11. **¿Qué tipo de regalo prefieres recibir?**

    Prefiero que me regal**en** dinero.
    SUBJUNCTIVE

12. **¿Y recibes regalos de tus parientes?**

    Sí. Mis abuelos siempre me dan ropa o algo así. El año pasado me regalaron una camiseta y un jersey.

13. **¿Cómo celebras tu cumpleaños?**

    Normalmente lo celebro en casa con mi familia. Mi madre prepara una cena especial y cocina un pastel riquísimo. Pone velas de muchos colores y yo tengo que soplar **hasta que** se apagu**en** todas.
    SUBJUNCTIVE

14. **Te diviertes mucho, ¿no?**

    Muchísimo. Siempre **lo paso muy bien**.
    (I have a good time)

> N.B.
> **Lo pasé bien** – *I had* a good time PAST
> **Lo pasaré bien** – *I'll have* good time FUTURE

15. **¿Me puedes describir cómo eres?**

    | Soy bastante | alto/**a** | delgado/**a** |
    | | baj**o/a** | moreno/**a** |
    | | perezos**o/a** *(lazy)* | |
    | | trabajador/**a** *(hard-working)* | |

    | Me considero | algo | serio/**a** |
    | | un poco | tímido/**a** *(shy)* |

    Casi siempre estoy de buen humor.

16. ¿Cómo es tu pelo?

Tengo el pelo

corto	y	negro
largo		rubio
lacio *(straight)*		
rizado *(curly)*		castaño
crespo *(frizzy)*	y	**suelto** *(loose)*

Soy pelirrojo/**a** *(red-haired)*. Muchos irlandeses lo son. También tengo la cara **pecosa** *(freckly)*.

17. ¿De qué color son tus ojos?

Tengo los ojos

azul**es**.
marron**es**.
verd**es**.
azul grisáceo.

18. ¿Eres muy deportista?

No **hago** mucho **deporte** este año.
   (play + sport)
Me gusta más bien ver los programas deportivos en la televisión.

19. ¿Qué haces para divertirte?

- Juego **al** baloncesto.
- Toco la guitarra.

N.B.	
jugar a	*to play + name of sport/game*
tocar	*to play + instrument*

- Escuchar música es lo que más me gusta.
- Prefiero quedarme en casa a leer porque soy muy hogareño/**a**.
- Me gusta salir con mis amigos.

20. ¿Te llevas bien con toda tu familia?

Sí, casi siempre. Claro que a veces hay discusiones, pero nada serio. Mis padres son muy **comprensivos** y tolerantes.   *(understanding)*

Track 2

Segunda Sección

ESCUCHA ESTAS CONVERSACIONES EN LA CINTA

- **¿Cómo te llamas?**
  Me llamo Peter.

- **¿Cuántos anos tienes?**
  Tengo diecisiete años ahora pero voy a cumplir los dieciocho años el mes que viene, el tres de mayo.

- **¿Eres el mayor de tu familia?**
  No, al contrario. Soy el menor. Tengo dos hermanos mayores y una hermana casada que ya no vive en casa con nosotros.

- **¿Entonces recibes muchos regalos de tus hermanos el día de tu cumpleaños?**
  Bueno, eso depende. Como mis dos hermanos mayores son estudiantes en la universidad casi nunca tienen dinero. Pero mi hermana Ana siempre me regala algo bonito. El año pasado, por ejemplo, me compró dos discos de mi grupo favorito.

- **¡Qué suerte! ¿Te llevas bien con toda tu familia?**
  Sí, sobre todo con mi hermano Michael. Nos dicen que somos muy parecidos. ¡El también es alto y guapo como yo! Compartimos la misma habitación y por eso, a veces, charlamos mucho juntos. **Casi nunca se queja.** *(He hardly ever complains.)* Creo que se lleva bien con todo el mundo.

Track 3

- **¿Quién eres?**
  Soy Marisa Kelly.

- **¿De qué nacionalidad eres?**
  Soy irlandesa pero mi madre es española. Tengo un apellido irlandés porque mi padre es de aquí.

- **¿Cuándo es tu cumpleaños?**
  Nací el diecinueve de abril de mil novecientos ochenta y uno. Así que voy a cumplir los dieciocho años dentro de unos días.

- **¿Y cómo vas a celebrar tu cumpleaños?**
  A lo mejor, este año iremos a cenar a un restaurante con mi hermano y mis padres. Cuando era pequeña unos amigos míos solían venir a mi casa. Pasábamos la tarde jugando en el jardín, comiendo caramelos, helados y pastelitos muy buenos que solía preparar mi madre. Lo pasábamos bomba. Ahora lo celebramos más bien en familia.

- **¿Ya sabes lo que te van a regalar?**
  Quiero que mis padres me compr**en** una bicicleta nueva. La que tengo es algo vieja y muy fea. Tampoco me gusta el color. En cuanto a mis dos abuelas, ellas siempre me regalan dinero. Con este dinero me compro ropa o perfume.

Tercera Sección

CONTESTA LAS SIGUIENTES PREGUNTAS

1. ¿Cómo te llamas?

   _____

   _____

2. ¿Eres de aquí?

   _____

   _____

3. ¿Cuántos años tienes?

   _____

   _____

4. ¿Cuándo cumpliste los diecisiete (dieciocho) años?

   _____

   _____

5. ¿En qué año naciste?

   _____

   _____

6. ¿Qué te regalaron para tu cumpleaños?

   _____

   _____

7. ¿Qué regalo te gustó más?

   _____

   _____

8. ¿Te gusta que te regalen dinero?

   _____

   _____

9. ¿Prefieres celebrar tu cumpleaños con tu familia o con tus amigos?

   _____

   _____

10. ¿Piensas que tus padres y abuelos recibían tantos regalos cuando eran jóvenes?

    _____

    _____

Cuarta Sección

☞ **A. ESCRIBE ABAJO 12 PALABRAS O EXPRESIONES DE ESTA UNIDAD QUE TÚ CONSIDERAS IMPORTANTES DE RECORDAR:**

1.. 2..

3.. 4..

5.. 6..

7.. 8..

9.. 10..

11.. 12..

B. ESCRIBE EL EQUIVALENTE EN ESPAÑOL DE ESTAS EXPRESIONES:

1. I'm 17 ....

2. My birthday is on the..

3. I'll be 18 very soon..

4. I turned 18 two months ago ....

5. I was born in 1980 ....

6. I'm the eldest in my family ....

7. My parents gave me ....

8. I had a good time ....

9. I have short fair hair ....

10. I have blue eyes ....

☞ **C. COMPLETA LAS SIGUIENTES FRASES CON LA PALABRA ADECUADA:**

Me _ _ _ _ _ _ Peter. Acabo de _ _ _ _ _ _ _ _ los dieciocho años. Mi cumpleaños

es _ _ dos _ _ marzo. Este año mis padres me _ _ _ _ _ _ _ _ _ _ una bicicleta.

El día de mi _ _ _ _ _ _ _ _ _ _ _ hubo una pequeña fiesta en mi _ _ _ _. Todos

mis _ _ _ _ _ _ vinieron y lo pasamos _ _ _ bien. Mi madre había preparado

un pastel rico con dieciocho _ _ _ _ _. Bailamos y cantamos hasta la madrugada.

_ _ _ acostamos muy tarde.

2. Mi familia

Primera Sección

1. **¿Cuántas personas hay en tu familia?**

   En mi familia **somos** tres.
   cuatro.
   cinco.

2. **¿Tienes hermanos?**

   - No tengo **ni** hermanos **ni** hermanas.
   - Soy hij**o** únic**o** *(an only child)*.
     hij**a** únic**a**.
   - Mis amigas dicen que como soy hija única estoy muy **mimada** *(spoilt)*. Pero eso no es verdad.
   - No tengo hermanos pero tengo una hermana mayor. Tiene veintidós años y está casada.
   - Tengo un hermano menor. Tengo dos hermanos mayor**es** y tres hermanas más pequeñas.

3. **¿Cuántos años tiene tu hermano menor?**

   Tiene catorce años. Tiene cuatro años menos que yo, pero mi hermana sólo tiene seis años.

4. **¿Cómo se llama tu hermana mayor?**

   Mi hermana mayor se llama …
   Hace dos años se casó y ya no vive en casa con nosotros.

5. **¿Cómo es su marido?**

   Se llama Felipe y es muy simpático. No viven muy lejos de nuestra casa. Así que nos vemos mucho.

6. **¿Qué hacen tus hermanos mayores?**

   Uno cursa estudios de ingeniería en la universidad el otro estudia **Informática** *(Computers)* para ser progamador.

7. **¿Te llevas bien con tus hermanos?**

   Me llevo bastante bien con mi hermano mayor.
   Casi nunca **nos peleamos**.
   　　　　(we fight)

   Mis hermanos y yo estamos todos muy unidos.

   Pero mi hermana menor está muy mimada. Siempre hay problemas con ella.

8. **¿En qué trabaja tu padre?** Mi padre es

médico	dentista
piloto	periodista
camarero	profesor
arquitecto	programador
abogado *(lawyer)*	
empleado de banco	
contable *(accountant)*	
director de una fábrica	
óptico	mecánico
ingeniero *(engineer)*	
funcionario *(civil servant)*	
director de empresa *(company director)*	
hombre de negocios *(business man)*	
agente de seguros *(insurance agent)*	
jefe de ventas *(sales manager)*	

tiene su propio negocio.
una tienda pequeña donde yo trabajo a veces.

9. **¿Trabaja tu madre?** No. Mi madre es **ama de casa** *(housewife)*.

10. **¿Antes de casarse en qué trabajaba ella?** Antes trabajaba de

secretaria.
peluquera.
enfermera *(nurse)*.
cajera.
recepcionista.
azafata *(air-hostess)*.
camarera.
profesora.
arquitecto.
abogada *(lawyer)*.

11. **¿Dónde solía trabajar antes de casarse?** **Solía** trabajar en
(She used to)

unos grandes almacenes.
una oficina.
una tienda.
un banco.
una fábrica.
un hotel.
un restaurante.
el aeropuerto.
una agencia de viajes.
la caja de un supermercado.

12. **¿Cómo son tus padres?**

- Son muy simpáticos y casi nunca están de mal humor. Me llevo muy bien con **los dos** *(both of them)*.
- Mi madre se enfada de vez en cuando, por ejemplo, cuando vuelvo a casa muy tarde o no **arreglo** *(tidy)* mi habitación.

13. ¿Viven tus abuelos?

Mi abuelo está muer**to**.
Mi abuela está muer**ta**.
Mis abuelos están muer**tos**.

14. ¿Tienes muchos parientes?

- Tengo muchos **parientes** *(relatives)* porque mi padre viene de una familia numerosa.

- Siempre hay gente en mi casa. Mis tíos y mis primos vienen a visitarnos con mucha frecuencia.

- **Nos reunimos mucho** *(We get together a lot)* durante el año para celebrar las fiestas familiares como los bautizos, **bodas** *(weddings)*, cumpleaños y cosas así. Y también nos reunimos en Navidad y en Semana Santa.

- El verano pasado fuimos todos a la boda de un primo mío. Se casó con una chica inglesa.

Segunda Sección

ESCUCHA ESTAS CONVERSACIONES EN LA CINTA

- **¿Cuántos sois en tu familia?**

  Somos cuatro. Mi madre, mi padre mi hermana pequeña y yo.

- **¿Cómo se llama tu hermana?**

  Se llama Nadine.

- **Es un nombre francés, ¿no?**

  Creo que sí. Viene del nombre ruso Nadja que significa "esperanza". A mi padre le gustaba mucho ese nombre.

- **¿Cuántos años tiene tu hermana?**

  Tiene quince años. Su cumpleaños es el treinta de junio.

- **¿Son de aquí tus padres?**

  No, son de un pueblo en el condado de Cork. Pero ya llevan años viviendo en esta ciudad.

- **¿Por qué decidieron venir a vivir aquí?**

  Porque a mi padre le ofrecieron un trabajo en una empresa. Por eso vinieron hace unos veinte años.

- **¿Vuelven a veces a su pueblo?**

  Claro. Vamos todos varias veces al año porque mis dos abuelas siguen viviendo allí. Tengo también dos tíos y una tía que están casados. Y vamos a visitarlos siempre que podemos.

Track 5

- **¿Qué tienes, hermanas o hermanos?**

  Tengo dos hermanas menores y un hermano mayor que está en la facultad en Galway.

- **¿Qué estudia allí?**

  Estudia Derecho. Acaba de terminar su primer año.

- **¿Entonces ya no vive en tu casa durante el curso?**

  No, ya no. Se aloja en una residencia estudiantil cerca de la universidad.

- **¿Cómo se ha adaptado a vivir allí?**

  Pues, al principio, se sentía muy solo. Pero ahora ya conoce a muchos estudiantes.

- **¿Le echas mucho de menos?** *(Do you miss him?)*

  Bueno, pues sí, pero mi madre es la que le echa más de menos. Mi madre llora cada vez que mi hermano se vuelve a ir a Galway después de haber pasado el fin de semana con nosotros.

- **¿En qué trabaja tu madre?**

  Es secretaria en una oficina de abogados. Pero sólo trabaja por las mañanas. Así que está en casa cuando volvemos del colegio.

- **¿A qué hora sale tu padre para ir a trabajar?**

  Bastante temprano, a eso de las siete y media. Trabaja en un banco en el centro de la ciudad y lo bueno es que puede llevarnos en coche al colegio.

Tercera Sección

CONTESTA LAS SIGUIENTES PREGUNTAS

1. ¿Cuántos sois en tu familia?

_____

_____

2. ¿Tienes hermanos?

_____

_____

3. ¿Cuántos años tiene tu hermano mayor?

_____

_____

4. ¿Sigue viviendo en casa?

_____

_____

5. ¿Cómo se llama tu hermana pequeña?

_____

_____

6. ¿Te llevas bien con todos tus hermanos?

_____

_____

7. ¿En qué trabaja tu padre?

_____

_____

8. ¿Trabaja tu madre fuera de casa?

_____

_____

9. ¿Crees que tus padres son muy estrictos?

_____

_____

10. ¿Vas a visitar a tus parientes muy a menudo?

_____

_____

Cuarta Sección

☞ **A. ESCRIBE ABAJO 12 PALABRAS O EXPRESIONES DE ESTA UNIDAD QUE TÚ CONSIDERAS IMPORTANTES DE RECORDAR:**

1.. 2...

3.. 4...

5.. 6...

7.. 8...

9.. 10..

11.. 12..

B. ESCRIBE EL EQUIVALENTE EN ESPAÑOL DE ESTAS EXPRESIONES:

1. There are four of us ....

2. I have a younger sister...

3. She is fourteen ....

4. He is married ....

5. He's at university..

6. I get on well with..

7. My mother is a housewife ....

8. When she was younger...

9. A cousin of mine got married..

10. My grandfather is dead ....

☞ **C. COMPLETA LAS SIGUIENTES FRASES CON LA PALABRA ADECUADA:**

_ _ _ _ _ cinco en mi familia. Mi hermana _ _ _ _ _ tiene doce años. Se _ _ _ _ _

Teresa. Tengo dos hermanos _ _ _ _ _ _ _. Uno está en la facultad donde

_ _ _ _ _ _ _ para ser ingeniero. El otro _ _ _ _ _ _ _ en una oficina en Londres.

Está casado _ _ _ una chica inglesa. Mi padre _ _ contable y trabaja en el centro

de la _ _ _ _ _ _. Sale muy temprano por la _ _ _ _ _ _ y me lleva al colegio

en _ _ _ _ _.

3. MIS AMIGOS

Primera Sección

1. ¿Cómo se llama tu mejor amigo/a?

Mi mejor amig**o/a** se llama …

2. ¿Le/la conoces desde hace mucho tiempo?

- Sí. { **Le** (MASC.) conozco desde hace muchos años. **La** (FEM.)

- Estuvimos en la misma clase en primaria.

3. ¿Cuántos años tiene?

- { **Él** (MASC.) también tiene diecisiete años. **Ella** (FEM.)

- Es un chic**o** de mi edad.

- Est**a** chic**a** tiene la misma edad que yo.

4. ¿Sabes cuál es la fecha de su cumpleaños?

Su cumpleaños es una semana antes del mío, a principios del mes de abril.

5. Descríbeme un poco cómo es.

Es alt**o** y rubi**o**.
alt**a** y rubi**a**.

Es bastante delgad**o**/delgad**a** *(thin)*.
moren**o**/moren**a** *(dark)*.

Es simpátic**o**/simpátic**a**.
inteligente.
divertid**o**/divertid**a**.
deportiv**o**/deportiv**a**.
trabajad**or**/trabajad**ora**.

Tiene el pelo rubio.
negro como el azabache *(jet-black)*.

6. ¿Cuáles son sus hobbys?

- **Le** gust**a** mucho   **la** música y tocar la guitarra.
  (*He AND She*)   **la** natación y ha ganado muchos
  + SING.   premios.
                        el fútbol.

- **Le** gust**an**   **los** deportes.
  (*He AND She*)   **los** coches.
  + PL.

7. ¿Son simpáticos sus padres?

Son muy simpáticos y, desde muy pequeño, voy una vez a la semana a comer en su casa. Luego él/ella viene a cenar conmigo otro día.

8. También tienes otros amigos ¿no?

- Sí. Tengo también otros amig**os** muy buen**os**. otr**as** amig**as** muy buen**as**.

- Existe una relación muy amistosa entre todos mis compañeros de clase.

- Tengo el mismo círculo de amigos desde hace seis años. Mis amigos juegan un papel muy importante en mi vida.

- Hay otra amiga que ya no está en el mismo colegio pero hablamos mucho por teléfono y podemos tirarnos horas y horas charlando.

9. ¿Conoces a algún chico español o chica española?

Sí. Hice un intercambio con un chico español y seguimos escribiéndonos. Escribo también a otros amigos españoles que conozco.

10. ¿Salís mucho juntos?

Casi siempre nos **reunimos** (*we meet*) los viernes por la noche. Algunas veces salimos al cine si ponen una película que queremos ver.

11. ¿Qué es lo que más les gusta hacer a tus amigos?

A todos **les** gusta   salir los viernes por la noche.
(*they*)   ir a las discotecas.
                   ir a una fiesta en casa de alguien.
                   ver un vídeo.
                   jugar al tenis.

12. ¿Tienes novio/a?

No. Por el momento prefiero salir con un grupo de amigos. Creo que soy demasiado joven para eso. ¿Verdad?

Segunda Sección

ESCUCHA ESTAS CONVERSACIONES EN LA CINTA

- **¿Cómo se llama tu mejor amigo?**

  Se llama Darragh y vive cerca de mi casa.

- **¿Tiene tu misma edad ?**

  El cumplió los dieciocho años el dos de febrero. Y yo los cumpliré el cuatro de junio. Así que sólo nos llevamos cuatro meses de diferencia.

- **¿Y cómo celebró su cumpleaños?**

  Pues, sus padres alquilaron una sala de fiestas cerca de su casa. Estuvimos todos allí. Había música, mucho de comer y beber. Pasamos una noche muy agradable y bailamos hasta la madrugada.

- **¿Recibió muchos regalos.**

  ¡Claro que sí! Cumplir dieciocho años es algo muy importante, como usted ya sabe. ¡A esta edad ya hemos dejado de ser niños! Sus padres le regalaron un reloj de oro precioso. También le dieron mucho dinero. Yo y otros dos amigos le regalamos una raqueta de tenis.

- **¿Practica muchos deportes?**

  Sí, es muy deportista. Juega al tenis y al baloncesto. También hace ciclismo y, a menudo, va a Wicklow a correr.

- **¿Ya sabe lo que va a hacer después de sus estudios?**

  Sí. Quiere trabajar en algo relacionado con los ordenadores.

- **¿Cómo se llaman tus amigas del colegio?**

  Mis dos mejores amigas se llaman Jenny y Elena aunque en mi clase todas somos buenas amigas.

- **¿Sales mucho con ellas los fines de semana?**

  No mucho. Porque ellas viven un poco lejos de mi casa. A veces nos reunimos en el centro de la ciudad para ir al cine o de compras. Pero cuando nos divertimos más es durante las vacaciones porque podemos pasar todos los días juntas.

- **¿Cómo es Jenny?**

  Es muy simpática e inteligente. Tiene el pelo muy corto y es muy delgada.

- **¿Hace tiempo que sois amigas?**

  Pues, nos conocimos en el primer año de primaria así que ya hace doce años que somos amigas.

- **¿Qué le gusta hacer en sus ratos libres?**

  Toca muy bien el piano y también le gusta dibujar. Algunos de sus dibujos están colgados por la casa. Como no tienen televisión en su casa también se entretiene leyendo.

- **¿Qué piensa hacer el año que viene?**

  Le gustaría ir a la facultad para estudiar música o francés. Siempre saca sobresaliente en el examen de francés. Creo que sería una lástima si no continuara estudiándolo porque lo domina perfectamente.

Tercera Sección

CONTESTA LAS SIGUIENTES PREGUNTAS

1. ¿Cómo se llama tu mejor amigo/a?

_____

_____

2. ¿Cuándo es su cumpleaños?

_____

_____

3. ¿Dónde vive?

_____

_____

4. ¿Qué tipo de persona es?

_____

_____

5. ¿Adónde vais los fines de semana?

_____

_____

6. ¿Cómo pasa sus vacaciones?

_____

_____

7. ¿Le gustan los deportes?

_____

_____

8. ¿Viene a tu casa con mucha frecuencia?

_____

_____

9. ¿Cómo son sus padres?

_____

_____

10. ¿Va a buscar un trabajo este verano?

_____

_____

Cuarta Sección

☞ **A. ESCRIBE ABAJO 12 PALABRAS O EXPRESIONES DE ESTA UNIDAD QUE TÚ CONSIDERAS IMPORTANTES DE RECORDAR:**

1.. 2..

3.. 4..

5.. 6..

7.. 8..

9.. 10..

11.. 12..

B. ESCRIBE EL EQUIVALENTE EN ESPAÑOL DE ESTAS EXPRESIONES:

1. My best friend is called ....

2. I've known her for six years..

3. Her birthday is on the 2nd May..

4. She is tall and thin..

5. He's hard-working and intelligent..

6. She likes to play the guitar ....

7. He likes sports ....

8. What he likes most is..

9. She is not in the same school..

10. We spend a lot of time chatting..

☞ **C. COMPLETA LAS SIGUIENTES FRASES CON LA PALABRA ADECUADA:**

Mi _ _ _ _ _ amiga se llama Elisa. No vive muy _ _ _ _ _ de mi casa. La

conozco desde _ _ _ _ siete años. Tiene el _ _ _ _ rubio y los _ _ _ _ azules.

Le _ _ _ _ _ mucho leer novelas policíacas. Sabe nadar y va a la piscina todos los

_ _ _ _ _ _ _. A veces vamos al centro de la _ _ _ _ _ _ donde nos gusta ir al

_ _ _ _. Estamos en el mismo colegio. Es muy trabajadora y _ _ _ _ _ _ _ _

mucho.

Track 8

4. El hogar

Primera Sección

1. ¿Dónde está tu casa?

Mi casa está | en el centro de la ciudad.
en las afueras de la ciudad.
bastante lejos del colegio.
muy cerca de aquí.
a unos diez minutos andando.
a ocho kilómetros más o menos de aquí
en otro pueblo al sur de la ciudad.

2. ¿Cómo es tu casa?

Es una casa | bastante grande.
pequeña.
vieja.
nueva.
moderna.
adosada (*terraced*).
de dos pisos.
independiente.

3. ¿Qué hay en la planta baja?

Abajo tenemos
(*Downstairs*)
una cocina muy bien amueblada.
un comedor al lado de la cocina.
un cuarto de baño.
el vestíbulo donde hay muchas plantas.
un salón cómodo donde tenemos el televisor.
un cuarto pequeño que sirve de oficina para mi padre.

4. ¿Cuántos dormitorios hay en tu casa?

Arriba (*upstairs*) hay cuatro dormitorios y **el cuarto de los huéspedes** (*guest room*).

5. ¿Hay mucho espacio para guardar cosas?

- Sí. Debajo del tejado está el **desván** (*attic*).

- Es allí donde guardamos un montón de cosas viejas, ropa usada, nuestros juguetes de hace muchos años, libros de mis padres y otras cosas inútiles.

- Allí no se ve casi nada porque no hay luz.

6. ¿Hay calefacción central?

Sí. Tenemos calefacción central por toda la casa. Así que siempre tenemos calor adentro.

7. ¿Hay jardín?

Sí. Tenemos
un jardín pequeño en la parte de delante.
un jardín más grande en la parte de atrás.
un **invernadero** *(greenhouse)* al fondo.
una caseta donde ponemos los útiles de jardinería.

8. ¿Prefieres el jardín en el verano o en el invierno ?

- Prefiero el verano y la primavera porque hay muchas flores en nuestro jardín.
- Cuando hace más calor tambien vienen muchas **mariposas** *(butterflies)* y **abejas** *(bees)*.

9. ¿Cómo es el jardín en el invierno?

- En el invierno muchos de los árboles están sin hojas y el jardín parece muy triste.
- Sin embargo, tiene un aspecto encantador cuando nieva y todo está cubierto de blanco.

10. ¿Te gusta trabajar en el jardín?

Bueno. Un poco. A veces corto el césped y recojo las hojas muertas en otoño.

11. ¿Y tenéis garaje?

- Sí. Está al lado. Lo usamos para el coche.
- Mi padre guarda allí también cajas y todas sus **herramientas** *(tools)*.

12. ¿Me puedes describir tu dormitorio?

Mi dormitorio es
grande.
pequeño.
cómodo.
tranquilo.

En mi dormitorio hay
una cama.
un armario **empotrado** *(built-in)*.
un **tocador** *(dressing-table)*.
un **espejo** *(mirror)* muy grande.
unas **estanterías** *(shelves)*.
mi guitarra con amplificador.
un ordenador.
mi mesita de noche.
un **despertador** *(alarm clock)*.
una lámpara.
mis **muñecas** *(dolls)*.

No cabe más. No caben más **cosas**.
(Nothing more can fit)

13. ¿Cómo son las paredes?
    (*walls*)

Las paredes están pintadas de azul.
tienen pósters de mis cantantes
y equipos favoritos.

14. ¿Tienes alfombra?

Sí. En el suelo hay una alfombra de color marrón.

15. ¿De qué color son las cortinas?

- Las cortinas son azules y muy bonitas.
- **La colcha** de mi cama (*bedspread*) es de la misma **tela** (*material*) que las cortinas.

16. ¿Tienes tu propio dormitorio?

Lo malo es que tengo que **compartir** (*share*) mi dormitorio con mi hermana menor.

17. Desde la ventana de tu dormitorio describeme lo que ves.

Da (*It looks on to*) **al** jardín de atrás.
al mar.
a la calle.
a un parque bonito.

Así que veo much**os** árboles.
barcos.
coches.
much**as** casas.
much**o** movimiento.

18. ¿Llevas mucho tiempo viviendo allí?

- Vivimos en esta casa desde hace diez años.
- Llevo **toda la vida** (*all my life*) viviendo en esta misma casa.
- Nunca he vivido en otra casa.
- Me gustaría cambiar de casa.

Segunda Sección

ESCUCHA ESTAS CONVERSACIONES EN LA CINTA

– **¿Dónde está tu casa?**

Mi casa está en las afueras, a unos ocho kilómetros de aquí.

– **¿Cómo es tu casa?**

Es una casa bastante moderna. En total tiene nueve habitaciones. Abajo está el comedor, y tiene una puerta que comunica con la cocina. En la planta baja están también el salón y un cuarto de baño pequeño. Arriba están los cuatro dormitorios y el otro cuarto de baño.

– **¿Tenéis muchos electrodomésticos en la cocina?**

Pues sí. Tenemos las cosas principales, la cocina eléctrica, el horno microondas, la lavadora, el lavavajillas y la nevera con congelador. También hay otras cosas que usamos mucho – la liquadora, la tostadora, la cafetera, y una exprimidora para el zumo.

– **¿Dónde haces los deberes?**

Arriba, en mi dormitorio. Tengo una mesa grande con una lámpara y al lado tengo dos estanterías llenas de libros, cuadernos y todo lo que me hace falta para el colegio.

– **Tu dormitorio, ¿es grande o pequeño?**

Es bastante grande pero tengo que compartirlo con mi hermano menor. Hay un armario empotrado pero casi siempre dejamos la ropa por todas partes. Cuando entra mi madre se enoja mucho. ¡La verdad es que a veces está muy desordenado! ¡Parece como si hubieran lanzado una bomba!

– **¿Vives cerca del colegio?**

Sí, mi casa está a unos dos minutos del colegio. Así que puedo venir andando todos los días.

– **¿Hace mucho tiempo que vives en esta casa?**

No. Sólo hace dos años que vivimos aquí. Antes vivíamos bastante lejos. Ésta era la casa de mi abuela y cuando murió mis padres decidieron venir a vivir aquí.

– **¿Es una casa nueva?**

No, es muy vieja. Creo que la construyeron en el siglo pasado. Es bastante grande con un jardín enorme en la parte de atrás y un jardín pequeño en la parte de delante.

– **¿Hay muchas flores en el jardín?**

Depende de la estación del año. A mí me gusta mucho en la primavera cuando está lleno de narcisos y tulipanes. Pero en verano también está muy bonito. ¡Lo malo es que casi siempre me toca a mí cortar el césped!

– **¿Cómo es tu dormitorio?**

No es muy grande pero es muy cómodo. Da al jardín de atrás, así que es muy tranquilo. Casi no se ve el empapelado porque he llenado las paredes con los pósters de mis actores favoritos. Las cortinas son verdes con rayas blancas y **hacen juego** (*match*) con el verde de la alfombra.

Tercera Sección

CONTESTA LAS SIGUIENTES PREGUNTAS

1. ¿Dónde vives?

_____

_____

2. ¿Qué tipo de casa es?

_____

_____

3. ¿Qué habitaciones hay en la planta baja?

_____

_____

4. ¿Cuántos dormitorios tiene la casa?

_____

_____

5. ¿Cómo es el desván?

_____

_____

6. ¿Tienes jardín?

_____

_____

7. ¿Compartes tu dormitorio con alguien?

_____

_____

8. ¿De qué color son las paredes?

_____

_____

9. ¿Da a la calle tu dormitorio?

_____

_____

10. ¿Vives en esta casa desde hace mucho tiempo?

_____

_____

Cuarta Sección

☞ **A. ESCRIBE ABAJO 12 PALABRAS O EXPRESIONES DE ESTA UNIDAD QUE TÚ CONSIDERAS IMPORTANTES DE RECORDAR:**

1.. 2..

3.. 4..

5.. 6..

7.. 8..

9.. 10..

11.. 12..

B. ESCRIBE EL EQUIVALENTE EN ESPAÑOL DE ESTAS EXPRESIONES:

1. I live far from school ....

2. It's an old house ....

3. The dining-room is beside the kitchen ....

4. The bathroom is upstairs ....

5. We have a small garage ....

6. There are a lot of flowers ....

7. My bedroom looks onto the garden ....

8. The curtains are white ....

9. I have to share a bedroom ....

10. Our house is very comfortable ....

☞ **C. COMPLETA LAS SIGUIENTES FRASES CON LA PALABRA ADECUADA:**

Vivo en una casa _ _ _ _ _ _ _ _ cerca de aquí. Abajo está la cocina, el

_ _ _ _ _ _ _, el salón y un cuarto de baño. _ _ _ _ _ _ hay tres dormitorios.

Tengo que _ _ _ _ _ _ _ _ _ mi dormitorio con mi hermana. Tenemos un

_ _ _ _ _ _ _ grande donde guardamos nuestra ropa. En las _ _ _ _ _ _ _ _ hay

muchos pósters. Me gusta mucho el jardín, sobre todo en el _ _ _ _ _ _ _ cuando

hace calor y hay muchas _ _ _ _ _ _ bonitas.

Primera Sección

1. **¿Está cerca de aquí el barrio donde vives?**

No. Vivo en las afueras de la ciudad, al lado del mar.

2. **¿Qué tipo de barrio es?**

Es un barrio

tranquilo	limpio
agradable	**ruidoso** *(noisy)*
bonito	antiguo
marítimo	residencial
peligroso *(dangerous)*	

Creo que es una zona bastante segura y no tenemos muchos problemas.

3. **¿Cómo son las calles?**

Las calles son **anchas** *(wide).*
estrechas *(narrow).*
limpias.
ruidosas.
tranquilas.

4. **¿Hay muchas distracciones?**

Cerca de mi casa hay
pistas de tenis.
un polideportivo.
un campo de fútbol.
una playa.
un cine.
un club juvenil.
un parque.
una escuela de equitación.
una discoteca.
una biblioteca.

5. **¿Adónde se puede ir para divertirse?**

Se puede ir

al parque	a jugar al tenis.
al cine	a bailar
al polideportivo	
a la discoteca	

6. **¿Hay mucho para los jóvenes?**

- Para los jóvenes hay mucho que hacer.

- Lo malo es que hay muy poco para los jóvenes.

7. ¿Hay un buen servicio de trenes y autobuses?

Sí la estación de tren me queda muy cerca.
Hay una parada de autobús al fondo de la calle.
Pero los autobuses nunca llegan a tiempo.
Por la mañana siempre van llenos.

8. ¿Hay algunas tiendas cerca de tu casa?

En la misma esquina de mi calle hay

una farmacia.
una peluquería.
una pequeña tienda.
un pequeño supermercado.

9. ¿Quién vive al lado?

Al lado vive

una pareja recién casada.
una pareja de personas mayores.
un **viudo** (*widow*).
una **viuda** (*widower*).
una familia con un chico de mi edad.
un **soltero** (*unmarried man*).
una **soltera** (*unmarried woman*).

10. ¿Cómo son los vecinos?

- Mis vecinos son muy simpáticos.
- Nos ayudan si hay algún problema.
- Cuidan la casa cuando vamos de vacaciones.

Segunda Sección

ESCUCHA ESTAS CONVERSACIONES EN LA CINTA

– **¿Cómo es tu barrio?**

Es un barrio bastante tranquilo con casas muy grandes.

– **¿Hay muchos lugares para los jóvenes?**

Sí, tenemos la suerte de tener muchas instalaciones deportivas en el barrio. Hay un polideportivo donde se puede practicar casi todos los deportes. También, se abrió una piscina climatizada hace poco y voy allí todos los viernes. Mis amigos del barrio y yo somos socios del club juvenil y nos divertimos mucho.

– **¿Tenéis algún cine o discoteca?**

No, para ir al cine o a la discoteca tenemos que ir al centro. Pero eso no es un gran problema. La parada del autobús está en la esquina de mi calle y la estación del tren está a unos cinco minutos de la parada de autobús.

– **¿Te gusta vivir en tu barrio?**

Sí. He vivido aquí toda mi vida. Es una zona muy tranquila con muy poco tráfico. Cuando era pequeño mis amigos y yo solíamos jugar al fútbol en la calle delante de la casa ya que sólo de vez en cuando pasaba algún coche.

– **¿Está tu casa cerca del colegio?**

No, está bastante lejos. Vivo en un pueblo al norte de la ciudad a unos veinte kilómetros de aquí.

– **¿Cómo es el barrio donde vives?**

Es muy tranquilo y bonito con muchos árboles y flores por las calles. Sólo hay tres o cuatro calles bastante largas. Aunque hay muy pocas tiendas interesantes tenemos una farmacia, una carnicería, una panadería y un pequeño supermercado.

– **¿Entonces vas mucho al centro de la ciudad?**

Sí, casi todos los fines de semana voy de compras. Me gusta ir a los grandes almacenes y a las tiendas de música.

– **No hay muchos lugares de diversión para los jóvenes, ¿verdad?**

Pues no. No hay nada para nosotros. Para divertirnos tenemos que ir en tren o en autobús al centro. Allí, podemos ir a las discotecas o al cine. Pero para volver a casa siempre tenemos problemas. A veces pasamos horas enteras buscando un taxi que nos lleve a casa.

– **¿Cómo son tus vecinos?**

Lo bueno es que todo el mundo en mi barrio se conoce. Si alguien tiene cualquier problema todos ayudan. En la casa de al lado vive **una pareja jubilada** *(a retired couple)* y yo les corto el césped cuando hace falta. Si voy a las tiendas les compro también lo que necesitan.

Tercera Sección

CONTESTA LAS SIGUIENTES PREGUNTAS

1. ¿Cómo es el barrio donde vives?

_____

_____

2. ¿Hace mucho tiempo que vives en este barrio?

_____

_____

3. ¿Está cerca del colegio?

_____

_____

4. ¿Es un barrio animado?

_____

_____

5. ¿Hay muchas tiendas cerca de tu casa?

_____

_____

6. ¿Hay muchas distracciones para los jóvenes?

_____

_____

7. ¿Qué es lo que más te gusta de tu barrio?

_____

_____

8. ¿Hay alguna desventaja de vivir allí?

_____

_____

9. ¿Es mejor coger el tren o el autobús para ir al centro desde tu barrio?

_____

_____

10. ¿Cómo son tus vecinos?

_____

_____

Cuarta Sección

☞ **A. ESCRIBE ABAJO 12 PALABRAS O EXPRESIONES DE ESTA UNIDAD QUE TÚ CONSIDERAS IMPORTANTES DE RECORDAR:**

1... 2...

3... 4...

5... 6...

7... 8...

9... 10..

11... 12..

B. ESCRIBE EL EQUIVALENTE EN ESPAÑOL DE ESTAS EXPRESIONES:

1. I live in a quiet district...

2. There are lots of nice gardens...

3. The streets are very narrow ....

4. There is a library near my house ....

5. Unfortunately there is no cinema ....

6. There is very little for young people ....

7. It's very noisy...

8. My neighbours are very helpful ....

9. They look after the house ....

10. I cut the grass for them ....

☞ **C. COMPLETA LAS SIGUIENTES FRASES CON LA PALABRA ADECUADA:**

Mi barrio _ _ _ _ en las afueras de la ciudad. Es un barrio _ _ _ _ _ _ _ _ _ _.

Las _ _ _ _ _ _ son anchas y tienen muchos _ _ _ _ _ _ _. Cerca de mi casa

hay un parque donde _ _ _ _ _ al fútbol con _ _ _ amigos. Vamos también _ _

club juvenil todos _ _ _ viernes. El ambiente es muy agradable allí. _ _ _ _ _ en

este barrio desde hace cuatro años. Lo único _ _ _ _ es que vivimos bastante

_ _ _ _ _ del centro de la ciudad.

6. Mi ciudad/Mi pueblo

Primera Sección

1. ¿Cuántos habitantes viven en esta ciudad? En mi ciudad hay unos

cuarenta
cincuenta
sesenta
setenta
ochenta
noventa

mil habitantes.

un millón y medio **de** ciudadanos.

2. ¿Qué tipo de ciudad es?

Es una ciudad

antigua	**y**	turistíca.
importante	**e**	interesante.
moderna	**e**	industrial.

El ambiente de la ciudad es muy agradable sobre todo cuando hay un partido importante de fútbol o de rugby.

3. ¿Cuáles son los edificios más importantes?

Hay muchos **edificios** *(buildings)* antiguos **e** importantes:

hoteles	restaurantes
cines	cafeterías
teatros	catedrales
bancos	colegios
universidades	talleres
un estadio de fútbol	
el **ayuntamiento** *(town hall)*	
fábricas	
iglesias que datan de la Edad Media.	

4. ¿Hay mucho para los turistas?

Para los turistas hay de todo

hoteles lujosos o baratos.
monumentos famosos.
una catedral enorme.
museos.
galerías de arte.
salas de exposiciones.
salas de conciertos.
excursiones organizadas.
parques bonitos.

**5. ¿Es una buena ciudad
   para las compras?**

Para ir de compras hay | tiendas elegantes de ropa.
unos grandes almacenes.
centros comerciales.
zonas **peatonales**.
(pedestrianised areas)
tiendas de **recuerdos**.
(souvenirs)

- Se puede **ir de escapartes** *(window-shop)*.

- El centro de la ciudad está reservado a los peatones.

- En las zonas céntricas siempre hay mucha gente.

6. ¿Se pueden practicar muchos deportes?

Si eres aficionado a los deportes puedes ir | a un centro deportivo.
al estadio de fútbol.
al campo de golf.
a la piscina.
a jugar al tenis.

**7. ¿Hay mucha industria en
   tu ciudad?**

Hay fábricas de

calzado	ropa
vidrio	productos químicos
muebles	cerveza
juguetes	objetos de plástico

También hay unas fábricas muy feas en los alrededores.

**8. ¿A tu parecer cuáles son los
   problemas más serios de la ciudad?**

Como en todas las grandes ciudades hay muchos problemas sociales como

- el paro – mucha gente que no tiene trabajo.

- el abuso del alcohol – dicen que los irlandeses beben demasiado.

- las drogas – es fácil conseguirlas en las discotecas e incluso por la calle.

- robos en domicilios – muchas veces contra la gente mayor.

- atracos en tiendas y otros establecimientos.

**9. El tráfico y el ruido son
también problemas, ¿no?**

Claro que sí. Además de los problemas sociales existen otros relacionados con la vida urbana, **tales como** *(such as):*

* la circulación – sobre todo a las horas punta por la mañana y por la tarde.
Hay que pasar muchas horas en los **atascos** *(trafffic-jams).*

* la contaminación – hay muchos humos sucios que salen de las fábricas y de los talleres.

* las calles están muy sucias – mucha gente echa basura en el suelo y no en las papeleras.

* el medio ambiente – existe muy poco interés en preservarlo.

* el ruido – con el volumen de coches en las calle todos los días, las alarmas que suenan a toda hora del día o de la noche, los teléfonos móviles por todos lados, la música y tantas otras cosas.

Segunda Sección

ESCUCHA ESTAS CONVERSACIONES EN LA CINTA

— **¿Vives en esta ciudad desde hace muchos años?**

Vivo aquí desde hace cinco años. Antes vivía en otra ciudad más pequeña.

— **¿Y cuál prefieres ?**

Esta, aunque al principio no me gustaba nada porque era una ciudad muy grande con mucho ruido y más tráfico. Pero ahora ya me he acostumbrado a todo esto y me gusta mucho el ambiente.

— **¿La gente de aquí es simpática?**

En general, sí que lo son. Pero se nota cada vez más que la gente lleva una vida más ajetreada y que tiene menos tiempo para charlar.

— **¿Crees entonces que hoy en día las personas que viven en ciudades tienen menos tiempo libre?**

Yo creo que sí. Los que trabajan en el centro de la ciudad tienen que salir muy temprano si van en coche. Y por la tarde siempre hay atascos. Mi padre regresa todos los días con los nervios destrozados.

— **¿Y por qué no coge el autobús o el tren para ir al trabajo?**

El problema es que no hay parada de autobús cerca de mi casa y tampoco nos sirve la línea del tren. A lo mejor vamos a cambiar de casa. Mi madre siempre dice que la vida sería más fácil para todos si pudiéramos usar el transporte público.

— **¿Has vivido en esta ciudad desde pequeña?**

Sí, siempre he vivido aquí. Pero me gustaría viajar y vivir quizás en Londres, París o Madrid.

— **¿Qué es lo que te atrae de estas ciudades?**

Hay siempre conciertos y espectáculos que pueden verse allí. Me lo ha dicho mi hermana que ha viajado mucho.

— **¿Entonces la vida de aquí te parece aburrida?**

Sí, un poco. Por Navidad cuando vuelve mi hermana me cuenta todo lo que ha hecho. Además, a mí me interesa mucho la moda y hay más oportunidades allí que aquí para estudiar la carrera de **diseñadora de modas** (*dress designer*).

— **¿Y qué piensan tus padres?**

Son muy comprensivos y siempre me apoyan. Creo que les ha influído mucho la situación de mi hermana y el hecho de que se haya encontrado tan a gusto viviendo en Londres. Además saben que viviría con ella y no me encontraría sola.

Tercera Sección

CONTESTA LAS SIGUIENTES PREGUNTAS

1. ¿Hace mucho tiempo que vives en esta ciudad?

   _____

   _____

2. ¿Cuántos habitantes hay en la ciudad?

   _____

   _____

3. ¿Qué tipos de edificios se pueden ver en el centro de la ciudad?

   _____

   _____

4. ¿Merece la pena visitar algunos lugares en particular?

   _____

   _____

5. ¿Cómo se puede uno divertir?

   _____

   _____

6. ¿Es un centro importante para el comercio?

   _____

   _____

7. ¿Existen muchas posibilidades para encontrar trabajo?

   _____

   _____

8. ¿Qué tipos de fábricas hay en la ciudad o en los alrededores?

   _____

   _____

9. ¿Es bueno el transporte público?

   _____

   _____

10. ¿A tu parecer cuáles son los problemas más graves de la ciudad?

    _____

    _____

Cuarta Sección

☞   **A. ESCRIBE ABAJO 12 PALABRAS O EXPRESIONES DE ESTA UNIDAD QUE TÚ CONSIDERAS IMPORTANTES DE RECORDAR:**

1.. 2..

3.. 4..

5.. 6..

7.. 8..

9.. 10..

11.. 12..

B. ESCRIBE EL EQUIVALENTE EN ESPAÑOL DE ESTAS EXPRESIONES:

1. There are 2 million inhabitants..

2. We have many interesting buildings ....

3. The pedestrianised areas are full of people ....

4. I like window-shopping..

5. The atmosphere is very pleasant ....

6. In the central parts ....

7. There are many factories ....

8. It is easy to get drugs ....

9. The traffic is very bad ....

10. There is noise everywhere..

☞   **C. COMPLETA LAS SIGUIENTES FRASES CON LA PALABRA ADECUADA:**

En mi _ _ _ _ _ _ hay unos setenta mil _ _ _ _ _ _ _ _ _ _. Tenemos muchos

_ _ _ _ _ _ _ _ _ importantes como la catedral y la universidad. Si quieres ir de

_ _ _ _ _ _ _ puedes ir a los grandes almacenes. También hay muchas

_ _ _ _ _ _ _ de recuerdos si buscas un regalo típico de este país. A las horas

_ _ _ _ _ hay problemas con los atascos.

7. Mi colegio

Primera Sección

1. ¿Cómo es tu colegio?

Mi colegio es   bastante

Es un edificio

grande.
pequeño.
moderno.
alto.
bajo.
de dos pisos.

2. Describe lo que hay en la planta baja.

En la planta baja tenemos:

la biblioteca.
muchas aulas.
la oficina del director.
la oficina de la directora.
la sala de arte.
el salón de actos.
el comedor.
varias oficinas.
la recepción.
el patio.
la sala de los estudiantes de sexto.

3. ¿Tenéis laboratorios de ciencias?

Sí. Los laboratorios de ciencias están en el primer piso.

4. ¿Cuáles son las salas más cerca de la entrada?

- La sala de profesores está situada cerca de la entrada.
- También la sala de ordenadores y la sala de trabajos manuales están situadas allí.
- Los servicios están en la planta baja.

5. ¿Hay muchas instalaciones deportivas?

Hay una   piscina cubierta.
un campo de fútbol.
varias pistas de tenis.
un gimnasio donde podemos practicar casi todos los deportes.
los vestuarios (*changing rooms*).

**6. ¿Se practican muchos deportes
en el colegio?**

Sí. Tenemos equipos de casi todos los
deportes, por ejemplo:

Se puede jugar | al tenis.
al baloncesto.
al fútbol.
al rugby.
al hockey.
al ping-pong.

hacer atletismo.
nadar.

7. ¿Y jugáis contra otros colegios?

Por supuesto. Participamos en muchos campeonatos
y torneos contra otros colegios.

8. ¿Cuándo se entrenan los equipos?

Los equipos **se entrenan** *(to train):*

los sábados por la mañana.
a la hora de comer.
todos los días.
a partir de las tres y media.

**9. ¿Además de los deportes
qué otras actividades hay?**

Además de los deportes se organizan
muchas otras actividades en el colegio.

Casi todos los departamentos ofrecen clubs.
Puedes pertenecer al club | de vídeo.
de **ajedrez** *(chess).*
de fotografía.

Hay muchos que toman parte en la sociedad
de idiomas y en los debates.

10. ¿Es un colegio mixto?

No. Nuestro colegio es | sólo de chicas.
sólo de chicos.

11. ¿Cuántos alumnos hay aquí?

En nuestro colegio somos **unos** *(about):*

quinientos alumnos.
seiscientos
setecientos
ochocientos
novecientos

12. ¿Cuántos sois en cada clase?

Normalmente hay | treinta | alumn**os/as.**
veinticinco

Para algunas asignaturas hay menos de veinte.

13. ¿Hay muchos profesores?

Creo que hay unos cuarenta profesores.

14. ¿Cómo son los profesores?

- Algunos profesores son **divertidos** *(amusing)*.
  simpáticos.
  entusiastas.
  exigentes *(demanding)*.
  comprensivos
  (understanding).
  abiertos.

  A mí me cae bien el profesor de orientación profesional.

- La mayoría de los profesores
  nos ayudan a aclarar los problemas.
  nos tratan bien.
  nos motivan mucho.
  nos dan muchos deberes.
  nos **castigan** *(punish)* si no nos portamos bien.
  explican bien las cosas.

- Casi todos se preocupan mucho por la marcha de nuestros estudios.

- Otros profesores son malos.
  incompetentes.
  aburridos.
  poco comprensivos.
  autoritarios.
  demasiado estrictos.

15. ¿Cómo castigan a los alumnos que se portan mal?

Si nos portamos mal:
- llaman a nuestros padres.
- el tutor del curso nos castiga dándonos ejercicios que copiar.
- nos **dice que** nos qued**emos** después de las clases.
  SUBJUNCTIVE
- tenemos que pagar una multa si nos encuentran fumando.

Segunda Sección

ESCUCHA ESTAS CONVERSACIONES EN LA CINTA

— **¿Dónde está tu colegio?**

Mi colegio está bastante cerca del centro de la ciudad y no muy lejos de mi casa. Por eso cada día vengo andando.

— **¿Es un edificio moderno?**

Como se ve, tiene partes bastante modernas como la sala de ordenadores y la sala de los estudiantes de sexto año. Sin embargo, la sección donde se encuentran la mayoría de las aulas es más antigua.

— **¿Cuántos alumnos hay en tu clase?**

Pues, eso depende de la asignatura. En la clase de inglés y en la de historia somos unos treinta. Pero en la clase de español sólo somos alrededor de quince estudiantes.

— **¿Te llevas bien con los profesores?**

Sí, con casi todos. La mayoría de ellos son muy simpáticos, sobre todo la profesora de español. Casi siempre está de buen humor y sus clases siempre son interesantes. Sin embargo en otras clases nos aburrimos mucho y entonces no le prestamos mucha atención al profesor. Hay unos profesores que **se enfadan** *(get angry)* por nada. Pero nosotros **nos reímos de ellos** *(we laugh at them)*.

— **Me parece muy grande este colegio. ¿Cuántos alumnos hay?**

Somos unos novecientos en total. Es un colegio mixto y la mayoría de los estudiantes son chicos. Antes era un colegio sólo de chicos y creo que por eso continúan viniendo más chicos.

— **¿Te gusta estar en un colegio mixto?**

Al principio no me gustaba nada. Algunos chicos siempre estaban haciendo tonterías. Hablaban mucho y no prestaban atención a la clase. Pero ahora lo prefiero así. Creo que es más normal. ¿No? Y nos llevamos muy bien. Lo bonito es que tengo amigos de ambos sexos. Nos gusta salir en grupo y nos ayudamos mucho con los estudios.

— **¿Tenéis muchas instalaciones deportivas?**

Sí, de todo tipo. Tenemos muchos campos de deportes y jugamos al rugby, al fútbol y al hockey. También jugamos al tenis y al baloncesto. El año pasado jugué en el equipo de baloncesto y tomamos parte en un campeonato. Llegamos a la final y nos pusimos muy contentas cuando ganamos el trofeo.

— **¿Qué otras actividades ofrece tu colegio?**

Hay una orquesta y un club de debates. A veces hacemos debates contra otros colegios. También yo voy todos los viernes al club de español. Nos reunimos para charlar sobre temas españoles. Y, además de divertirnos, siempre aprendemos algo.

Tercera Sección

CONTESTA LAS SIGUIENTES PREGUNTAS

1. ¿Cómo es tu colegio?

_____

_____

2. ¿Es un edificio moderno?

_____

_____

3. ¿Qué facilidades tenéis para los deportes?

_____

_____

4. ¿Perteneces a algún equipo?

_____

_____

5. ¿Cuántas veces a la semana tienes que hacer entrenamiento?

_____

_____

6. ¿Crees que los deportes son importantes para los jóvenes de tu edad?

_____

_____

7. ¿Cuántos alumnos hay aquí?

_____

_____

8. ¿Cómo son los profesores?

_____

_____

9. ¿Qué castigos se emplean en tu colegio?

_____

_____

10. ¿Cuáles son las ventajas y las desventajas de un colegio mixto?

_____

_____

Cuarta Sección

☞ **A. ESCRIBE ABAJO 12 PALABRAS O EXPRESIONES DE ESTA UNIDAD QUE TÚ CONSIDERAS IMPORTANTES DE RECORDAR:**

1.. 2..

3.. 4..

5.. 6..

7.. 8..

9.. 10...

11.. 12...

B. ESCRIBE EL EQUIVALENTE EN ESPAÑOL DE ESTAS EXPRESIONES:

1. My school is quite old ....

2. We have a computer-room ....

3. There is an indoor swimming-pool ....

4. There are many sports facilities...

5. We have eight tennis courts...

6. We train twice a week ....

7. Many other activities are organised...

8. I belong to the Spanish club ....

9. There are about 500 students...

10. Some teachers are very demanding ....

☞ **C. COMPLETA LAS SIGUIENTES FRASES CON LA PALABRA ADECUADA:**

Voy a un _ _ _ _ _ _ _ de chicas. _ _ un edificio bastante moderno. Todas las

_ _ _ _ _ y la sala de los profesores están en la _ _ _ _ _ _ baja. Tenemos muchas

_ _ _ _ _ _ _ _ _ _ _ para los deportes. Jugamos _ _ baloncesto y _ _ tenis. Nos

entrenamos tres _ _ _ _ _ a la semana y tomamos parte en campeonatos con otros

_ _ _ _ _ _ _. La mayoría de los profesores _ _ _ muy simpáticos y nos tratan

_ _ _ _.

8. MIS ASIGNATURAS

Primera Sección

1. ¿Cuáles son las asignaturas que estudias este año?

En el colegio estudio inglés.
irlandés.
matemáticas.

Estas tres asignaturas son obligatorias.

La mayoría de los alumnos estudian otro idioma:

el español	el alemán
el francés	el italiano

Mis otras asignaturas son

la geografía
la historia

la **contabilidad**
(accounting)

las ciencias   los **estudios empresariales**
la química   *(Business Studies)*
la física   la economía
la biología   la **informática** *(computers)*

la religión   el dibujo
los estudios clásicos   el dibujo técnico

la música   el **hogar** *(Home Economics)*
la educación física   – deportes

los trabajos manuales   – carpintería
soldadura

2. ¿Qué asignatura prefieres?

• Me gusta más **el** francés ⎧ **Lo**
MASC

Prefiero **la** biología. **La** encuentro muy fácil.
FEM útil.

• A mí la asignatura que más me gusta es …
• Mi materia favorita es …
• Lo que más me gusta estudiar es …

(contd.)

- Me gust**an** más **los** idiomas.

> Creo que son muy importantes.
> Me parece que son muy útiles.
> Me resulta fácil hablarlos.
> Lo que es difícil es escribirlos.

Voy a seguir estudiándolos el año que viene.
Entiendo el francés mejor que el español.

Se me dan bien las matemáticas *(I do well in)*.

3. ¿Cuál es la asignatura que menos te gusta ?

- No me gust**a el** irlandés. Lo encuentro muy difícil. Lo que menos me gust**a** es **la** historia.
- Tampoco me gust**an las** matemáticas. Son muy difíciles/aburridas.

- **Lo más** | difícil / aburrido | **es** tener que | aprender todos los verbos. / leer tantas páginas.
- **Lo** | malo | | estudiar todos los poemas.

Tengo que trabajar mucho para salir adelante.
Tengo **la cabeza como un colador**.
(head like a sieve)

4. ¿Desde hace cuántos años estudias el francés?

Estudio el francés **desde hace** seis años.
OR
Llevo seis años **estudiando** el francés.

NOTE PRESENT TENSE = *I've been studying for . . .*

5. ¿A qué nivel estudias el irlandés?

Lo estudio al nivel superior.
bajo.

6. ¿Cuántas clases tienes al día?

- Tenemos ocho clases **al día** *(per day)* **menos** *(except for)* el miércoles cuando sólo hay clases por la mañana.
- Estudiamos cada asignatura cuatro veces **a la semana** *(per week)*.

7. ¿Cuántas asignaturas tienes que estudiar?

- Casi todos los alumnos estudian siete **u** ocho asignaturas.
- **Eso quiere decir** *(that means)* que tenemos un horario supercargado.

8. **¿Hay un tutor para cada clase?**

Sí. A primera hora todos los días estamos con el tutor de nuestra clase.

9. **¿A qué hora empiezan las clases?**

- Las clases emp**ie**zan a las nueve menos diez de la mañana.
- Terminan a las tres y media o a las cuatro de la tarde.

10. **¿Por la mañana cuántas clases hay?**

Hay dos clases por la mañana antes del recreo y tres después.

11. **¿Y cada clase dura cuánto tiempo?**

Cada clase dura cuarenta / cuarenta y cinco minutos.

12. **¿Hay clases por la tarde todos los días?**

- El miércoles no hay clases por la tarde.
- Tampoco hay clases los días de reunión de padres y profesores.

13. **¿Todos los alumnos vuelven a casa a la misma hora?**

- Algunas personas se quedan en el colegio por la tarde para estudiar en la biblioteca.
- También hay muchos que hacen deporte.

14. **¿Te dan muchos deberes?**

Sí. Todos los días tenemos muchos deberes **que** hacer.

> N.B.
> **Mucho que hacer** *(a lot to do)*

15. **¿Qué tipo de alumno eres?**

- Soy buen alumn**o** / buen**a** alumn**a** / perezoso/a / trabajador/**a**
- Casi siempre saco sobresaliente / buenas notas / malas notas en mis exámenes.
- Estoy muy centrad**o/a** en mis estudios.

16. **¿Cómo reaccionan tus padres si no apruebas en los exámenes?**

Si no apruebo en los exámenes mis padres se enfadan mucho y **me riñen**.
(give out to me)

Segunda Sección

ESCUCHA ESTAS CONVERSACIONES EN LA CINTA

– **¿Cuántas asignaturas estudias?**

Este año estudio ocho asignaturas, seis de nivel superior y dos de nivel bajo.

– **¿Cuáles son tus asignaturas de nivel bajo?**

Pues, el irlandés y las matemáticas. Estas dos asignaturas las encuentro bastante difíciles.

– **¿Cuál te gusta más?**

Mi asignatura favorita es la historia. Me interesa mucho lo que ocurrió antes. Siempre he tenido interés en otras épocas.

– **¿Tienes muchos deberes que hacer cada noche?**

¡Claro que sí. Todos los profesores nos exigen mucho. Piensan que sólo tenemos que estudiar su asignatura y por eso nos dan muchos deberes. Casi cada noche estudio cuatro horas antes de irme a dormir.

– **¿Los fines de semana tienes tiempo para descansar?**

¡Qué va! Es cuando tenemos más que hacer. Los trabajos más difíciles, por ejemplo, los análisis de obras literarias tenemos que hacerlos el sábado y el domingo.

– **¿Hay alguna asignatura que no te gusta?**

La que menos me gusta es la química. La encuentro muy difícil. Me aburro mucho durante esa clase y casi nunca le presto atención al profesor.

– **¿Cuáles son las asignaturas que estudias para el Leaving?**

Pues, este año hago siete asignaturas: inglés, irlandés y matemáticas que son las obligatorias. Después, también estudio español, geografía, biología y física.

– **¿Cuál es tu asignatura preferida?**

Pues se me dan bien las ciencias, sobre todo la biología. Me fascina el estudio del cuerpo humano y aprender cosas sobre la naturaleza. Algunas chicas de mi clase aborrecen el estudio de los gusanos y las ranas sobre todo cuando tenemos que diseccionarlos. En cambio a mí, es algo que me interesa muchísimo.

– **¿Y te gustan los idiomas?**

Sí, mucho. Estudio el irlandés desde hace unos catorce años y he ido varias veces a un colegio irlandés durante el verano. Por eso lo hablo bastante bien y entiendo casi todo lo que dice la profesora en clase.También me gusta el español y llevo aprendiéndolo desde hace seis años. Y además, me encanta el estilo de vida español. Durante el año de Transición hice un intercambio con una chica de Madrid. Nos llevamos muy bien y sigo escribiéndole.

Tercera Sección

CONTESTA LAS SIGUIENTES PREGUNTAS

1. ¿Cuántas asignaturas estudias este año?

2. ¿Qué asignatura te gusta más?

3. ¿Hay alguna asignatura que encuentras más difícil?

4. ¿Cuántos idiomas estudias ?

5. ¿Cuántos años llevas estudiando español?

6. ¿Crees que es importante saber hablar otros idiomas?

7. ¿En inglés prefieres estudiar obras de teatro, novelas o poesía?

8. ¿Qué tipo de notas sacas en los exámenes?

9. ¿Cuántas horas estudias cada noche?

10. ¿Hay alguna asignatura que no puedes hacer en el colegio y que te gustaría estudiar?

Cuarta Sección

☞ **A. ESCRIBE ABAJO 12 PALABRAS O EXPRESIONES DE ESTA UNIDAD QUE TÚ CONSIDERAS IMPORTANTES DE RECORDAR:**

1... 2...

3... 4...

5... 6...

7... 8...

9... 10...

11... 12...

B. ESCRIBE EL EQUIVALENTE EN ESPAÑOL DE ESTAS EXPRESIONES:

1. I study eight subjects this year ....

2. My favourite subject is ....

3. I prefer history ....

4. I study it at higher level ....

5. I don't like maths..

6. What I like least is ....

7. The most difficult thing is ....

8. Four times a week..

9. Seven or eight subjects ....

10. I'm hard-working ....

☞ **C. COMPLETA LAS SIGUIENTES FRASES CON LA PALABRA ADECUADA:**

Este año estudio ocho _ _ _ _ _ _ _ _ _ _ _. El irlandés, el inglés y las

matemáticas son _ _ _ _ _ _ _ _ _ _ _ _. También aprendo otros dos

_ _ _ _ _ _ _ el español y el francés. _ _ _ _ _ cinco años estudiando español.

Mi asignatura favorita es la historia. _ _ encuentro muy interesante. No me

_ _ _ _ _ nada la química. Es muy _ _ _ _ _ _ _.

9. La vida cotidiana

Primera Sección

1. **¿A qué hora te despiertas los días de colegio?**

   Me despierto a las siete y cuarto los días de colegio.
   un poco antes de las siete.
   un poco después de las ocho.
   lo más tarde posible.
   bastante temprano.

   Pongo el **despertador** (*alarm*) para las siete.

2. **¿Qué haces después de levantarte?**

   Voy al cuarto de baño a ducharme
   a bañarme.
   a lavarme los dientes.
   a **afeitarme** (*shave*).
   a **peinarme** (*brush my hair*).

3. **¿Dónde te vistes?**

   Me visto (*get dressed*) en mi habitación.
   Me arreglo para el colegio

4. **¿Haces tu cama antes de desayunar?**

   Sí. Siempre hago mi cama antes de bajar a la cocina.

5. **¿Qué desayunas?**

   - Desayuno muy poco.
   - Tomo un desayuno bastante fuerte.
   - Desayuno cereales.
     tostadas con mantequilla y mermelada.
     un **huevo duro** (*boiled egg*).
     un huevo frito con **beicón** (*bacon*).
     huevos revueltos (*scrambled eggs*).

6. **¿Y qué bebes por la mañana?**

   Para beber tomo un zumo de naranja.
   té con azúcar.
   un vaso de leche fría.
   chocolate caliente.

7. **¿Tus padres, se levantan antes o después que tú?**

   Los dos se levantan más temprano y mientras desayuno mi madre me prepara los bocadillos para el colegio.

8. ¿A qué hora sales de casa?

Me despido de mis padres
(I say goodbye to)
y salgo de casa a eso de las ocho y cuarto.
hacia

9. ¿Cómo vienes al colegio?

- Como vivo cerca del colegio vengo andando todos los días.
en bicicleta.
- Puesto que mi casa se encuentra un poco alejada del colegio casi siempre vengo en coche con mi padre.
- Casi siempre cojo el autobús.
el tren.
- Mi padre me lleva en coche.

10. ¿A qué hora llegas al colegio?

Llego al colegio a eso de las nueve menos cuarto.

11. ¿Qué haces después de llegar al colegio?

- Al llegar al colegio entro en mi clase y hablo con mis amigos.
- Voy a mi **taquilla** *(locker)* a sacar los libros que me hacen falta para ese día.

12. ¿Tienes un descanso por la mañana?

Sí, a las diez y media.
Durante el recreo salimos todos al patio si hace buen tempo.
comemos algo dentro de la clase si llueve.
tomamos un refresco si tenemos sed.

13. ¿Te quedas en el colegio a la hora de comer?

- Sí. Me quedo aquí a la hora de comer.
- Como en el comedor del colegio.
- No. Salgo a las tiendas a comprar algo.
- Cojo mi bocadillo y lo como **afuera** *(outside).*

14. ¿Qué sueles hacer en cuanto terminan las clases?

Salgo	**disparado/a** *(rush away)* del colegio.
Vuelvo	a casa **en seguida** *(right away).*
Estoy	muy cansad**o/a** normalmente.
Me quedo	un rato a hablar con mis amigos.
Estudio	en la biblioteca antes de volver a casa.

15. ¿A qué hora vuelves a casa?

Vuelvo a eso de las cinco.

16. ¿Meriendas algo al volver a casa?

Sí. Meriendo **galletas** *(biscuits).*
un bollo de chocolate.
zumo de fruta.

17. ¿Y empiezas a estudiar en seguida?

No. Para descansar un poco:

escucho la radio.
salgo al jardín.
veo **dibujos animados** *(cartoons)*
en la televisión.
voy a la tienda a comprar caramelos.
hablo con mi amiga que vive al lado.

18. ¿Cuándo empiezas a hacer la tarea?

Subo a mi habitación donde empiezo la
tarea antes de cenar.
después de cenar.
a eso de las siete.

19. ¿Te acuestas temprano?

- Me ac**ue**sto un poco después de las once.
  (ac**o**starse – RADICAL-CHANGING VERB)

- Les **doy** las buenas noches a mis
  padres antes de acostarme.

- Empiezo a **tener mucho sueño** a eso
  de las once *(get very sleepy)*.

20. ¿Te duermes en seguida?

- No. Leo un poco en la cama antes de acostarme.

- Me gusta escuchar la radio.

- D**ue**rmo **como un lirón** *(sleep like a log)*.
  (d**o**rmir – RADICAL-CHANGING VERB)

- A veces **no pego ojo**.
  (I have a sleepless night)

> **N.B.**
> **RADICAL-CHANGING VERBS**
>
> | | | |
> |---|---|---|
> | desp**e**rtarse | – | **me** desp**ie**rto | e > ie |
> | mer**e**ndar | – | mer**ie**ndo | |
> | emp**e**zar | – | emp**ie**zo | |
> | | | | |
> | s**o**ler | – | s**ue**lo | o > ue |
> | v**o**lver | – | v**ue**lvo | |
> | d**o**rmir | – | d**ue**rmo | |
> | ac**o**starse | – | me ac**ue**sto | |
> | | | | |
> | *BUT* v**e**stirse | – | **me** v**i**sto | e > i |

Segunda Sección

ESCUCHA ESTAS CONVERSACIONES EN LA CINTA

– **¿A qué hora te levantas por la mañana?**

Los días de colegio tengo que levantarme bastante temprano, a las siete.

– **¿Te gusta madrugar?**

¡Ni hablar! Soy muy dormilón y no me gusta nada madrugar sobre todo en invierno. Cuando suena el despertador todavía parece de noche.

– **¿Qué haces antes de desayunar?**

Intento ir al cuarto de baño antes que mi hermana porque ella tarda mucho tiempo en arreglarse. Y casi nunca queda agua caliente para ducharme. Después me visto de prisa y bajo a desayunar.

– **¿Qué desayunas?**

Desayuno muy poco, pan tostado y zumo de naranja. A esa hora de la mañana no me apetece comer mucho .

– **¿A qué hora sales de casa para venir al colegio?**

Normalmente salgo de casa a eso de las ocho y cuarto. Como no vivo muy lejos vengo en bicicleta. Pero, cuando llueve tengo que coger el autobús, entonces salgo más temprano.

– **¿A qué hora vuelves a casa**

Salgo a las tres y media y llego a casa un poco antes de las cuatro. Meriendo algo ligero y hago dos horas de deberes antes de que regrese mi padre a eso de las seis. Entonces cenamos todos juntos. Y después subo otra vez a mi habitación para seguir trabajando sin levantar cabeza hasta las diez.

– **¿Quién se levanta primero en tu casa?**

Mi madre siempre se levanta antes y luego me despierta a mí.

– **¿Y te levantas en seguida?**

Sí, casi siempre. Prefiero no tener que apresurarme por la mañana.

– **¿Cómo vienes al colegio?**

Cojo el tren todos los días. Pero lo malo es que hay tantas personas esperando que suben al tren **a empujones** (*push their way in*).

– **¿Adónde vas primero al llegar al colegio?**

Lo primero que hago es ir a mi taquilla para sacar los libros que me hacen falta. Después voy a mi clase donde charlo con mis amigas.

– **¿Te cansa tener que estudiar tanto?**

Sí, sobre todo este año. Me quedo aquí en la biblioteca estudiando. Así que no vuelvo a casa hasta las diez. Y como los profesores nos exigen cada vez más trabajo siempre vuelvo a casa completamente rendida.

– **¿Y qué haces para relajarte?**

Toco la guitarra un poco. Me ayuda mucho a olvidarme de los estudios y luego tengo más ánimos para estudiar .

Tercera Sección

CONTESTA LAS SIGUIENTES PREGUNTAS

1. ¿A qué hora te levantas normalmente?

2. ¿Qué haces después de levantarte?

3. ¿Qué tomas para el desayuno?

4. ¿A qué hora sales de casa?

5. ¿Cómo vienes al colegio?

6. ¿Al llegar al colegio qué haces?

7. ¿Te quedas en el colegio a la hora de comer?

8. ¿A qué hora vuelves a casa?

9. ¿Cenáis todos juntos?

10. ¿Sales por la noche durante la semana?

Cuarta Sección

A. ESCRIBE ABAJO 12 PALABRAS O EXPRESIONES DE ESTA UNIDAD QUE TÚ CONSIDERAS IMPORTANTES DE RECORDAR:

1.. 2..

3.. 4..

5.. 6..

7.. 8..

9.. 10..

11.. 12..

B. ESCRIBE EL EQUIVALENTE EN ESPAÑOL DE ESTAS EXPRESIONES:

1. I get up just after 7.00 a.m...

2. Before I get dressed ....

3. I have a light breakfast ....

4. I leave home at ....

5. I take the bus...

6. When I arrive at school ....

7. At lunch-time...

8. I go home right away...

9. I begin my homework...

10. I go to bed quite late ....

☞ **C. COMPLETA LAS SIGUIENTES FRASES CON LA PALABRA ADECUADA:**

Todos _ _ _ días me levanto a _ _ _ siete. _ _ ducho en el _ _ _ _ _ _ _ de baño

y después me _ _ _ _ _ en mi habitación. Para el _ _ _ _ _ _ _ _ _ tomo tostadas

_ _ _ mantequilla y mermelada. Bebo un _ _ _ _ de leche _ _ _ _. Voy _ _

colegio en tren pero cuando llueve mi padre me _ _ _ _ _ en coche. Estoy muy

_ _ _ _ _ _ _ cuando terminan las clases. Vuelvo a casa y descanso un poco

_ _ _ _ _ de hacer la tarea.

10. Las tareas domésticas

Primera Sección

1. ¿Ayudas mucho a tus padres en casa?

Sí. Ayudo mucho a mis padres.
casi siempre
a menudo
a veces
de vez en cuando

Ayudo con numerosas tareas domésticas.

Nunca ayudo con la limpieza de la casa.
No ayudo **nunca**.

En mi casa todos **echamos una mano**.
(to help out)

2. ¿Qué haces para ayudar?

- Todos los días hago mi cama.
  saco al perro por la tarde.
  voy a la tienda a comprar lo
  que nos hace falta.

- Mi hermana y yo nos encargamos de poner y
  quitar la mesa todas las noches.

- Durante la semana no hago muchos quehaceres
  domésticos.

3. ¿Qué tareas haces los fines de semana?

Arreglo mi dormitorio y quito el polvo.
Paso la aspiradora en mi dormitorio.

Tengo que **barrer el suelo** *(sweep the floor)*.
Limpio la cocina.
Ayudo a preparar las comidas.
Lavo los platos.
Pongo/Quito la mesa.
Pongo los platos en el lavavajillas.
Saco todo del lavavajillas.

Pongo la lavadora.
Tiendo la ropa **para que** se **seque** *(to dry)*.
                                    SUBJUNCTIVE
Salgo a hacer la compra con mis padres.
Corto el césped.

4. ¿Qué es lo que menos te gusta hacer?

- Lo que menos me gusta es lavar **las sartenes**.
  ¡Qué asco!   *(frying-pan)*
- No me gusta nada tender la ropa.
  Nunca limpio el cuarto de baño.

5. ¿Qué es lo que más te gusta hacer?

- Lo que más me gusta es ayudar con la plancha.
  No me importa **planchar** *(ironing)*.

> N.B.
> **No me importa** + INFINITIVE *(I don't mind verb+ing)*

6. ¿Quién corta el césped normalmente?

A mí   no me
A mi padre/madre   no le   importa cortarlo.
A mis hermanos   no les

7. ¿Ayudan tus hermanos tanto como tú con las tareas domésticas?

Sí. En nuestra casa compartimos entre nosotros todas las tareas de la casa.

8. ¿Cómo se reparten tus padres las tareas domésticas?

Mi padre   es   el que   se ocupa más bien:
Mi madre   la que

de lo adentro   la cocina.
                la ropa.
                la plancha.

de lo de afuera   del jardín.
                  de cortar la hierba.
                  de lavar el coche.

de arreglar las cosas de la casa.

9. ¿Crees que los hombres hoy en día dedican más tiempo a las faenas del hogar?

Creo que sí.
En estos últimos años ha cambiado mucho la situación. Hoy en día los hombres dedican más tiempo al hogar y es más probable que repartan el trabajo de la casa con su esposa.

10. ¿Por qué ha habido este cambio?

El hombre ha dejado de ser el único proveedor económico de la familia. Ahora hay muchas mujeres que trabajan fuera de casa y entonces no tienen tanto tiempo como antes para las tareas del hogar.

Segunda Sección

ESCUCHA ESTAS CONVERSACIONES EN LA CINTA

– **¿Cómo ayudas a tus padres en casa?**

Pues, la verdad es que de momento no hago muchos quehaceres domésticos porque vuelvo muy tarde del colegio todos los días. Lo único que hago es quizás quitar la mesa o ir a por pan a la tienda de la esquina. A veces saco el cubo de la basura a la calle los martes por la noche.

– **Entonces, ¿tienes más tiempo los fines de semana para echar una mano?**

Sí, por supuesto. Los sábados por la mañana lo primero que hago es arreglar un poco mi habitación. La ropa limpia la pongo en mi armario en vez de dejarla encima de la silla y pongo la ropa sucia en la lavadora. Además mi hermana y yo nos turnamos para pasar la aspiradora.

– **¿Quién cocina en la casa?**

Entre semana es mi madre la que cocina porque vuelve primero de su trabajo. Sin embargo, los domingos por la noche a mi padre le encanta cocinar algo especial. Hace una paella muy rica o prepara algo de pescado.

– **¿A ti te gusta cocinar?**

No mucho. A veces hago espaguetis con carne picada o una tortilla de jamón. Cuando mis padres salen me gusta mucho llamar a telepizza o a un restaurante chino y encargar comida para llevar.

– **¿Vas a hacer algo este fin de semana para ayudar a tus padres?**

Claro que sí. El viernes por la noche iremos todos al supermercado a hacer la compra de la semana. Mientras mi padre hace cola en la carnicería yo voy a comprar las verduras y la fruta. Mi hermano casi siempre se encarga del resto. Y así terminamos antes.

– **El sábado, ¿qué piensas hacer?**

Este fin de semana mi padre me ha pedido que le ayude en el jardín. A lo mejor cortaré la hierba y vamos a plantar rosales nuevos y otras flores.

– **¿Quién se ocupa de la limpieza de la casa?**

Mi madre es ama de casa y durante la semana ella pasa su tiempo arreglando y limpiando casi todo. También prefiere lavar la ropa y plancharla. Pero yo casi siempre plancho mis vaqueros y camisetas.

– **¿Ayuda tu hermano con las tareas de la casa?**

Bueno, pues, un poco. Pone la mesa de vez en cuando y ayuda a fregar los platos. Pero no le gusta nada colgar la ropa ni plancharla. A mi parecer los chicos no hacen tanto en casa como las chicas. Siempre buscan alguna razón por no hacer nada.

Tercera Sección

CONTESTA LAS SIGUIENTES PREGUNTAS

1. ¿Ayudas a menudo con los quehaceres domésticos?

_____

_____

2. ¿Qué trabajo de la casa es lo que menos te gusta hacer?

_____

_____

3. ¿Eres tú quién hace la limpieza de tu dormitorio?

_____

_____

4. ¿Quién cuida el jardín?

_____

_____

5. ¿Se hace una compra grande cada semana en tu casa?

_____

_____

6. ¿Ayudan mucho tus hermanos con las tareas domésticas?

_____

_____

7. ¿Crees que es importante que todos echen una mano en casa?

_____

_____

8. ¿Cómo ayuda tu padre con las tareas del hogar?

_____

_____

9. ¿Te gusta cocinar?

_____

_____

10. ¿Hay cierta época del año cuando se hace una limpieza a fondo en tu casa?

_____

_____

Cuarta Sección

☞ **A. ESCRIBE ABAJO 12 PALABRAS O EXPRESIONES DE ESTA UNIDAD QUE TÚ CONSIDERAS IMPORTANTES DE RECORDAR:**

1.. 2..

3.. 4..

5.. 6..

7.. 8..

9.. 10...

11... 12...

B. ESCRIBE EL EQUIVALENTE EN ESPAÑOL DE ESTAS EXPRESIONES:

1. I help out a lot at home ....

2. I nearly always set the table ....

3. My dad looks after the ....

4. The household jobs..

5. My brother hoovers upstairs...

6. We have to empty the dishwasher ....

7. We share all the housework..

8. What I least like is ....

9. My mum doesn't mind ....

10. The truth is...

☞ **C. COMPLETA LAS SIGUIENTES FRASES CON LA PALABRA ADECUADA:**

Yo _ _ _ _ _ bastante con los _ _ _ _ _ _ _ _ _ _ domésticos sobre todo los

fines de _ _ _ _ _ _. Los sábados por la mañana tengo que _ _ _ _ _ _ _ _ mi

habitación porque casi siempre _ _ _ _ muy desordenada. _ _ _ _ la aspiradora

y limpio el cuarto de baño. Lo que _ _ _ _ _ me gusta es planchar. Nunca aliso

bien la ropa y prefiero que mi madre lo _ _ _ _. Lo que más me _ _ _ _ _ es salir

_ _ compras con mis padres.

11. El dinero y el trabajo

Primera Sección

1. ¿Cuánto dinero te dan tus padres a la semana?

Mis padres me dan cinco libras a la semana para mis gastos personales.

2. ¿Haces algún trabajo para ganar un poco más dinero?

- No. A mis padres no les gusta que trabaj**e**.
  Mis padres prefieren que no trabaj**e**.
  <small>SUBJUNCTIVE</small>
- Sí. Trabajo cerca de mi casa.

3. ¿Cuándo empezaste a trabajar?

- Hace dos meses más o menos empecé a trabajar.
- Durante el año de Transición tuve la oportunidad de trabajar dos semanas para tener cierta **experiencia laboral** *(work experience)*.

4. ¿Dónde trabajas?

Trabajo en una pequeña tienda cerca de mi casa.
un garaje en las afueras de la ciudad.
un supermercado.
un hotel como recepcionista.
un restaurante.
una peluquería.
para mis vecinos como canguro.
una escuela de vela.

5. ¿En qué consiste el trabajo?

Paso toda la mañana trabaj**ando**.
sirv**iendo** a los clientes.
contest**ando** al teléfono.
apunt**ando** detalles.
dej**ando** recados para los huéspedes.
hac**iendo** tareas distintas.
lav**ando** los coches.
pon**iendo** los comestibles en los estantes.

6. ¿Te pagan bien?

Son muchas horas de trabajo y **me pagan** bastante bien.
pocas *(I'm paid)* mal.

Gano mucho dinero.
poco.
dos libras la hora.

7. **¿Cuántas horas trabajas?**

- Estoy allí desde que abren a las nueve hasta que cierran a las cinco.
- Empiezo a trabajar a las cinco de la tarde y termino a las ocho.

8. **¿Trabajas todos los días?**

No. Sólo trabajo

los fines de semana.
el viernes por la noche.
el sábado a partir de las nueve.
el domingo por la tarde **hasta** *(until)* las seis.
a tiempo parcial.
dos días a la semana.
durante las vacaciones.

9. **¿Cómo es el trabajo?**

El trabajo es

difícil	interesante
fácil	aburrido/pesado

10. **¿Tus amigos trabajan también?**

Algunos amigos míos hacen el mismo tipo de trabajo.

11. **¿Es preciso que trabajes para ganar dinero?**

SUBJUNCTIVE

Si no trabaj**ara** no tend**ría** bastante dinero para mis gastos.

12. **¿Has trabajado antes?**

- Nunca he trabajado en otro sitio.
- Durante el año de Transición trabajé con una compañia de **seguros** *(insurance)*.

13. **¿Gastas todo tu dinero?**

Gasto casi todo mi dinero en

cigarillos	cine
CDs	cintas
discotecas	vídeos
revistas	libros
conciertos	ropa
caramelos	cerveza

14. **¿Ahorras algo?**

Ahorro *(I save)* la mitad de lo que gano porque

quiero comprar una moto.
quisiera ir de vacaciones con mis amigos.
pienso regalarle algo bonito a mi novi**o/a**.
pongo mi dinero en una cuenta bancaria.

Segunda Sección

ESCUCHA ESTAS CONVERSACIONES EN LA CINTA

– **¿Ganas algún dinero?**

Sí, los fines de semana trabajo en un restaurante cerca de mi casa.

– **¿Cuántas horas trabajas?**

Trabajo ocho horas los viernes y los sábados.

– **Son muchas horas de trabajo. ¿Qué haces exactamente?**

Bueno, hago de todo. Al llegar, lo primero que hago es preparar las mesas. Luego, ayudo en la cocina a pelar las patatas y a preparar las verduras. Después, cuando los camareros traen los platos sucios a la cocina tengo que lavarlos. ¡Eso es lo que menos me gusta del trabajo!

– **¿Hace tiempo que trabajas allí?**

No. Hace muy poco. Sólo desde el verano pasado. Fue entonces cuando decidí buscar algo porque quería ir a un concierto de mi grupo favorito. Sabía que mis padres se quejarían mucho si les pidiera el dinero para la entrada. Así que busqué en los periódicos y vi un anuncio para ese trabajo.

– **¿Te pagan bien?**

Sí, bastante bien. Gano cuatro libras por hora.

– **Tus padres, ¿están contentos de que trabajes tanto?**

No. Dicen que debería estudiar más. Creo que tienen razón. Por eso voy a dejar el trabajo después de Semana Santa.

– **¿Quién te da dinero para tus gastos personales?**

Suelo recibir dinero de mis padres cada semana y a veces me presta dinero mi hermano mayor.

– **¿Cuánto dinero recibes a la semana?**

Bueno, depende. Normalmente recibo unas quince libras.

– **¿Cómo gastas tu dinero?**

Cada semana tengo que comprar los billetes de autobús. Con lo que me queda, me compro caramelos y CDs. Pero si me hacen falta cosas caras, como zapatos o vaqueros, les pido el dinero a mis padres y me lo dan sin problema.

– **¿Y no tienes ningún empleo?**

Antes sí que tenía, pero de momento no trabajo. Creo que no podría estudiar bien si tuviera que ir a trabajar. Tampoco me dejarían mis padres. Mi madre siempre dice que tendré toda la vida después para trabajar y que ahora me dedique a los estudios. Lo malo es que ya no tengo dinero.

– **¿Dónde trabajabas antes?**

Durante el año de Transición hay un programa de experiencia laboral y yo pasé dos semanas trabajando en una fábrica de ropa de mujer. Después, durante las vacaciones del verano me ofrecieron un empleo fijo. Gané mucho dinero y me compré una bicicleta nueva.

Tercera Sección

CONTESTA LAS SIGUIENTES PREGUNTAS

1. ¿De quién recibes dinero para tus gastos?

_____

_____

2. ¿Cuánto dinero te dan tus padres?

_____

_____

3. ¿En qué lo gastas?

_____

_____

4. ¿Tienes empleo ahora o has trabajado antes?

_____

_____

5. ¿Dónde trabajas?

_____

_____

6. ¿Cuándo empezaste a trabajar por primera vez?

_____

_____

7. ¿En qué consiste tu trabajo?

_____

_____

8. ¿Qué tal te pagan?

_____

_____

9. ¿Ahorras algún dinero o lo gastas todo?

_____

_____

10. ¿Cuántas horas a la semana tienes que trabajar?

_____

_____

Cuarta Sección

☞ **A. ESCRIBE ABAJO 12 PALABRAS O EXPRESIONES DE ESTA UNIDAD QUE TÚ CONSIDERAS IMPORTANTES DE RECORDAR:**

1.. 2..

3.. 4..

5.. 6..

7.. 8..

9.. 10...

11... 12...

B. ESCRIBE EL EQUIVALENTE EN ESPAÑOL DE ESTAS EXPRESIONES:

1. My parents don't like me working ....

2. They give me £10 a week ....

3. I began working ....

4. I only work at the weekends..

5. I spend the evening serving the customers ....

6. The work is hard..

7. I'm paid quite well ....

8. I used to work in a shop..

9. I spend my money on ....

10. I save half my money ....

☞ **C. COMPLETA LAS SIGUIENTES FRASES CON LA PALABRA ADECUADA:**

Mis padres no me dejan _ _ _ _ _ _ _ _ este año. Prefieren darme algo cada

semana para mis _ _ _ _ _ _ personales. El _ _ _ _ _ _ _ pasado busqué un trabajo

en un garaje. Era muy difícil y tuve _ _ _ trabajar muchas horas seguidas sin

descansar. Lo único bueno era que me _ _ _ _ _ _ _ _ muy bien y podía comprarme

un ordenador con el dinero que _ _ _ _.

12. La moda y la ropa que llevo

Primera Sección

1. ¿Hay que llevar uniforme en tu colegio?

Sí. En este momento

llevo puesta	una blusa azul.
	una falda gris.
	una camisa blanca
	de manga larga.
	una corbata azul.
	una chaqueta marrón.
llevo puesto	un jersey verde oscuro.
	un pantalón negro.
llevo puestos	calcetines grises.
	zapatos negros.
llevo puestas	medias negras.

2. ¿Te gusta el uniforme?

- No. No me gusta el uniforme. Es muy feo. Me gustaría más bien llevar la ropa que **está de moda** *(is fashionable)* ahora.
- Sí. A mi parecer el uniforme es muy práctico.
- A mí **me da igual** llevar uniforme o no. *(it's all the same to me)*

3. ¿Podéis venir al colegio vestidos como queráis?

- Hay que venir bien vestido.
- No nos permiten llevar vaqueros ni zapatos deportivos.
- No llevamos uniforme aquí.
- Podemos llevar lo que queramos.
- Casi todo el mundo lleva **ropa vaquera**.
  (denim clothes)

4. ¿Está permitido llevar joyas al colegio?

Están prohibidas las joyas llamativas salvo los relojes de pulsera.

Algunas chicas llevan
| **pendientes** *(earrings)*. |
| **anillos** *(rings)*. |
| **pulseras** *(bracelets)*. |
| collares de plata o de oro. |
| broches. |

5. ¿En este colegio hay reglas sobre el peinado de los alumnos?

- No nos permiten llegar con el pelo mal peinado.
- Hay que venir con el pelo bien arreglado.
- Algunos alumnos llegan al colegio con un peinado muy raro.
- Otros **se tiñen el pelo** *(dye their hair).*
- Unos tienan el pelo muy corto.

6. ¿Las chicas pueden venir con mucho maquillaje?

- No pasa nada si llegas con sombras de ojos y un poco de **pintalabios** *(lipstick).*
- Algunas chicas vienen con las uñas muy largas y pintadas con esmalte de colores.

7. ¿Qué te pones cuando llueve?

Si llueve me pongo un **impermeable**.
un **chubasquero** *(raincoat).*
salgo siempre con **paraguas** *(umbrella).*

8. ¿Cómo te vistes en verano?

- Me gusta vestirme de verano.
- En verano me visto en prendas ligeras.
pantalones cortos.
una falda de algodón.
una **camiseta** *(tee-shirt).*
un bañador.
- Salgo con **alpargatas** o **zapatillas** cómodas.
(sandals)

9. ¿Qué tipo de ropa llevas en el invierno?

En invierno cuando hace mucho frío llevo

ropa **de lana** *(woollen).*
un abrigo grueso y largo.
un **plumífero** *(anorak).*
una **gorra** *(cap).*
una bufanda.
guantes de punto.
botas **con cordones**.
(with laces)

10. ¿Qué tipo de ropa está de moda ahora?

Están de moda los pantalones amplios.
las blusas largas.
las camisetas ajustadas.
los colores oscuros.

11. ¿Cómo prefieres vestirte los fines de semana?

Los fines de semana me visto con ropa más cómoda. Me siento más a gusto con:

una camisa	amplia.
	sencilla.
una camiseta	de cuadros.
	a rayas.
una blusa	de manga corta.
	con **bolsillos grandes** (*big pockets*).

una chaqueta de cuero.
un chandal (*tracksuit*).
vaqueros (*jeans*).
calzado deportivo.

12. ¿Para salir de noche te arreglas mucho?

Para salir a la discoteca me gusta **vestirme a la última moda** (*dress in the latest fashion*). Entonces me pongo:

una falda	de **seda** (*silk*).
	de **terciopelo** (*velvet*).
	de **algodón** (*cotton*).
	de color negro
	con **cinturón**.
	con **chaleco**.

una minifalda **ajustada** (*tight*).
unos zapatos de plataforma con **tacones altos** (*high heels*).

13. ¿Te vistes en las mejores tiendas?

- A veces. Pero la ropa allí es muy cara.
- Gasto mucho dinero en ropa porque creo que la buena presencia es muy importante.
- Prefiero ir a los grandes almacenes cuando hay rebajas y donde la ropa me sale más barata.

14. ¿Te gusta que tus padres te compren ropa?

- No. **Prefiero que** me d**en** dinero para que yo pued**a** eligir lo que qu**iera**.   SUBJUNCTIVE
- Siempre me compran ropa que no está de moda y tengo que ir a cambiarla.

Segunda Sección

ESCUCHA ESTAS CONVERSACIONES EN LA CINTA

– **¿Te gusta llevar uniforme?**

A mi no me importa mucho. Quizás es mejor llevar uniforme. De esa manera no tienes que pensar en la ropa que te vas a poner cada día. Así, no hay problema. Todo el mundo se viste igual.

– **¿Todos los alumnos tienen el mismo uniforme?**

Más o menos. Vestimos camisa blanca con corbata azul, pantalones grises, zapatos de cuero, y nunca nos ponemos zapatillas de deporte. Lo único que diferencia a los mayores es el jersey. Durante los dos últimos años podemos llevar un jersey de un color distinto al que llevan los alumnos de los tres primeros años.

– **¿Qué pasa si llegas un día sin uniforme**

En ese caso tienes que venir con una carta de tus padres explicando por qué no lo llevas. Y si no, llaman a tus padres o te mandan a casa diciendo que no regreses hasta que te vistas correctamente.

– **¿Tú has tenido que volver a casa alguna vez por eso?**

Yo no. Pero, hace poco, un amigo mío vino un día con bambas y sin los pantalones del uniforme. ¡Se armó un escándalo espantoso y le dijeron que no volviera jamás vestido de esa manera.

– **¿Prefieres vestirte de uniforme para venir al colegio?**

No. No me gusta nada llevar uniforme todos los días y a mis amigas tampoco les gusta llevarlo. ¡Qué lástima que no nos dejen llevar la ropa que nos gusta!

– **¿Por qué preferirías no tener que llevar uniforme?**

Primero, porque esta falda es muy larga y además está pasada de moda. Me parece que es mejor que nos vistamos con ropa cómoda y con los colores que preferimos. Otra cosa es el precio. El uniforme cuesta mucho y sólo se puede comprar en tiendas especializadas. Y nunca hay rebajas de uniformes.

– **¿Qué tipo de ropa prefieres llevar?**

Casi siempre llevo vaqueros, una camiseta y un jersey. Aunque depende de lo que haga y de adónde vaya. Por ejemplo, si voy con mis padres a un restaurante bueno mi madre quiere que me vista bien. En esas ocasiones casi siempre llevo una falda, una blusa y una chaqueta. A veces me pongo un vestido bonito que compré hace poco. Es muy bonito, largo con estampado de flores.

– **¿Te gusta que tus padres te compren ropa?**

¡Qué va! ¡De ninguna manera! Antes solían regalarme ropa para mi cumpleaños pero ahora no tienen la menor idea de lo que está de moda. Por eso, prefiero que me den dinero y así compro la ropa que más me gusta.

Tercera Sección

CONTESTA LAS SIGUIENTES PREGUNTAS

1. ¿Te gusta llevar uniforme?

_____

_____

2. ¿Todos los alumnos llevan el mismo tipo de uniforme?

_____

_____

3. ¿Y podéis llevar anillos, pendientes u otras joyas?

_____

_____

4. ¿Qué pasa si vienes un día al colegio sin llevar uniforme?

_____

_____

5. ¿Si no tuvieras que llevar uniforme qué te pondrías para venir al colegio?

_____

_____

6. ¿Gastas mucho dinero en ropa?

_____

_____

7. ¿En qué tipo de ropa te sientes más cómodo/a?

_____

_____

8. ¿Cómo te vistes para ir a la discoteca?

_____

_____

9. ¿Llevas la misma ropa en invierno como en verano?

_____

_____

10. ¿Compras ropa durante las rebajas de enero?

_____

_____

Cuarta Sección

☞ **A. ESCRIBE ABAJO 12 PALABRAS O EXPRESIONES DE ESTA UNIDAD QUE TÚ CONSIDERAS IMPORTANTES DE RECORDAR:**

1.. 2..

3.. 4..

5.. 6..

7.. 8..

9.. 10..

11.. 12..

B. ESCRIBE EL EQUIVALENTE EN ESPAÑOL DE ESTAS EXPRESIONES:

1. We have to wear a uniform ....

2. I'm wearing a white short-sleeved shirt ....

3. White shoes and black socks ....

4. Clothes which are in fashion ....

5. I like to wear jeans and runners ....

6. We can wear what we want ....

7. In winter I wear a heavy coat and scarf ....

8. I don't like my parents buying clothes for me...

9. When there are sales ....

10. I feel more comfortable in ....

☞ **C. COMPLETA LAS SIGUIENTES FRASES CON LA PALABRA ADECUADA:**

En nuestro colegio nos obligan a _ _ _ _ _ _ uniforme. Llevo _ _ _ _ _ _ una

blusa azul con una corbata. Mi falda _ _ gris igual que mi jersey. A mí no me

_ _ _ _ _ nada llevar uniforme. Me siento más _ _ _ _ _ _ en vaqueros y

camisetas. Tampoco me gustan los zapatos del colegio y los fines de _ _ _ _ _ _

siempre llevo mis _ _ _ _ _ _ _ _ _. Para comprar mi ropa prefiero ir a los

grandes _ _ _ _ _ _ _ _ _ en el centro de la ciudad.

13. Ir de compras

Primera Sección

1. **¿Acompañas a tus padres cuando hacen la compra?**

   - Les acompaño de vez en cuando.
   - Voy de compras con mis padres los viernes por la noche.

2. **¿Hay algunas tiendas cerca de tu casa?**

   Sí. Hay muchas tiendas buenas cerca de mi casa:

   un supermercado – donde hacemos la compra de la semana:

té	carne	**galletas** *(biscuits)*
café	yogur	
leche	verduras	**congeladas** *(frozen)*
azúcar	jamón	
mermelada	salchichas	
mantequilla	huevos	
cereales	**un gran surtido** *(a big choice)* **de vino**	

   una carnicería – donde hay carne muy buena:

   chuletas de cerdo *(pork chops)*
   cordero *(lamb)*
   carne picada *(mince meat)*
   ternera *(veal)*

   una pescadería – donde se puede comprar pescado fresco del día:

   bacalao *(cod)*
   gambas *(prawns)*
   truchas
   salmón
   mejillones *(mussels)*

   un mercado – Los sábados por la mañana voy allí con mis amigos.
   Siempre hay mucho **jaleo** *(bustling)*.
   una muchedumbre que busca
   artículos **a precio de saldo** *(bargain)*.

   la tienda del barrio –

   - Puedes comprar todos los comestibles básicos aquí.
   - Todos los días compramos el periódico en esta tienda.
   - Aquí se vende de todo pero los precios son un poco altos.

(contd.)   una frutería –   Siempre compramos toda la fruta y todas las
verduras aquí:

naranjas	peras	lechuga	guisantes
manzanas	uvas	tomates	zanahorias
plátanos	melocotones	cebollas	col
fresas	melones	patatas	coliflor
frambuesas	limones	aguacates	puerros

Nos gusta comprar ajo y finas hierbas aquí también:

el perejil *(parsley)*	**el tomillo** *(thyme)*
la albahaca *(basil)*	**el romero** *(rosemary)*

una panadería/pastelería –Aquí voy a por
pan
panecillos
pasteles deliciosos

una ferretería – Se venden las herramientas de carpintería y los
útiles de jardinería.

una librería

• Me gusta hojear los libros y mirar las revistas
y tarjetas postales.
• Venden también libros baratos.

una tienda de música – Se pued**en** comprar
Pl.

CDs.
libros de música.
cintas.
guitarras.
flautas.
tambores.
(drums)

Se pued**e** escuchar música con auriculares.
Sing.

una farmacia

• Vamos aquí cuando nos hace falta una
medicina con **receta** *(prescription)*.
• También compramos jabón, pasta de dientes,
perfume, **tiritas** *(elastoplast)*.

unos grandes almacenes y un centro comercial – Aquí se encuentra todo lo
necesario para amueblar la casa: muebles, **telas** *(material)* y también ropa y
juguetes *(toys)*.

3. ¿Dónde se encuentran los grandes almacenes?

Se encuentran en el centro de la ciudad.
una zona peatonal.
las calles céntricas.

4. ¿Te gusta ir de compras allí?

Por supuesto. Hay tanta variedad y en cada planta hay muchos departamentos distintos.

5. ¿Hay alguna época del año cuando es mejor ir allí?

Prefiero ir: durante las vacaciones.
cuando hay **grandes rebajas**.
(big reductions)
antes de Navidad para ver
los **escaparates** *(shop-windows)*.
si necesito comprar algo especial.
un día **de descanso/de fiesta**.
(a day off school)

6. ¿Hay mucha gente comprando?

Siempre hay cola en los grandes almacenes:

en la caja – para pagar.
en el aparcamiento – para aparcar.
en los **probadores** – para probar ropa.
(changing-rooms)

En la sección de alimentación la mayoría de los clientes tiene**n** su carrito lleno.

Segunda Sección

ESCUCHA ESTAS CONVERSACIONES EN LA CINTA

— **¿Qué hiciste el viernes pasado?**

Fuimos de compras al centro comercial. No me gustó nada porque había un montón de gente. Además, mi madre pasó horas enteras comprando lo que nos hacía falta e incluso algunas cosas de promoción a las que no se pudo resistir. Al llegar a casa tuve que sacar todas las bolsas del coche para ponerlas en la cocina. Me quedé **hecho polvo** *(exhausted)*.

— **¿En tu casa siempre hacéis la compra los viernes por la noche?**

No. Lo bueno es que ahora el supermercado de al lado de casa está abierto todos los días de la semana hasta las nueve de la noche. Por eso podemos ir a comprar a cualquier hora.

— **¿Prefieres ir a otros tipos de tienda?**

Sí. Por ejemplo hay una frutería cerca de nuestra casa. Dice mi madre que la fruta allí es mucho más barata que en el centro comercial. El dueño es una persona muy simpática y le gusta bromear. Casi siempre nos hace algún regalo, una manzana, una pera o algo así. Tampoco hay que esperar mucho tiempo para que nos sirva.

— **¿Adónde vas a comprarte la ropa?**

Pues depende de lo que busque. Si me hace falta ropa de diario voy al centro comercial de las afueras. Allí venden camisas y pantalones a buen precio. También hay muchas tiendas de ropa. Pero si busco algo especial casi siempre voy a los grandes almacenes del centro de la ciudad.

— **¿Quién hace la compra en tu casa?**

Mi madre, cuando regresa del trabajo. La hace dos o tres veces por semana en un centro comercial. Los otros días si nos hace falta algo voy a la tienda del barrio. Allí venden pan, leche, mantequilla, huevos, jamón y otras cosas.

— **¿Te gusta ir de compras con tus padres?**

Sí, me encanta, sobre todo con mi padre porque casi siempre me compra algo. Algún sábado le acompaño a ir de compras. Por ejemplo, la semana pasada nos fuimos a la pescadería cerca del puerto. Allí tienen puestos de pescado muy fresco que venden a mitad de precio.

— **¿Qué tipo de tienda prefieres?**

Creo que los grandes almacenes son los más interesantes. Hay tantas secciones distintas. Voy primero a la sección de perfumería donde se puede probar los perfumes. Después, subo a la primera planta donde tienen los discos. Casi siempre encuentro a alguna amiga allí y escuchamos juntas nuestros discos favoritos.

Tercera Sección

CONTESTA LAS SIGUIENTES PREGUNTAS

1. ¿Te gusta salir de compras con tus padres?

_____

_____

2. ¿Quién hace la compra normalmente en tu casa?

_____

_____

3. ¿Qué tipo de tiendas hay en tu barrio?

_____

_____

4. ¿Compran mucha fruta en tu casa ?

_____

_____

5. ¿Dónde se puede comprar pan y tartas de manzana?

_____

_____

6. ¿Con qué frecuencia vas a las tiendas?

_____

_____

7. ¿Prefieres ir a las tiendas pequeñas o a los grandes almacenes?
   ¿Por qué?

_____

_____

8. ¿Adónde irías si quisieras comprar un regalo especial para alguien?

_____

_____

9. ¿Vas muchas veces a las librerías?

_____

_____

10. ¿Cuál es tu tienda favorita?

_____

_____

Cuarta Sección

☞ **A. ESCRIBE ABAJO 12 PALABRAS O EXPRESIONES DE ESTA UNIDAD QUE TÚ CONSIDERAS IMPORTANTES DE RECORDAR:**

1.. 2..

3.. 4..

5.. 6..

7.. 8..

9.. 10..

11.. 12..

B. ESCRIBE AL LADO EQUIVALENTES EN ESPAÑOL DE ESTAS EXPRESIONES:

1. I like to go shopping ....

2. There is a small shop near my house ....

3. My dad buys fresh fish every Saturday ....

4. All the vegetables are cheaper there ....

5. They sell everything ....

6. My mum prefers to buy ....

7. The owner of the corner shop ....

8. I go to the big stores ....

9. During the January sales ....

10. Half the normal price ....

☞ **C. COMPLETA LAS SIGUIENTES FRASES CON LA PALABRA ADECUADA:**

El viernes pasado salí _ _ compras con mis padres. Fuimos al _ _ _ _ _ _

comercial que está situado no muy lejos de _ _ _ _ _ _ _ casa. Mientras mi

_ _ _ _ _ se fue a comprar _ _ _ en la panadería _ _ padre y yo nos acercamos

a la _ _ _ _ _ _ _ _ _ _. Había chuletas de cerdo muy buenas y mi padre pidió

un kilo y medio. También queríamos _ _ _ _ _ _ _ pescado pero había demasiada

_ _ _ _ _ haciendo cola y no podíamos esperar.

14. Las comidas y la alimentación

Primera Sección

1. ¿Qué tomas para el desayuno?

Para el desayuno tomo un zumo de naranja.
cereales.
tostadas con mantequilla
y mermelada.
huevos fritos con jamón..
un huevo duro.
un huevo pasado por agua.

2. ¿Te gusta comer bocadillos?

Durante la semana como bocadillos de jamón.
atún.
ensalada.
tomate.
queso.

3. ¿Para el almuerzo qué tomas normalmente?

Los fines de semana para el almuerzo como –
sopa.
muchas verduras.
una tortilla de champiñones.
una ensalada mixta.
espaguetis.

4. ¿Qué te gusta comer de postre?

De postre siempre hay fruta.
flan.
yogur.
helados.
una tarta de manzana.

5. ¿Comes mucha fruta?

- Sí. Según mi madre hay que tomar por lo menos una pieza de fruta fresca al día.
- Es muy buena para la **salud** *(health)*.

6. ¿Tienes mucha hambre cuando vuelves a casa después del colegio?

Al volver del colegio estoy muerto de hambre y lo primero que hago es merendar.

7. ¿Qué tomas para la merienda?

Meriendo un bocadillo de queso.
un pastelito.
unas galletas con chocolate caliente.

8. ¿Qué se bebe en tu casa con las comidas?

En nuestra casa bebemos –

leche fría	sidra	té o café
refrescos	cerveza	agua con gas
zumo natural	vino	agua sin gas

Mis padres toman bebidas alcohólicas.

9. ¿A qué hora cenas?

Cenamos a eso de las siete cuando mi padre vuelve del trabajo. Es la comida principal del día para mi familia y comemos todos juntos.

10. ¿Qué cenaste anoche?

Cené pescado con patatas fritas.
filete de ternera con zanahorias.
pollo con arroz.
una pizza.
salchicas con huevo y **alubias** *(beans)*.

11. ¿Qué tipo de comida prefieres?

Prefiero comer carne.
pescado.
las comidas chinas.
la comida vegetariana.

12. ¿Sabes guisar?

• Sí. Pero no guiso mucho.

• Hago una tortilla de tomates y jamón.

• Mi madre tiene un montón de libros de recetas. A veces saco uno para preparar algo delicioso.

13. ¿Sales a veces a comer con tus padres?

• Salimos muy a menudo a comer en un restaurante

chino	indio
francés	italiano

• Cuando es el cumpleaños de alguien en mi familia siempre lo celebramos afuera, en un buen restaurante.

• De vez en cuando salgo con mis amigos.

14. ¿Te gusta comer al aire libre?

- Cuando éramos niños solíamos hacer una merienda en el campo en el verano.

- Ahora tenemos la barbacoa afuera y me encanta comer carne a la brasa.

15. ¿Crees que los jóvenes comen demasiada comida rápida?

- Sí. Es verdad. Hoy día se come mucha comida rápida –

  hamburguesas
  patatas fritas
  refrescos de cola

- No son sólo los jóvenes los que comen esa alimentación.

16. ¿Es importante seguir un régimen equilibrado?

Claro que sí. Para la salud y para mantenerse en forma hay que comer bien. Los cardiólogos siempre **advierten del** *(warn of the)* riesgo del consumo excesivo de grasas animales.

A mi parecer sería mejor también reducir el consumo de sal.

17. ¿Crees que las chicas se preocupan demasiado por la línea?

- Quizás. Yo, por ejemplo, me preocupo bastante por la línea.

- Quiero perder peso y por eso estoy a dieta.

- La delgadez es un tema muy importante entre las chicas.

- Lo malo es que puede conducir a casos extremos como la anorexia y la bulimia.

18. ¿Has probado la comida española?

He probado varios platos españoles. El que más me gusta es:

el gazpacho	– una sopa de verduras que se toma fría. Está riquísima.
la tortilla española	– está hecha de huevos, patatas, cebollas y aceite de oliva.
la paella	– es el arroz amarillo con mariscos, pescado, trocitos de carne o pollo. Está muy rica.

Segunda Sección

ESCUCHA ESTAS CONVERSACIONES EN LA CINTA

– **¿Desayunas mucho antes de salir para el colegio?**

Sí. En mi casa nos hemos acostumbrado a desayunar bastante bien por la mañana. Mis padres dicen que el desayuno es la comida más importante del día. Tomamos primero zumo de naranja y luego cereales. Después también me gusta tomar huevos revueltos con tostadas.

– **¿Cuál es la comida principal del día en tu casa?**

Es la cena. Al mediodía sólo como bocadillos y algo de fruta. A la hora de cenar todos estamos en casa y nos gusta comer bien.

– **¿Cuál es tu plato preferido?**

Es difícil de decir porque me gusta casi todo. Aunque prefiero la comida italiana, las pizzas y los espaguetis. También tengo debilidad por los postres y mi madre nos prepara algunos riquísimos.

– **¿Qué piensas de la comida española?**

El año pasado fui por primera vez a España y pude probar cada día algo distinto. ¡Qué variedad de verduras! El plato que más me gustó fue el gazpacho que es una sopa que se sirve fría. Era tan sabrosa. También comí mucho pescado, calamares, gambas, atún, merluza y unas tapas de pulpo muy ricas.

– **¿Qué bebéis en tu casa con las comidas?**

Mi hermano y yo casi siempre bebemos agua mineral, y a mis padres también les gusta el agua. Sin embargo, los fines de semana mi padre casi siempre abre una botella de vino tinto o vino blanco y nos echa un poco en nuestros vasos.

– **¿Cuál es tu plato favorito?**

Prefiero comer pollo o pescado con verduras o ensalada mixta. De postre suelo tomar fruta fresca porque acabo de empezar una dieta bastante estricta y sólo como los alimentos que tienen un bajo contenido en calorías.

– **¿Crees que las chicas de hoy día se preocupan mucho por la línea?**

Sí. Casi todas mis amigas están a dieta La delgadez es muy importante para nosotras. Pero unos chicos que conozco también se preocupan por mantenerse en forma. Por eso van al gimnasio muy a menudo.

– **¿Vas a comer en restaurantes de comida rápida?**

De vez en cuando pero cada vez menos. Sólo puedes pedir una hamburguesa con patatas fritas. Esos alimentos engordan mucho y te dejan con sensación de hambre.

Tercera Sección

CONTESTA LAS SIGUIENTES PREGUNTAS

1. ¿Qué tomas normalmente para desayunar?

_____

_____

2. ¿Al mediodía comes algo fuerte?

_____

_____

3. ¿Eres muy goloso/a?

_____

_____

4. ¿Cuál es tu plato preferido?

_____

_____

5. ¿Me podrías describir algún plato típico irlandés?

_____

_____

6. ¿Se come mucha fruta en tu casa?

_____

_____

7. ¿Qué les gusta beber a tus padres con la cena?

_____

_____

8. ¿Qué opinas de la comida rápida?

_____

_____

9. ¿Has probado alguna vez un plato español? ¿Cómo era?

_____

_____

10. ¿Crees que hay mucha diferencia entre la comida española y la de Irlanda?

_____

_____

Cuarta Sección

☞ **A. ESCRIBE ABAJO 12 PALABRAS O EXPRESIONES DE ESTA UNIDAD QUE TÚ CONSIDERAS IMPORTANTES DE RECORDAR:**

1.. 2..

3.. 4..

5.. 6..

7.. 8..

9.. 10..

11.. 12..

B. ESCRIBE EL EQUIVALENTE EN ESPAÑOL DE ESTAS EXPRESIONES:

1. I have a light breakfast ....

2. I usually take orange juice and toast ....

3. My mother prepares ham sandwiches for me...

4. My sister always drinks cold milk...

5. My parents open a bottle of red wine ....

6. Fruit is very good for your health...

7. I have some biscuits for a snack ....

8. I prefer chicken and vegetables ....

9. My favourite dish is...

10. I have never tried Spanish omelette ....

☞ **C. COMPLETA LAS SIGUIENTES FRASES CON LA PALABRA ADECUADA:**

Por la mañana no desayuno mucho. Sólo _ _ _ _ zumo de naranja y algunas

_ _ _ _ _ _ _ _ _. Al mediodía cojo mis _ _ _ _ _ _ _ _ _ _ _ de jamón y los como

en el patio. Al _ _ _ _ _ _ del colegio tomo la merienda con mis dos hermanos.

La cena es la _ _ _ _ _ _ principal del día para mi familia. Por la noche prefiero

cenar pollo con patatas fritas. De postre casi _ _ _ _ _ _ _ _ tomo fruta. Es muy

_ _ _ _ _ para la salud.

15. El ocio – los pasatiempos

Primera Sección

1. ¿Cuál es tu pasatiempo preferido?

Mi distracción preferida es

la lectura	la pesca
el dibujo	la música
la pintura	el deporte
la fotografía	la natación

2. ¿Cómo sueles pasar tu tiempo libre?

Durante mis ratos libres **suelo** (*I usually*):

leer mucho –

Me entretengo mucho leyendo una buena novela.
Devoro una novela entera en muy pocos días.
Leo revistas y periódicos.
Antes me encantaba leer **tebeos** (*comics*).
En el colegio tenemos que leer novelas, poemas, obras de teatro.

ir de pesca –

Salgo de pesca con mi padre.
Como regalo de cumpleaños mis padres me regalaron una caña de pescar.
A veces alquilamos una barca para pescar en el mar.
Si no, vamos de pesca a un río en las montañas.
Una vez pesqué una trucha enorme.
Lo malo es que puedes esperar mucho tiempo sentad**o/a** en la orilla sin que ningún pez **pique el anzuelo**.
(swallow the bait)

dibujar o **pintar** –

El dibujo me encanta.
Paso horas enteras dibujando retratos de caras interesantes que veo.
Prefiero pintar paisajes al óleo **sobre lienzo** (*on canvas*).

montar a caballo – Voy al campo los fines de semana.

El Español Bien Hablado

(contd.)

hacer una excursión en **bicicleta todo terreno**.
(mountain bike)

sacar fotos – Siempre salgo con mi máquina fotográfica.
Saco fotos siempre y cuando pueda.
Tengo unas fotos maravillosas de **fut bolistas** famosos.
Mis padres me regalaron mi máquina cuando cumplí dieciocho años.

3. ¿Tienes otros pasatiempos?

También me encanta:

coleccionar cosas – monedas de otros países.
muñecas.
tarjetas telefónicas.
sellos de todos los países del mundo.

modelar con arcilla – con un molde.

construir maquetas – Empecé muy joven.
Ahora debo tener unas doscientas maquetas de avión.
Las guardo en un armario en mi dormitorio.

ir al club juvenil – Hay un montón de actividade allí.
Voy con unos amigos míos.
unas amigas mías.
Nunca nos aburrimos.

salir al cine/al teatro/a un concierto.

4. ¿Practicas mucho deporte?

- Soy muy aficionado al deporte.
- **Hago** mucho deporte – Me encantan los deportes de todo tipo.
- Soy **socio** *(a member)* de un club deportivo.
- Casi todos los viernes voy a la bolera con mis amigos – juego a los bolos.

Juego al billar – Hay una sala de billar en mi barrio.
Pasamos el sábado por la mañana jugando allí.

Me gusta nadar – La natación es muy buena para la salud.
Cuando era más joven iba a clases de natación todos los sábados.
Por eso sé nadar muy bien.
Hice un cursillo de salvamento y socorrismo.
Trabajé de socorrista el año pasado.

(contd.)

Practico el atletismo.
el ciclismo.
la vela.
los deportes acuáticos.

BUT Hago atletismo.

El atletismo es otro de mis aficiones.

5. ¿Prefieres hacer deporte al aire libre a cubierto?

- En verano casi siempre estoy al aire libre –
me gusta pasear en el parque.
voy de excursión en bicicleta.
- Cuando hace más frío hago entrenamiento con **pesas** *(weights)* en el gimnasio.

6. ¿Has ido alguna vez a esquiar?

El invierno pasado fui a esquiar a los Pirineos.

7. No tienes mucho tiempo este año para practicar deporte, ¿verdad?

Sí. Tiene usted razón. Pero trato de hacer algo de deporte. Es importante descansar/relajarse.

15. (A) LA LECTURA

1. ¿Cómo prefieres pasar tus ratos libres? Soy muy aficionado a la lectura.

2. ¿Qué género de lectura te gusta más? Me interesan más las novelas de ciencia-ficción.
de amor.
históricas.
divertidas.
policíacas.

Prefiero las novelas que tratan de un crimen.
una aventura.
un tema amoroso.

Me entretengo también leyendo obras de teatro.
poesía.
periódicos.
revistas.

3. ¿Qué te gustaba leer cuando eras más joven?

Cuando era pequeño/a me entusiasmaban:
- los **tebeos** *(comics)*.
- los libros de la naturaleza.
- libros que trataban de los planetas.
- **los cuentos de hadas** *(fairy-tales)* como "Blancanieves y los siete enanitos" y "Cenicienta".

4. ¿Cuáles son los libros de literatura
que tenéis que estudiar este año?

Hay ciertos libros de la literatura clásica
señalados *(set)* para el examen de inglés:

(a) La obra de teatro es del dramaturgo Shakespeare. Se llama ....

(b) La novela que estudiamos se llama ....

(c) En la sección de poesía nos concentramos en **los** poem**as** de **los** poet**as** irlandeses y ingleses

....

N.B.
el poeta   **el** poema

5. ¿Dónde transcurre la historia?

• La novela está situada en Inglaterra.
                                    los Estados Unidos.

• **Los sucesos** *(events)* ocurren en España.

6. ¿De qué trata?

El tema principal de la obra es el amor.
                                    el racismo.
                                    la relación entre …
                                    el conflicto entre …

7. ¿Cómo se llama el protagonista?

La heroína   se llama …
El héroe

8. ¿Qué tipo de carácter es?

Es una persona | fuerte | débil
| simpática | desagradable
| comprensiva | **celosa** *(jealous)*
| valiente | cobarde
| buena | mala
| seria | burlona
| indecisa | **emprendedora**
| | *(go-ahead)*

9. ¿Cuéntame lo que pasa?

La historia empieza con …

Al final **nos damos cuenta de que** …
          (we realize that)

Tiene un **desenlace** *(ending)* triste ≠ feliz.

10. ¿Es una buena novela?

Esta novela la encuentro muy aburrida.
                                    emocionante.
                                    trágica.
Siempre lloro en las partes tristes de un libro.

11. ¿A tus padres también les gusta leer?

En nuestra casa leemos todos y tenemos muchas estanterías para libros.

12. ¿Eres socio/a de una biblioteca?

- Sí. Soy socio/a de la biblioteca de mi barrio y voy allí dos o tres veces al mes.
- Con mi tarjeta de biblioteca me dejan sacar hasta tres libros a la vez.

13. ¿Te compras muchos libros?

- Cuando recibo **un vale** *(token)* para comprar libros voy en seguida a la librería.
- A veces voy a una librería a comprar libros **de ocasión** *(second-hand).*

15. (B) EL DIBUJO Y LA PINTURA

1. ¿Estudias el arte para el Leaving?

- Sí. El arte es mi asignatura favorita en el colegio.
- Paso casi todo mi tiempo libre dibujando o pintando.
- Aprovecho cualquier momento para dibujar aunque sólo sean unas horas.

2. ¿Siempre te ha gustado pintar y dibujar? Sí. Desde muy pequeño/a me ha interesado el arte.

3. ¿Necesitas muchos materiales para este hobby?

La verdad es que sí. Para este pasatiempo me hacen falta muchos materiales:

> los lápices
> el **caballete** *(easel)*
> el papel especial
> los pinceles
> el **lienzo** *(canvas)*
> los óleos
> las **acuarelas** *(water-colours)*

Gasto mucho dinero comprándolos en las tiendas de arte.

4. ¿Qué temas tratas en tus pinturas?

Los temas que trato son

> paisajes de invierno.
> marinas.
> retratos y figuras.
> **bodegones**.
> *(still-life paintings)*

Hago también cuadros y **bosquezos** *(sketches)* de mi familia. Prefiero pintar

> al óleo.
> al acuarela.
> con acuarelas.
> a **la cera** *(wax).*

5. **Me imagino que es un pasatiempo muy relajante, ¿verdad ?**

Sí. Es un pasatiempo perfecto para poder olvidarse completamente de todas las preocupaciones de este año.

6. **¿Has ido alguna vez a la Galería Nacional?**

- Claro que sí. Me encanta ir a ver las exposiciones que ponen en la Galería Nacional.
- Lo maravilloso es que puedes meterte allí a pintar o dibujar **si te da la gana** *(if you feel like it).*

7. **¿Conoces los museos famosos de Madrid y de París?**

- Sí. Hace dos años tuve la oportunidad de ir a Madrid y aproveché mi visita para ir al Museo del Prado.
- Allí se ven cuadros de todos los pintores famosos como Goya, El Greco, y Velázquez.
- En el Centro de Arte Reina Sofia me conmovió mucho la obra impresionante de Picasso – El Guernica. Es un cuadro enorme que muestra todo el sufrimiento del pueblo de Guernica al ser bombardeado por los alemanes.
- También he visto las obras maravillosas del Museo del Louvre en París. Allí se pueden ver cuadros de pintores como Goya y los Impresionistas.

8. **¿Piensas hacer algo relacionado con la pintura después de terminar al colegio?**

Quisiera seguir mis estudios de arte el año que viene en el colegio de Bellas Artes.

15. (C) LA FOTOGRAFÍA

1. **¿Estás interesado en la fotografía?**

- Sí. Me encanta la fotografía.
- Creo que mi interés por la fotografía **lo he heredado** de mi padre. *(I inherited it)*
- Con las fotos me parece que se pueden guardar los recuerdos aún más vivos.

2. **¿Tienes una buena máquina fotográfica?**

Hace dos años mis padres me regalaron una buena máquina fotográfica de la mejor marca para Navidad.

Antes, solía sacar fotos con una máquina **desechable** *(disposable).*

3. ¿De qué cosas te gusta más sacar fotos?

Lo que más me interesa es sacar fotos –

> de mi familia.
> de mi perro.
> de lugares extranjeros.
> durante las vacaciones.

4. ¿Tienes muchas fotos?

- Tengo un montón de fotos. Las que prefiero las hago ampliar y después **las enmarco** (*I frame them*).
- Escribo la fecha y el lugar por detrás de la foto.

5. ¿Dónde las guardas?

- Creo que es importante guardarlas en un álbum.
- Si no, es muy fácil perderlas o **estropearlas**.
  (*damage them*)
- Paso mucho tiempo mirando mis álbumes.

6. ¿Tienes que gastar mucho dinero para este pasatiempo?

La verdad es que sí. Es un pasatiempo bastante caro porque hay que comprar los **carretes** (*films*) y pagar el revelado.

7. ¿Hay alguna foto que prefieres sobre todas las demás?

Mi fot**o** preferid**a** tiene que ser la de –

> un encuentro que tuve con un futbolista famoso.
> mi tercer fiesta de cumpleaños.
> la boda de mi tía cuando yo era **la damade honor** (*bridesmaid*).
> un día al zoo cuando yo daba de comer a los monos. Esa foto **se hizo** en otoño.
> (*was taken*)

8. ¿Eres socio de algún club de fotografía?

- No. Es una lástima. En mi colegio no hay tanto interés. Pero el año que viene, si voy a la facultad me gustaría hacerme socio del club de fotografía.
- Entonces podré revelar mis propias fotos.

15. (D) LA PESCA

 Note the IMPERFECT TENSE to convey what you **used to do**.

1. ¿Cuál era tu pasatiempo preferido cuando eras más pequeño?

Desde muy pequeño/a mi pasatiempo favorito ha sido la pesca.

2. ¿Con quién ibas a pescar?

Solía ir de pesca todos los sábados con mi padre y algunos amigos.

3. ¿Pasabas el día entero a orillas del río?

Salíamos a primera hora y no **regresábamos** hasta el anochecer.

4. ¿Qué materiales teníais que llevar?

Teníamos que llevar todos los materiales:

las cañas de pescar	**el cebo** *(bait)*
una cesta grande	botas de goma
un paraguas enorme	un impermeable

5. ¿Cómo os preparabais para la pesca?

Lo primero que **hacíamos** al llegar a la orilla del río **era** poner el cebo en el **anzuelo** *(hook)*.

6. ¿Qué tipo de peces había en ese río?

Pescábamos peces como trucha
caballa *(mackerel)*

7. Es un pasatiempo que requiere mucho tiempo, ¿verdad?

Sí. Es verdad y hay que tener mucha paciencia también. Cuando íbamos allí **teníamos** que esperar muy callados **hasta que** algún pez pic**ara** el anzuelo.
IMPERFECT SUBJUNCTIVE

8. ¿Siempre cogías algo?

- Casi siempre **volvíamos**

  cargados de peces.
  sin haber cogido ningún pez.

- Mi madre **se ponía** contenta cuando **llegábamos** a casa con el pescado y lo cocinaba para la cena.

- A veces **hacíamos** un fuego en el campo para cocinar el pescado allí.

15. (E) LOS SELLOS

1. ¿Cómo te gustaba pasar tu tiempo libre cuando eras pequeño/a?

- **Me divertía** mucho coleccionando sellos.

- Empecé a coleccionarlos cuando **tenía** unos siete años.

- Cuando **era** más joven **pasaba** mucho tiempo coleccionando sellos.

2. ¿Qué tipos de sellos te gustaban más?

- Los que más **me interesaban eran** los sellos de Australia y de América Latina.

- La mayoría **eran** de flores y de animales.
  Para mí **eran** los sellos más bonitos del mundo.

3. ¿Y tus amigos tenían el mismo interés?

- Unos amigos míos/Unas amigas mías **se entusiasmaban** también con los sellos y **solíamos** cambiarlos entre nosotros/nosotras.

- Cuando estuve en Madrid **solía** ir a la Plaza Mayor todos los domingos por la mañana.

- Allí **había** muchísimos puestos de vendedores de sellos y de monedas antiguas.

- Me encantaba pasar horas y horas allí mirando y comprando sellos interesantes.

4. ¿Qué haces con todos tus sellos?

Tengo álbumes llenos de sellos de todos los países del mundo.

5. ¿Tus padres te han dado este interés por los sellos?

Creo que me interesa tanto la filatelía a causa de un tío mío. El tiene una colección preciosa de unos veinte álbumes y me encanta mirarlos cada vez que voy a su casa.

6. ¿De dónde vienen los sellos?

Se venden los sellos en **sobres** *(envelopes)* según el tema, o sea, de países.
animales.
flores.

- Cuando llega una carta del extranjero siempre miro primero el sello y lo despego al vapor.

- Todos mis parientes me ayudan con mi colección.

- Por ejemplo cuando van al extranjero siempre envían sus cartas o tarjetas con sellos de muchos colores.

Segunda Sección

ESCUCHA ESTAS CONVERSACIONES EN LA CINTA

– **¿Qué sueles hacer en tu tiempo libre?**

Voy al club de jóvenes los domingos por la noche.

– **¿Qué se puede hacer ahí?**

Hay de todo. Se practican muchos deportes y también tenemos una sala grande para juegos distintos. Por ejemplo, se puede jugar a los dardos, al billar o al ajedrez.

– **¿Tienes que pagar entrada?**

Sí, pagamos veinte peniques al llegar y después tenemos el derecho al uso de todas las facilidades.

– **¿Va mucha gente joven?**

Depende, durante las vacaciones siempre somos muchos, pero otras veces no hay nadie. Muchos dejan sus deberes para el domingo y por eso no tienen tiempo de salir.

– **¿Crees que es importante tener un pasatiempo?**

Sí, sobre todo este año, debido al gran esfuerzo que requiere el Leaving. Si no pudiera olvidarme de los estudios me volvería loco. Me siento más relajado y con más ganas de estudiar después de haber hecho algún deporte.

– **¿Cómo sueles pasar tu tiempo libre?**

Los fines de semana me encanta hacer cosas de cerámica.

– **¿Dónde aprendiste?**

Hace dos años durante el verano me matriculé en un curso de verano en la escuela de arte.

– **¿Qué tipo de cosas haces?**

Prefiero hacer jarros pequeños y platos. Después los pinto. Acabo de terminar un juego de té precioso.

– **Necesitas mucho espacio para este pasatiempo, ¿no?**

Sí que se necesita. Mis padres me han ayudado mucho. Tengo una caseta al fondo del jardín donde guardo la arcilla y el torno. Lo único que no tengo es el horno. Pero una amiga de mi madre tiene uno y siempre me deja cocer mis jarros en su horno.

– **¿Es éste un pasatiempo que cuesta mucho dinero?**

Sí, ése es el problema. Para mi cumpleaños mis amigos y mis parientes siempre me regalan cosas relacionadas con la arcilla, o me dan dinero. Ahora estoy ahorrando para comprarme mi propio horno.

– **¿Qué haces con todos los platos y jarros que tienes?**

La mayoría los guardo en casa. A veces en Navidad regalo algunas cosas a mis amigas. Y de vez en cuando vendo algunos.

Tercera Sección

CONTESTA LAS SIGUIENTES PREGUNTAS

1. ¿Qué te gusta hacer en tus ratos libres?

_____

_____

2. ¿Te gusta leer?

_____

_____

3. ¿De qué trataba el último libro que leíste?

_____

_____

4. ¿Prefieres leer obras de teatro o novelas?

_____

_____

5. ¿Sabes tocar algún instrumento?

_____

_____

6. ¿Cuánto tiempo llevas aprendiendo a tocarlo?

_____

_____

7. ¿Te gusta más estar al aire libre o adentro durante tu tiempo libre?

_____

_____

8. ¿Eres socio de algún club deportivo?

_____

_____

9. ¿Cómo te diviertes los sábados por la tarde?

_____

_____

10. ¿Te interesa coleccionar cosas?

_____

_____

Cuarta Sección

  A. ESCRIBE ABAJO 12 PALABRAS O EXPRESIONES DE ESTA UNIDAD QUE TÚ CONSIDERAS IMPORTANTES DE RECORDAR:

1.. 2..

3.. 4..

5.. 6..

7.. 8..

9.. 10..

11.. 12..

B. ESCRIBE EL EQUIVALENTE EN ESPAÑOL DE ESTAS EXPRESIONES:

1. During my free time ....

2. I have just started to play the guitar ....

3. I enjoy reading historical novels ....

4. I spend hours painting landscapes ....

5. I take a lot of photos when I'm on holidays ....

6. I'm interested in music ....

7. I used to go fishing when I was younger ....

8. My friends and I play a lot of sport ....

9. I collect foreign coins ....

10. In summer I do a lot of cycling ....

  C. COMPLETA LAS SIGUIENTES FRASES CON LA PALABRA ADECUADA:

Hago muchas cosas durante mis _ _ _ _ _ libres. Cada viernes voy a la biblioteca

a sacar un _ _ _ _ _. Después paso _ _ _ _ _ enteras en mi dormitorio leyéndolo.

Me encantan las _ _ _ _ _ _ _ románticas e intento leerlas de un tirón. Otro de

mis pasatiempos es la fotografía. Me divierto mucho sacando _ _ _ _ _ y he

llenado por lo menos diez álbumes. La foto que más me _ _ _ _ _ es la de un

futbolista argentino.

16. Los deportes

Primera Sección

1. **¿Eres muy deportista?**

    Sí. **Hago** mucho deporte. *(I play + SPORT)*
        BUT
    Juego al tenis. *(I play + NAME of Sport)*

- Soy muy aficionad**o/a** al deporte.
- Tengo mucha afición

- Soy bastante deportist**a**. (MASC.+ FEM.)

- Me encantan los deportes de todo tipo.

    No. No me | gusta | nada el deporte.
              | interesa |

- No soy muy deportist**a**.

- Sólo me interesan los grandes acontecimientos deportivos como los Juegos Olímpicos y la Copa Mundial.

- Prefiero ser espectador.

2. **¿Perteneces a algún equipo?**

En el colegio pertenezco a un equipo de:

    fútbol
    baloncesto
    tenis
    natación
    rugby

Se practican muchos deportes en mi colegio.
Llevo cinco años jugando al rugby.

Fuera del colegio | soy socio de un club deportivo.
               | no pertenezco a ningún equipo deportivo.

3. **¿Cuántas veces a la semana tienes que entrenarte?**

Nos entrenamos | todos los días.
            | hasta tres horas diarias.

4. ¿Haces deporte todos los días?

Sólo juego **al** fútbol dos **o** *(or)* tres veces a la semana.
al baloncesto los miércoles por la tarde.
al tenis los sábados por la mañana.
al rugby a la hora de comer.
al golf durante las vacaciones.

5. ¿Adónde vas para practicar tu deporte favorito?

Los fines de semana voy al polideportivo.
al gimnasio.
al estadio.
a la piscina.
al campo de golf.

6. ¿Juegas bien al golf?

No, juego muy bien pero me encanta.

7. ¿Qué deportes haces en verano?

En verano suelo jugar al tenis.
hacer atletismo.
hacer footing en el parque.
practicar la natación.

8. ¿Has ido alguna vez a esquiar?

El invierno pasado fui a una estación de esquí en los Pirineos.

9. ¿Cuál es tu deporte preferido?

Me encantan esquiar   - el esquí
montar a caballo   - la equitación
nadar   - la natación
salir en bicicleta   - el ciclismo
salir de paseo en barco   - la vela
correr en el maratón   - el footing
     - el atletismo

Me encantan los deportes acuáticos.
de invierno.
de equipo.

• La vela y el esquí son mis actividades preferidas.

• Saco mi barco todos los sábados.

• Salgo a hacer vela.

10. ¿Te gusta montar a caballo?

Sí. Hago equitación en el campo.
el monte.

11. ¿Quién es tu deportista favorito?

Mi deportista favorito es el tenista …
el futbolista …
el atleta …
el jugador de golf …

12. ¿Eres hincha de algún equipo de fútbol?

El Real Madrid es mi equipo favorito de fútbol.

13. ¿Crees que es importante que los jóvenes practiquen algún deporte?

- Sí. Después del **agobio** *(pressure)* de la rutina diaria hace falta **desahogarse** *(to relax)*.

- El deporte ayuda mucho para aliviar el agobio.

14. ¿Por qué el deporte se ha hecho tan importante?

- Creo que el deporte se ha hecho tan importante en el mundo de hoy porque muchas personas ganan mucho dinero por medio del deporte.

- Lo malo es que el dinero y las grandes empresas controlan el mundo del deporte.

- Casi todos los deportistas a nivel profesional ganan muchísimo dinero.

15. ¿Qué piensas de los deportistas que toman drogas?

- Es verdad que hoy en día el deporte está relacionado muchas veces con el mundo de la droga.

- Es una lástima que haya tantos deportistas que tomen drogas para mejorar sus posibilidades de ganar.

16. ¿Cómo influye la política en el deporte?

Hay los que mezclan el deporte en la política. Por ejemplo, se aprovechan de los grandes acontecimientos deportivos para atraer la atención del mundo a ciertos problemas políticos que existen.

Segunda Sección

ESCUCHA ESTAS CONVERSACIONES EN LA CINTA

– **¿Te gustan los deportes?**

Sí. Soy muy deportista pero la verdad es que no hago tanto deporte ahora a causa de mis estudios.

– **¿Qué deporte prefieres?**

Mi deporte preferido es el fútbol. Pero sólo juego el sábado por la mañana. Soy miembro de un equipo del barrio y todos los fines de semana nuestro entrenador organiza un partido con otro equipo.

– **¿Eres un buen jugador de fútbol?**

A veces juego bien. El sábado pasado, por ejemplo, jugamos con un equipo muy bueno y fui yo el que marcó los dos goles de mi equipo. El resultado final fue de empate a dos.

– **¿Ha ganado tu equipo alguna vez un campeonato o un torneo?**

Sí, esta última temporada llegamos a la final y nuestro club ganó un trofeo precioso. A cada jugador también nos dieron una medalla de plata y estamos muy orgullosos.

– **¿Cuál es tú equipo favorito?**

Soy un aficionado **acérrimo** *(staunch)* del Atlético de Madrid. Hace dos años hice un intercambio con un chico de Madrid y fuimos al estadio Vicente Calderón a verlos jugar. Desde entonces sigo de cerca las azañas de mis ídolos y mi amigo español me envía el periódico **Marca** cada vez que hay un artículo sobre el equipo.

– **María, ¿te gustan los deportes?**

Sí, soy muy deportista. Voy a la piscina dos o tres veces a la semana y también voy a un gimnasio que queda cerca de mi casa.

– **¿Y qué haces allí?**

Se pueden hacer muchas cosas. Tienen todo tipo de máquinas para hacer ejercicio. A mí, lo que más me gusta es hacer ciclismo. Hay una de esas bicicletas que puedes progamar para diferentes niveles de dificultad.

– **¿No te cansas después de tanto ejercicio?**

Sí, un poco. Pero cuando termino me ducho y a veces tomo una sauna. Después me siento muy relajada.

– **¿Crees que el deporte es importante para los jóvenes?**

No sólo para los jóvenes. Todo el mundo tiene que hacer algo para mantenerse en forma. La mayoría de los ciudadanos tienen un trabajo sedentario y por eso es importante que hagan algo de deporte.

– **¿Entonces tus padres también son deportistas, ¿no?**

Sí. Los dos se divierten mucho jugando al tenis. Y mi padre es el capitán del club. Juegan por lo menos tres veces a la semana y aún más durante las vacaciones.

Tercera Sección

CONTESTA LAS SIGUIENTES PREGUNTAS

1. ¿Eres muy aficionado/a a los deportes?

_____

_____

2. ¿Qué deportes se practican en tu colegio?

_____

_____

3. ¿Qué deporte prefieres?

_____

_____

4. ¿Desde cuándo practicas este deporte?

_____

_____

5. ¿Prefieres hacer un deporte de equipo o un deporte individual?

_____

_____

6. ¿Cuáles son las ventajas de un deporte de equipo/individual?

_____

_____

7. ¿Perteneces a algún club deportivo?

_____

_____

8. ¿Has visto alguna vez a un deportista famoso? Describe la situación.

_____

_____

9. ¿Crees que es importante que los jóvenes de tu edad hagan deporte?

_____

_____

10. ¿Qué instalaciones deportivas hay en tu barrio?

_____

_____

Cuarta Sección

☞ **A.** **ESCRIBE ABAJO 12 PALABRAS O EXPRESIONES DE ESTA UNIDAD QUE TÚ CONSIDERAS IMPORTANTES DE RECORDAR:**

1.. 2...

3.. 4...

5.. 6...

7.. 8...

9.. 10..

11... 12..

B. **ESCRIBE EL EQUIVALENTE EN ESPAÑOL DE ESTAS EXPRESIONES:**

1. I'm very keen on sport...

2. I like to play tennis ....

3. I'm a member of a football team ....

4. We train three times a week ....

5. My friends also enjoy doing exercice..

6. We go to the Sports Centre at the weekend...

7. Outside of school I don't play much sport ....

8. I love swimming ....

9. We usually do athletics in summer...

10. My parents love water sports...

☞ **C.** **COMPLETA LAS SIGUIENTES FRASES CON LA PALABRA ADECUADA:**

A mi me apasionan casi todos los _ _ _ _ _ _ _ _. Juego _ _ tenis en un club no

muy lejos de mi _ _ _ _ .Voy también a la _ _ _ _ _ _ _ a nadar los viernes

_ _ _ la noche. Los sábabos me gusta ver los _ _ _ _ _ _ _ _ _ deportivos en la

televisión. Mi _ _ _ _ _ _ favorito de fútbol es Manchester United y el verano

_ _ _ _ _ _ fui a verlos jugar. Fue un _ _ _ _ _ _ _ emocionante.

17. La música

Primera Sección

1. **¿Te gusta la música?**

Sí. Me gusta mucho la música rock.
encanta
moderna.
pop.
de los años sesenta.
folklórica.
clásica.

También soy aficionado al jazz. Creo que he heredado mi afición por la música de mi padre.

2. **¿A los jóvenes les gusta el jazz?**

- Sí. Creo que el jazz tiene cada vez mayor presencia en la vida de los jóvenes.
- Hay un festival de jazz en casi todas las grandes ciudades.

3. **¿A tus padres les gusta la música?**

Sí. Sobre todo la música clásica.
Van a menudo a los conciertos en la Sala de Conciertos. ¡Qué aburrido! ¿Verdad?

4. **¿Tienes muchos CDs?**

- Sí. Tengo un montón de CDs y de cassettes.
- Los tengo en una estantería en mi habitación.
- En nuestra casa tenemos una gran variedad de épocas y tendencias musicales.

5. **¿Gastas mucho dinero comprando CDs?**

- Sí. Tristemente cuestan mucho – unas quince libras por CD.
- Ahorro todo el dinero que me regalan y me compro los CDs que quiero.

6. **¿Adónde vas para escuchar música?**

- Lo más normal, la escucho en mi habitación. Tengo mi propio estéreo.
- A veces pongo la radio y la escucho con mis auriculares.
- Si hay un concierto voy con mis amigos. Voy a la discoteca los viernes por la noche.

7. ¿Cómo se llama tu grupo o cantante favorito?

Se llama …
Es un grupo | americano.
cantante | inglés.
| irlandés.

8. ¿Qué instrumentos tocan?

Hay uno que toca la guitarra y otro que toca el piano.

9. ¿Cuántas personas hay en el grupo?

Hay tres miembros en el grupo: | un guitarrista.
| un bajista.
| un cantante.

El guitarrista que **se destaca** *(stands out)* por encima de los demás en la actualidad es …

10. ¿Has ido alguna vez a un concierto de un grupo conocido?

Sí. El verano pasado fui a ver al grupo …
Iniciaron su **gira** *(tour)* europea en Irlanda.

11. ¿La entrada era muy cara?

Sí. Eso era el problema. El billete me costó veintiocho libras.

12. ¿Tus padres te dieron el dinero?

No. Como me enteré **con anticipación** *(in advance)* que iban a venir pude ahorrar mi dinero.

13. ¿Qué tal fue el concierto?

- Fue un espectáculo | maravilloso.
| emocionante.
| inolvidable.
- Los sonidos y el ambiente eran fenomenales.
- El escenario era espectacular.
- Los efectos especiales eran increíbles.

14. ¿Qué tipo de canciones había?

Había de todo – canciones viejas y algunas nuevas.
Cantaron todos sus éxitos.

15. ¿ Tú sabes tocar algún instrumento?

- Sí. Sé tocar el piano y el clarinete.
- Estudié el piano hasta tercer grado.
- Ahora aprendo a tocar la guitarra.
- Llevo dos meses aprendiendo a tocarla. Voy a clases particulares.

Segunda Sección

ESCUCHA ESTAS CONVERSACIONES EN LA CINTA

– **¿Te gusta la música?**

Sí. Durante mis ratos libres me gusta mucho escuchar música. Suelo escucharla en mi habitación porque mis padres no tienen los mismos gustos musicales. Si escucho la radio en la cocina tengo que bajar el volumen porque si no, se enfada mucho mi madre.

– **¿Qué tipo de música prefieres?**

Prefiero la música rock pero también me encanta la música tradicional irlandesa. La encuentro muy interesante.

– **¿Tienes muchos CDs?**

Sí. Debo tener por lo menos cien CDs. La mayoría de mis CDs los he comprado pero casi siempre me regalan CDs por mi cumpleaños.

– **¿Cuál es tu grupo/cantante favorito,?**

Es un grupo irlandés. Se llama U2. Hay un guitarrista, un batería, un bajista y el cantante. Los ritmos de sus canciones son sensacionales.

– **¿Has ido alguna vez a verles?**

No. Nunca les he visto actuar en directo, pero van a tocar aquí en verano. Naturalmente no me voy a perder su actuación.

– **¿Le interesa la música a tu familia?**

Sí. En mi casa a todos nos apasiona la música, sobre todo la de los años sesenta. Mis padres son muy aficionados a los Beatles y a los Rolling Stones. Y yo compro muchos CDs y cintas de música pop.

– **¿Te gusta ver los programas musicales de la televisión?**

No veo mucho la televisión este año pero de vez en cuando veo el canal musical. Hoy en día lo que vale no es sólo la música, sino el que vaya acompañada de un vídeo.

– **¿Ahora qué canción es el número uno?**

Creo que la última canción de Boyzone encabeza la lista de éxitos.

Es el nuevo estreno del grupo más éxitoso en este momento.

– **¿Sabes tocar algún instrumento?**

Sí, en mi familia todos tocamos un instrumento distinto. Yo, por ejemplo, toco el violín bastante bien y mi hermano sabe tocar la batería. Mi padre toca la guitarra y mi madre el piano.

– **¿Os juntáis para dar algún concierto?**

Sí. Pero sólo cuando no están nuestros vecinos. Les volveríamos locos con **una mezcla tan espantosa** (*such a terrible mixture*) de instrumentos y sonidos. Nos divertimos bastante el año pasado durante la Navidad, pues, hicimos un pequeño concierto. Fue muy divertido y todo el mundo participó. Aprovechamos la ausencia de nuestros vecinos durante esas fechas.

Tercera Sección

CONTESTA LAS SIGUIENTES PREGUNTAS

1. ¿Qué piensas de la música moderna?

_____

_____

2. ¿Compras muchos CDs?

_____

_____

3. ¿Dónde prefieres escuchar música?

_____

_____

4. Descríbeme tu grupo favorito.

_____

_____

5. ¿Has ido a algún concierto de música moderna?

_____

_____

6. ¿Había mucha gente allí?

_____

_____

7. ¿Cómo era el ambiente?

_____

_____

8. ¿Te gusta la música que ponen en las discotecas?

_____

_____

9. ¿Sabes tocar algún instrumento?

_____

_____

10. ¿Desde hace cuánto tiempo aprendes a tocarlo?

_____

_____

Cuarta Sección

☞   **A. ESCRIBE ABAJO 12 PALABRAS O EXPRESIONES DE ESTA UNIDAD QUE TÚ CONSIDERAS IMPORTANTES DE RECORDAR:**

1..   2..

3..   4..

5..   6..

7..   8..

9..   10..

11..   12..

B. ESCRIBE EL EQUIVALENTE EN ESPAÑOL DE ESTAS EXPRESIONES:

1. I like all kinds of music ....

2. My parents don't have the same tastes ....

3. I spend a lot of money buying CDs ....

4. My favourite singer is English ....

5. I went to a pop concert two years ago ....

6. It was a marvellous evening ....

7. I had to save all my money to buy a ticket ....

8. I've been learning the guitar for three months ....

9. I play it quite well...

10. I turn my parents mad with the noise ....

☞   **C. COMPLETA LAS SIGUIENTES FRASES CON LA PALABRA ADECUADA:**

Para mí la música _ _ muy importante. Lo primero que hago al volver del colegio

es poner _ _ radio en la cocina. Siempre escucho música mientras meriendo. Los

jueves veo los veinte principales _ _ _ _ _ _ en la televisión. En _ _ _ _

programa se pueden ver todos los grupos más famosos. También _ _ _ _ _ _ _ _ a

tocar la guitarra clásica. Acabo de empezar y por eso la _ _ _ _ bastante _ _ _.

18. Los medios de comunicación y el cine

Primera Sección

18. (A) LA TELEVISIÓN

1. ¿Ves mucha televisión?

Veo la tele | todos los días.
antes de empezar mis deberes.
sólo media hora los días de colegio.
unas dos horas al día.
los viernes por la noche.
cuando me interesa un programa.

En cuanto entro en casa **la enciendo.**
(As soon as)   *(I turn it on)*

2. ¿Qué tipo de programas prefieres?

Me interesan más	los programas	deportivos. de música. de risa.
Me entusiasman	las películas	de guerra. románticas. policíacas. **divertidas.** *(funny)*
Me aburren *(I get bored by)*	los dibujos animados. las telecomedias como ...	
No aguanto *(I can't stand)*	los **culebrones** *(soaps).* los conciertos. los anuncios.	
Me resultan muy aburridos.		
Estoy muy interesado/a en	los documentales. las noticias. las entrevistas.	

- Me parecen muy importantes porque son muy educativos.
- Es importante mantenerse informado de los sucesos que ocurren a diario.
- Suelo ver una serie juvenil cada semana.
- Una de mis series preferidas es ...
- La encuentro muy divertida/realística.

3. **¿Qué día de la semana
    ponen este programa?**

    Lo ponen todas las noches de ocho a ocho y media.

4. **¿Consultas siempre la programación
    antes de encender la tele?**

    No. Enciendo primero y **hago zapping** *(I flick)*
    hasta que encuentro algo que me interese.

5. **¿Apagas la televisión si
    no te interesa el programa?**

    - Lo que hago casi siempre es cambiar de cadena
      para buscar un programa más interesante.

    - A veces me quedo pegad**o/a** al televisor y mis
      padres se enfadan mucho.

6. **¿Cuántas cadenas tienes?**

    - Tenemos todas las principales. Es decir, RTE
      Uno y Dos y las cadenas británicas de la BBC.

    - Además de éstas tenemos varias cadenas de
      televisión por satélite – una emite un servicio de
      información las 24 horas del día y hay otra que se
      dedica exclusivamente a los deportes.

    - Es verdad que los telespectadores en la actualidad
      tienen mucha selección.

7. **¿Hay que abonarse para
    tener este servicio?**

    Para éstas no. Pero existen otras, como la de las
    películas que sólo pueden ser difundidas a hogares
    particulares si se abona uno.

8. **¿Has visto alguna vez
    un programa en español?**

    Sí. A veces veo el Telediario por la noche.
    Es interesante y siempre aprendo cosas nuevas.

9. **¿Tienes vídeo?**

    Sí. Lo usamos mucho. Lo bueno es que podemos
    grabar *(record)* un programa si no estamos en casa
    o si mis padres quieren ver otro programa que ponen
    a la misma hora.

10. **¿Hay un videoclub
    cerca de tu casa?**

    Sí. Casi todos los fines de semana alquilamos un
    vídeo. Puedes quedarte con él una noche pero hay
    que **devolverlo** *(return it)* antes de las ocho y media
    del día siguiente. Lo bueno es que puedes ver las
    últimas películas a precios muy bajos.

18. (B) LA RADIO

1. ¿Te gusta escuchar la radio?

Sí. Tengo mi propia radio.

La pongo | mientras me arreglo por la mañana.
cuando estoy en la cama antes de dormirme.
en la cocina.

2. ¿Qué emisora prefieres?

- Escucho casi siempre las emisoras de música como 98FM.
- De esa manera estoy al corriente de los CDs nuevos que salen **de día en día** *(from day to day)*.
- Escucho los programas de **tertulia** *(chat)*.
- Se aprende mucho sobre las inquietudes de la gente.

3. ¿Crees que la radio tiene alguna ventaja sobre la televisión?

- Sí. Lo bueno es que puedes escucharla mientras haces otra cosa.
- La radio es un medio de expresión para la gente de la calle.
- Hay muchos programas donde la gente puede expresarse y quejarse.
- Otra ventaja es que la puedes oír en cualquier sitio – en el jardín, en el cuarto de baño, en el extranjero – **dondequieras** *(wherever you want)*.

4. ¿Te gusta escuchar la radio cuando te encuentras en otro país?

- Sí. Por supuesto. Siempre me la llevo cuando voy al extranjero.
- He podido comprar unos CDs estupendos que no los hubiera conocido de no haberlos escuchado primero por la radio.
- Es, además, un medio de estar al corriente de lo que pasa.

18. (C) LA PRENSA

1. ¿Lees el periódico todos los días?

- Sí. Cada noche **echo un vistazo** al periódico.
  (glance)
- Sólo leo los titulares de las noticias.
- A mi parecer es importante estar al día de lo que pasa en nuestro país y en el mundo entero.
- Tienes que leer el periódico para **enterarte de** lo que ha pasado.   *(find out about)*

- Creo que la mitad de mi clase no lee diarios.

2. ¿Qué páginas del periódico prefieres leer?

Estoy más interesad**o/a** en –

los artículos sobre el deporte.
las noticias internacionales.
los escándalos políticos o económicos.
las páginas sobre la moda.
las cartas al Director.
los reportajes sobre los conciertos.
los artículos editoriales.

- Para mí las más leídas son las páginas de …

- Los artículos que más me llaman la atención son sobre …

3. ¿Hay algún periodista que prefieres leer?

- Prefiero leer los artículos de …

- Es un periodista que expone sus ideas y valora los acontecimientos desde un punto de vista muy personal.

- Escribe de una manera muy divertida.

4. ¿Por qué crees que los periódicos sensacionalistas son tan populares?

A muchos lectores les gusta el **chismorreo** *(gossip)* sobre la vida de los famosos.

5. ¿Lees también algunas revistas?

Sí. **Me abono a** *(subscribe to)* una revista

semanal/mensual de música.
del corazón.
del motor.
de moda.

18. (D) EL CINE

1. ¿Vas mucho al cine?

Voy al cine dos o tres veces al mes.
sólo cuando echan una película nueva que quiero ver.

2. ¿Con quién vas?

A veces voy con mis padres.
mi mejor amig**o/a**.
mi novi**o/a**.

3. **¿Qué tipo de película prefieres?**

Me gusta ver las películas | de horror.
de amor.
de espionaje.
de intriga.
de aventuras.
de acción.
de risa.
históricas.
de ciencia-ficción

4. **¿Te gustan las novelas adaptadas al cine como …?**

A mi parecer, la versión para la pantalla casi siempre pierde algo.

5. **¿Cuál fue la última película que viste?**

• Fui al estreno de …

6. **¿Qué tal estuvo?**

• Estuvo muy bien. De veras merece la pena verla.

7. **¿De qué se trata?**

• Se trata de un **asesinato** *(murder)*.
    un crimen
    la vida de …

Es una película sobre | la droga y el racismo.
la juventud y la amistad.
el paso del tiempo.
temas sociales.

8. **¿En qué período transcurre?**

La película está **ambientada** *(set)* en los años cincuenta.

9. **¿Dónde se rodó la película?**

La película **se rodó** *(was filmed)* en distintos escenarios de Los Estados Unidos.

10. **¿Cuánto tiempo duró?**

Duró dos horas.

11. **¿Tienes una película preferida?**

• Sí. Se llama …

• Es una comedia musical en la que apenas hay diálogos.

• Es uno de los títulos más taquilleros de los años noventa.

• Es uno de los proyectos más ambiciosos del cine americano.

12. ¿Quién era el protagonista?

El papel principal lo interpretó …
Es un actor   de mucho talento.
   una actriz
- Es una de las mejores estrellas de cine.
- Es una película en la que sobresale la actuación de …

13. ¿Cómo eran los actores secundarios?

La actriz … tenía un papel destacado.
… es un actor prometedor.

14. ¿Prefieres ver una película en la pequeña pantalla o ir a a verla en el cine?

Me encanta el ambiente del cine con la pantalla grande. En la oscuridad del cine te olvidas de todos los problemas de **la vida cotidiana** *(everyday life)*.

15. ¿Has visto algunas películas españolas?

- Sí. A veces las ponen en la televisión.
  Las echan con subtítulos. Así que es más fácil saber de qué se tratan.

- También nuestra profesora de español nos ha dejado ver algunas en clase.

- En España casi todas las películas extranjeras están **dobladas** *(dubbed)*.
  Este doblaje lo encuentro muy molesto.

16. ¿Te acuerdas del nombre de alguna película española?

Sí. Me acuerdo de varias:

Como Agua Para Chocolate, dirigido por Alfonso Arus.
El Espíritu de la Colmena, por el cineasta Victor Erice.
El Jardín de las Delicias, dirigido por Carlos Saura.
Mujeres al Borde de un Ataque de Nervios, por Pedro Almodóvar.
El Encanto Discreto de la Burguesía, de Luis Buñuel.
También vi la película mexicana *El Mariachi* de Roberto Rodriguez.

17. ¿Sabes cómo se traduce al español alguna película de habla inglesa?

Lo que el Viento Llevó	*Gone with the Wind*
Fiebre del Sábado Noche	*Saturday Night Fever*
Tres Solteros y un Biberón	*Three Men and a Baby*
El profesor Chiflado	*The Nutty Professor*
interpretado por Jerry Lewis	
Regreso al Futuro	*Back to the Future*
Tiburón	*Jaws*
El Padrino	*The Godfather*
Ciento y un Dálmata	*101 Dalmatians*
Con Faldas y a lo Loco	*Some like it Hot*

Segunda Sección

ESCUCHA ESTAS CONVERSACIONES EN LA CINTA

— **¿Te gusta ver la televisión?**

Sí, la veo un poco todos los días. Pero la veo mucho más los fines de semana – que es cuando ponen los programas que a mí me interesan.

— **¿Qué programas te gustan más?**

Los sábados me entretengo con los programas de deportes. Y los martes dan una serie que se llama "Urgencias" que nunca me la pierdo. Acaba de empezar su segunda temporada.

— **¿De qué trata?**

Trata de la vida cotidiana en un hospital. Examina la responsabilidad médica y nos muestra las negligencias que suceden de vez en cuando. Vemos la vida de los médicos, los cirujanos y los pacientes. La verdad es que yo la encuentro fascinante y emocionante.

— **¿Les gusta también esta serie a tus padres?**

Sí, un poco. Pero creo que prefieren ver las noticias y los programas de debate como "Preguntas y Respuestas".

— **¿Y escuchas la radio a veces?**

Sí, mucho. La pongo siempre que estoy en mi habitación.

— **¿Qué tipo de emisoras escuchas?**

Pues, de todo. Música, entrevistas, noticias, tertulias, lo que sea. Me encanta escuchar la radio antes de dormirme.

— **¿Te gusta ir al cine?**

Sí. ¡Me apasiona!

— **¿Vas a menudo allí?**

Voy por lo menos tres o cuatro veces al mes y si hay una festival de cine voy con más frecuencia.

— **¿Hay un cine cerca de tu casa o vas al centro de la ciudad?**

Prefiero ir a los cines del centro. Siempre hay películas de estreno, el ambiente es más agradable y el sonido es mejor. El cine que está cerca de mi casa es muy pequeño y a veces es difícil conseguir entradas, sobre todo si es una película de estreno.

— **¿Con quién vas al cine?**

Voy con dos o tres amigos. Primero vamos a la taquilla a comprar las entradas y después compramos palomitas y caramelos.

— **¿Crees que la gente, ahora, ya no va tanto al cine?**

No. Hace unos diez años se temía que los cines cerraran porque la televisión era como tener el cine en casa. Pero en los últimos diez años la situación ha cambiado y el público vuelve a ir al cine otra vez. Muchos cines se han modernizado y se están construyendo multicines que tienen hasta quince salas.

Tercera Sección

CONTESTA LAS SIGUIENTES PREGUNTAS

1. ¿Ves la televisión todos los días?

_____

_____

2. ¿Cuál es tu programa preferido?

_____

_____

3. ¿Qué día de la semana ponen este programa?

_____

_____

4. ¿Qué programas de televisión viste este fin de semana?

_____

_____

5. ¿Qué piensas de los culebrones?

_____

_____

6. ¿Quién elige en tu casa la cadena y lo que se ve en la televisión?

_____

_____

7. ¿Te quedas pegado/a delante de la tele, pongan lo que pongan?

_____

_____

8. ¿Qué tipo de emisora de radio te interesa más?

_____

_____

9. ¿Cómo se llama la última película que viste?

_____

_____

10. ¿De qué trata?

_____

_____

Cuarta Sección

☞ **A. ESCRIBE ABAJO 12 PALABRAS O EXPRESIONES DE ESTA UNIDAD QUE TÚ CONSIDERAS IMPORTANTES DE RECORDAR:**

1.. 2..

3.. 4..

5.. 6..

7.. 8..

9.. 10...

11... 12...

B. ESCRIBE EL EQUIVALENTE EN ESPAÑOL DE ESTAS EXPRESIONES:

1. During the week I don't watch much ....

2. There are too many sports programmes ....

3. I can't stand soap operas ....

4. In our house the television is turned off at. ....

5. Many people have satellite channels ....

6. I used to buy a lot of video games..

7. My mum likes to rent a video...

8. The first thing I do is turn on my radio ....

9. I saw a very funny film last weekend...

10. The main character was ....

☞ **C. COMPLETA LAS SIGUIENTES FRASES CON LA PALABRA ADECUADA:**

No voy _ _ cine muy a menudo. Prefiero _ _ _ _ _ _ _ _ un vídeo para verlo en

casa. Es más cómodo y no tienes _ _ _ hacer cola para sacar las entradas. Sin

embargo a mi hermana le encanta _ _ cine. Va al cine en el centro dos o tres

_ _ _ _ _ al mes. Hace poco se fue al estreno de una nueva _ _ _ _ _ _ _ _ _.

Me dijo que _ _ _ muy divertida. _ _ apasionan todos los personajes de Disney.

19. Las vacaciones

Primera Sección

1. ¿Qué vas a hacer después de los exámenes?

- Tenemos una casa de **verano** *(summer house)* en el oeste de Irlanda y a lo mejor pasaré gran parte de mis vacaciones allí.
- Me quedaré aquí y trataré de encontrar un trabajo.

2. ¿Te quedas en casa durante las vacaciones o vas a otro sitio?

- Suelo ir con mis padres a visitar a mis abuelos.
- Aprovechamos el verano para ir de vacaciones **al extranjero** *(abroad)*.
- Nos alojamos en un hotel o **un parador** en España. Los paradores están **enclavados** *(set)* en monumentos históricos como palacios, conventos o castillos.
- Alquilamos un apartamento con vistas al mar.
- Estos dos últimos años he hecho un intercambio con un/a chic**o/a** español/**a**.
- Cuando era pequeñ**o/a** solía pasar un período de tiempo en un colegio irlandés para mejorar el idioma.

3. ¿Con quién vas de vacaciones?

- Todos los veranos voy con toda la familia a un país diferente.
- Sin embargo, este verano me apetece hacer camping con unos compañeros del colegio.

4. ¿Cómo vais de vacaciones?

Vamos en | coche | en avión
| barco | en tren
| autocar |

Alquilamos bicicletas.

5. ¿Prefieres ir a la playa o al monte?

- Lo ideal para mí es …
- A mi me gusta más la costa.
- Me encanta estar en la playa. **Hay tanto que hacer** *(so much to do)*.
- Me encantan los deportes acuáticos, como la vela y el windsurfing.

(contd.)

Paso mucho tiempo	nadando y **buceando** *(diving)*
Mi hermana se divierte	construyendo **castillos de arena**. *(sand-castles)*

- Si hace mucho sol me pongo muy moreno**/a** porque **tomo el sol** *(I sunbathe)* todos los días.
- En España se organizan muchos juegos junto al mar.
- En estos **lugares de veraneo** *(holiday resorts)* hay más distracciones para la juventud:

> discotecas.
> espectáculos al aire libre.

6. ¿Cómo te diviertes en el campo?

- Lo que más me gusta es ir al campo.
- Es muy tranquilo y puedes pasear por las carreteras sin ver a nadie.
- Es muy agradable oír los animales como las vacas y las ovejas.
- Allí se puede respirar bien.

7. ¿Tienes una tarjeta de albergue juvenil?
(youth hostel)

- Sí. Es muy útil y resulta muy barato.
- El verano pasado fui a un concierto de música pop y me alojé en un albergue.
- Otra cosa que es muy agradable es que aquí en Irlanda la mayoría de estos albergues se encuentran en sitios muy pintorescos y aislados.

PAST TENSE

1. ¿Has hecho camping alguna vez en el extranjero?

- Sí. Hace dos años **nos quedamos** una semana en un camping en Francia.
- Lo **pasamos** muy bien.
- **Había** muchos otros turistas.
- **Había** muchas facilidades como:

> piscina
> supermercado
> restaurante
> lavandería

- **Conocí** a muchos jóvenes de mi edad.
- **Nos reuníamos** para salir juntos.

2. ¿Qué tiempo hacía?

- Afortunadamente **hacía** buen tiempo.
- **Había** un cielo despejado todos los días.
- Desafortunadamente **llovía** mucho.
- **Era** muy desagradable cuando teníamos que montar o doblar la tienda bajo la lluvia.

3. **¿Te quedaste en tu casa durante las vacaciones de Navidad?**

Sí. No salimos nunca de Irlanda durante esa época del año.

4. **¿Y cómo pasaste las vacaciones de Semana Santa?**

- Este año **me quedé** en casa porque **tenía** que estudiar para los exámenes.

- **Hice** un repaso de todo para el Leaving.

> Note the uses and tenses of **haber** below:
> **Hay** – *there is/are*
> **Había** – *there was/were*
> **Habrá** – *there will be*

FUTURE TENSE

1. **¿Irás de vacaciones a principios del verano o al final de las vacaciones?**

Voy a ir a las Islas Canarias con un grupo de amigos en el mes de septiembre.

2. **¿Y qué harás antes de ir de vacaciones?**

Para pagar los gastos del viaje **tendré** que buscar trabajo antes.

3. **¿Llevarás mucho equipaje contigo?**

Sólo **voy a llevar lo imprescindible**.
(what's necessary)

una maleta.
un maletín de mano.
un bolso ligero.

Llevaré de casa las cremas bronceadoras.
una sola prenda de lana.
ropa ligera.
ropa de dormir.
calzado cómodo.

Meteré en mi maleta un minibotiquín con medicinas.
un pequeño costurero.
la bolsa de aseo.

4. **¿ A qué hora sale el avión?**

Sale a las nueve de la noche.

CONDITIONAL TENSE + SUBJUNCTIVE

1. **¿Si pudieras escoger
   adónde irías de vacaciones?**

   - **Me encantaría** recorrer toda América Latina **si tuviera** bastante dinero.
   - **Sería** un viaje inolvidable.
   - !Ojalá que **fuera** posible!

2. **¿Tus padres te darían el dinero
   para un viaje muy largo?**

   - **Si trabajara** todo el verano **tendría** el dinero para comprar mis billetes de avión. De esa manera no **sería** necesario que me **dieran** mucho dinero.

3. **¿Qué harías si te quedaras
   en Irlanda todo el verano?**

   - **Si no saliera** del país **aprendería** a conducir y trataría de sacarme el carné.

Segunda Sección

ESCUCHA ESTAS CONVERSACIONES EN LA CINTA

– **¿Dónde pasas normalmente las vacaciones?**

Todos los años vamos a un sitio diferente. A veces nos quedamos en Irlanda y aprovechamos el verano para ir a sitios que todavía no hemos visitado.

– **¿Prefieres veranear en Irlanda o en el extranjero?**

A mi me encanta ir al extranjero, sobre todo a países mediterráneos porque sabes que no va a llover. Esto hace que sea muy diferente. Me encanta el estilo de vida de esos países.

– **¿Y qué tal la comida?**

Es bastante diferente. Se come casi todo a base de aceite de oliva y se cocina con mucho ajo. Pero la comida es otra cosa que me encanta. A toda mi familia nos gusta probar los platos regionales de otros países.

– **¿Dónde os alojáis?**

Lo que hacemos casi siempre es reservar con mucha anticipación un apartamento. En cuanto salen los folletos de las agencias de viajes los miramos y acordamos dónde ir.

– **¿Y quién decide por fin?**

Pues, lo hablamos hasta que nos ponemos de acuerdo. Pero al fin y al cabo es mi padre el que lleva la voz cantante.

– **¿Cómo pasaste las vacaciones el verano pasado?**

Primero, me fui a un colegio irlandés en Donegal para mejorar mis conocimientos del idioma.

– **¿Y aprendiste mucho?**

Creo que sí. Al principio lo encontré bastante difícil porque entendía muy poco del idioma. Pero los profesores nos ayudaron mucho y he mejorado bastante.

– **¿Cuánto tiempo te quedaste allí?**

Me quedé las tres primeras semanas del mes de junio y viví con una familia irlandesa.

– **¿Y has ido a España alguna vez?**

Sí. He visitado España varias veces. El verano pasado, por ejemplo, mi familia hizo uno de esos viajes organizados con vuelo chárter y nos alojamos en un apartamento. Pero lo que más me gustó fue el viaje que hice a Madrid durante el año de Transición.

– **¿Cuándo fue eso?**

Hace dos años hice un intercambio con una chica madrileña que era muy simpática y con la que me llevé muy bien. Además, iba cada día a clases y aprendí muchísimo. Hicimos excursiones a Toledo y a Segovia. Al final de mi estancia no tenía ganas de regresar a Irlanda.

Tercera Sección

CONTESTA LAS SIGUIENTES PREGUNTAS

1. ¿Adónde vas de vacaciones normalmente?

_____

_____

2. ¿Cuántas semanas de vacaciones tiene tu padre en verano?

_____

_____

3. ¿Prefieres pasar las vacaciones a orillas del mar o en el campo?

_____

_____

4. ¿Cómo puede uno divertirse junto al mar?

_____

_____

5. ¿Te gusta ir de camping? ¿Por qué? ¿Por qué no?

_____

_____

6. ¿Qué hiciste el verano pasado?

_____

_____

7. ¿Has ido alguna vez de vacaciones al extranjero?

_____

_____

8. ¿Te gustaría ir a España este verano?

_____

_____

9. ¿Has ido alguna vez a un colegio de irlandés? ¿Cómo era?

_____

_____

10. ¿Qué piensas hacer este verano, después de los exámenes?

_____

_____

Cuarta Sección

A. ESCRIBE ABAJO 12 PALABRAS O EXPRESIONES DE ESTA UNIDAD QUE TÚ CONSIDERAS IMPORTANTES DE RECORDAR:

1.. 2..

3.. 4..

5.. 6..

7.. 8..

9.. 10..

11.. 12..

B. ESCRIBE EL EQUIVALENTE EN ESPAÑOL DE ESTAS EXPRESIONES:

1. I usually stay in Ireland ....

2. During the summer holidays ....

3. It's better to travel abroad ....

4. It's sunny every day ....

5. I love being at the beach..

6. We sometimes rent a car ....

7. Last year I went camping ....

8. It was very uncomfortable..

9. We never go on holidays at Christmas ....

10. I'll work to pay for the expenses ....

☞ **C. COMPLETA LAS SIGUIENTES FRASES CON LA PALABRA ADECUADA:**

A principios del verano me quedo aquí y salgo muy a menudo con mis amigos. Los fines de semana, si _ _ _ _ buen tiempo, vamos de excursión a algún sitio de interés que no se _ _ _ _ _ _ _ _ muy lejos. Hacemos una merienda en el campo y volvemos a casa a _ _ _ de las seis. Después, en el mes de _ _ _ _ _ o agosto, pasamos unos días en casa de mis abuelos en el campo. Pero lo que _ _ _ me gusta es pasar una quincena en otro _ _ _ _.

20. Proyectos para el futuro

Primera Sección

**1. ¿Qué piensas hacer
el año que viene?**

Quisiera   ir a la universidad.

Me gustaría seguir estudiando.

Espero   buscar trabajo.
    pasar un período de tiempo
    viajando por los Estados Unidos.

2. ¿Qué estudios vas a cursar?

Me interesa más la Economía.
    la Medicina.
    la Informática.
    la Ingeniería.
    el Derecho.

Quisiera **licenciarme** en Letras.
    (get a degree) Ciencias.
    Ciencias Sociales.
    Economía.

Me gustaría **sacar el título de**   médico.
    (to qualify as a)   ingeniero.

Voy a cursar   estudios empresariales.
    ciencias políticas.
    dedicarme a los negocios.

**3. ¿Es difícil matricularse
en este curso?**

Sí. Bastante. Todo **depende de** los puntos que se
sa**que** en el Leaving.
¡Ojalá que yo con**siga** los puntos necesarios!
Subjunctive

**4. ¿Si no sacas la nota
necesaria dejarás tus estudios?**

A lo mejor tendré que repetir el examen.
Trataré de encontrar trabajo en algún sitio.

Haré algún cursillo de ordenadores.
    mecanografía.
    (typing)

**5. ¿Cuántos años tendrás que
seguir estudiando?**

- Por lo menos tres o cuatro años para obtener un
título universitario *(degree)*.
- La Licenciatura es de cuatro años de duración.
- ¡Así que no voy a graduarme hasta el año dos mil
tres!

**6. ¿Cuando hayas terminado
el curso qué harás?**

- Una vez terminada la carrera buscaré un puesto
de trabajo.
- Espero hacer entrevistas.
- **Espero que** me llam**en** para algo que me interes**e**.
       SUBJUNCTIVE   SUBJUNCTIVE
- Haré un curso de formación profesional.
- A lo mejor seguiré un curso a nivel de posgraduado.
- Si no encuentro trabajo en Irlanda tendré que
trabajar en el extranjero.
- Después de sacarme la Licenciatura espero tener
más posibilidades de trabajo.

7. ¿Cómo quieres ganarte la vida?
        (earn your living)

Tengo ganas de trabajar como …

Busco un trabajo | fijo.
estable.
rutinario.
variado.

Lo más importante para mí es | tener un buen sueldo.
estar al aire libre.
trabajar **por mi propia cuenta**.
        (for myself)
hacer algo útil en la vida.
No me importaría tener horario de noche.

**8. ¿Cómo podrás asegurarte para que
te llamen para un puesto de trabajo?**

- Lo primero es tener **las aptitudes requeridas**.
        (necessary qualifications)
- Tendré que escribir una carta persuasiva para
conseguir captar el interés.
- Enviaré un buen currículum breve y fácil de leer.

**9. ¿Antes de ir a una entrevista
cómo te prepararías?**
(how would you prepare yourself?)

- Intentar**ía** informarme de cómo es el sitio en el
que quiero entrar.
- Llegar**ía** puntual y bien vestid**o/a**.
- Tratar**ía** de mostrar confianza en mi mismo y
mantenerme relajad**o/a**.

**10.¿Si fracasas en una entrevista
cómo te sentirás?**
(how will you feel?)

- Sin duda me sentiré algo deprimido/a.

- Pero intentaré sacar provecho de la experiencia.

**11. ¿Te apetece la idea de
ir a vivir en otro país?**

- No me importaría ir a vivir algunos años a otro país.

- Ganaría mucha experiencia antes de instalarme aquí.

- Los licenciados tienen posibilidades de encontrar un mejor puesto de trabajo en la Unión Europea.

- Preferiría *(I'd prefer)* seguir viviendo en Irlanda.

- Si pudiera elegir me gustaría vivir en España.

**12. ¿Te gustaría trabajar en algo
relacionado con los idiomas?**

- Sí. Me encantan los idiomas.

- Tengo cierta facilidad para los idiomas.

- Hoy día es importante que entiend**as** y **sepas** hablar un idioma extranjero.   SUBJUNCTIVE

- Entre los requisitos de muchos puestos figura el conocimiento de dos idiomas.

- Preferir**ía** trabajar en el campo científico. Así que no tendr**ía** tantas posibilidades para usar los idiomas.

**13. ¿Crees que el sueldo
es un factor importante?**

- Para mí lo más importante es tener un trabajo en el cual me sentiría a gusto.

- A mi parecer es imprescindible tener un trabajo con posibilidades de promoción donde pudiera ganar bastante dinero.

**14. ¿Ha cambiado mucho el papel de
la mujer en el mundo laboral ?**

Creo que sí. Hoy día, las chicas tienen las mismas posibilidades de educación que los chicos y tienen también oportunidades de conseguir buenos puestos de trabajo. Así que es cada vez mayor el número de mujeres que trabajan fuera de casa.

Toda mujer trabajadora tiene derecho a un período **de baja** maternal.
(leave)

Segunda Sección

ESCUCHA ESTAS CONVERSACIONES EN LA CINTA

40

– **¿Te gustaría continuar tus estudios el año que viene?**

Sí. Se me dan bien las ciencias y me gustaría mucho ir a la universidad para estudiar una carrera en este campo.

– **¿Cuántos años más tendrías que estudiar?**

Para sacarme la licenciatura creo que tendría que seguir estudiando unos cuatro años y quizás otro año más si quiero hacer un curso especializado de posgraduado.

– **¿Crees que habrá mucha diferencia entre la vida universitaria y la vida que llevas este año?**

Va a ser completamente diferente. Lo bueno de la universidad es que sólo estudias las dos o tres asignaturas que te interesan. También tienes mucha más libertad. Esto es bueno pero puede resultar fatal a los jóvenes que no sepan organizar sus estudios y sus pasatiempos.

– **¿Seguirás viviendo con tu familia o tendrás que buscar alojamiento cerca de la universidad?**

Como vivo bastante lejos tendré que quedarme en un apartamento o en una residencia universitaria. Mis padres preferirían que me hospedara en una pensión donde preparan las comidas.

– **¿Crees que va a ser difícil encontrar trabajo cuando termines el curso?**

Pues, no sé. Si me encontrara en paro trataría de encontrar trabajo en el extranjero.

– **¿Ya sabes en qué quieres trabajar después de terminar tus estudios?**   41

Sí. Me gustaría trabajar de recepcionista en un hotel de cuatro o cinco estrellas.

– **¿Y tienes alguna experiencia?**

Pues, sí. Durante el año de Transición pasé una semana trabajando en un hotel de cinco estrellas en el centro de la ciudad.

– **¿En qué consistía el trabajo?**

Era bastante variado. Tenía que contestar el teléfono y atender al público. A veces mandaba los fax y aprendí a usar el ordenador. Sí había algún problema serio, otra recepcionista se encargaba de resolverlo pero ahora creo que podría asumir esta responsabilidad.

– **¿Por qué has eligido este trabajo para ganarte la vida?**

Desde muy pequeña me ha gustado tener mucha gente a mi alrededor, por lo que me gustaría trabajar en un sitio donde siempre hay gente de paso.

– **En este tipo de trabajo no vas a tener horarios fijos, ¿verdad?**

No, pero no me importaría porque si trabajara por la noche tendría más tiempo libre durante el día.

Tercera Sección

CONTESTA LAS SIGUIENTES PREGUNTAS

1. ¿Vas a seguir estudiando el año que viene?

_____

_____

2. ¿Cuántos puntos te hacen falta para entrar en la facultad?

_____

_____

3. ¿Conoces a alguien que haya cursado los mismos estudios?

_____

_____

4. ¿Después de terminar la carrera qué harás?

_____

_____

5. ¿Si no vas a la universidad qué piensas hacer el año que viene?

_____

_____

6. ¿Preferías trabajar solo/a o con otras personas?

_____

_____

7. ¿Te importaría trabajar muchas horas, incluso los fines de semana?

_____

_____

8. ¿ Qué harías si no pudieras encontrar trabajo en Irlanda?

_____

_____

9. ¿Cuáles son los inconvenientes de vivir en otro país?

_____

_____

10. ¿Si te tocase el gordo seguirías trabajando?

_____

_____

Cuarta Sección

☞ **A. ESCRIBE ABAJO 12 PALABRAS O EXPRESIONES DE ESTA UNIDAD QUE TÚ CONSIDERAS IMPORTANTES DE RECORDAR:**

1... 2...

3... 4...

5... 6...

7... 8...

9... 10...

11... 12...

B. ESCRIBE EL EQUIVALANTE EN ESPAÑOL DE ESTAS EXPRESIONES:

1. I'd like to go to university ....

2. It's very difficult to get into that course ....

3. I'll continue studying next year...

4. I hope to do a degree in science ....

5. If I don't get good results ....

6. My parents want me to look for a job ....

7. The most important thing for me is ....

8. I wouldn't mind working at night..

9. I'd prefer to work abroad...

10. I'd like to earn a good salary ....

☞ **C. COMPLETA LAS SIGUIENTES FRASES CON LA PALABRA ADECUADA:**

A lo mejor seguiré _ _ _ _ _ _ _ _ _ _ el año que viene. Me gustaría ir a la

_ _ _ _ _ _ _ _ _ _ _ para licenciarme en Aplicaciones Informáticas. En esta

carrera se aprende a programar _ instalar medios informáticos en las empresas. La

licenciatura _ _ _ _ cuatro años. Después de terminar preferiría trabajar por mi

_ _ _ _ _ _ cuenta por que no quiero atarme a un horario fijo. Creo que ganaré

un buen _ _ _ _ _ _.

PART 2: Role-plays

ADVICE FOR THE ROLE-PLAYS

This part of the oral examination takes place after the general conversation. Here candidates are assessed on their ability to deal with everyday situations and problems that may arise while visiting Spain. Some of the likely role-play situations that occur are:

- booking accommodation (in a hotel, youth hostel or camp-site)
- asking for information in a tourist office
- ordering a meal (perhaps dealing with some problem regarding the food or service)
- arriving in Spain by car or aeroplane

The examiner chooses one of the five situations selected by the individual school and the student will be given one minute to prepare. During this time think of yourself in the situation. Imagine you really are in that restaurant or at the airport. This will help the conversation to unfold more naturally. Remind yourself of the basic vocabulary and the correct parts of the verbs that you will require.

Decide before you begin on the correct form of address for the chosen role-play. Although the familiar form of address is becoming very common, there are situations where you should still use the polite form. Ask yourself if this is a role-play where you should address the other person as **usted**, using the verb endings for the third person singular. You will also have to use the possessive pronouns, like **su** and **sus**, in such a role-play and the polite form of the commands if these are required. This would be the case, for example, in the role-plays where an adult is helping you deal with a particular problem.
If you are talking to a friend, use the **tú** form of the verb and the corresponding possessive adjectives **tu** and **tus** . The familiar form of the imperative of the verb must also be used where necessary. When you have decided which form to use remember to be consistent throughout the role-play.

The candidate's card clearly indicates who has to initiate the conversation. Before the examiner continues with this final part of the oral examination he or she may ask you **¿estás listo/a?** or a similar question. Answer appropriately, **sí, podemos empezar ahora**. If it is indicated for you to begin, do so confidently. As the role-play develops, try to look at the examiner on occasion so that the conversation becomes more than the reading of a prepared script. The examiner will ask one final question, relevant to the situation, to which you will respond. This is to test your ability to respond to something that has not been prepared in advance. If you consider carefully the role-plays, you should be able to think of possible additional questions. For example, in the role-play **En el restaurante**, the examiner might conclude by asking:

¿Le gustaría un cigarillo español?
¿Necesita una cerilla?
Veo que no son de aquí. ¿De dónde son ustedes?
¿Cuánto tiempo llevan ustedes aquí?
¿Les gusta la comida española?

As you prepare the role-plays presented in *El Español Bien Hablado* you should gain the necessary confidence and practice to deal effectively with the situation that is chosen. However, do not feel the role-play presented is the only way to respond to the situation. For example, you could choose different food in the restaurant situation (Role-play 1) and give a different description of the brief-case (Role-play 5) or suitcases (Role-play 8).

Finally, listen to the role-plays recorded on tape and try to imitate the intonation and pronunciation. Notice differences in tone to show emotions like annoyance, confusion, curiosity or frustration.

As you finish your oral examination you should come out of the room feeling confident and relaxed, in the knowledge that you were thoroughly prepared and have achieved a high percentage of marks allocated for this part of your Leaving Certificate Examination.

A large amount of the material included for the oral examination will also help the Leaving Certificate candidate with the rest of the Spanish examination.

1. En el restaurante

You are in a restaurant in Spain with a friend. You are about to finish your meal. You call the waiter or waitress.

The Examiner is the waiter/waitress.

WAIT FOR THE WAITER/WAITRESS TO SPEAK

1. Camarero Ask whether they have finished their meal or if they would like something else.

1. Tú Order one black coffee and one white coffee and ask for the bill.
AWAIT RESPONSE

2. Camarero Serve the coffee, present the bill and say you hope they enjoyed the meal.

2. Tú Say the first course and the desserts were fine and so was the fish course that you yourself had. Say what your friend's main course was and why she didn't like it much.
AWAIT RESPONSE

3. Camarero Say that's unfortunate. Ask if they liked the wine you recommended.

3. Tú Say yes, that it was very good; but you only had half a bottle and you see from the bill that you have been charged for a full bottle.
AWAIT RESPONSE

4. Camarero Say there must be a mistake, perhaps it's the wrong bill.

4. Tú Say yes, you see now that it's not your bill. Say what courses you had and what courses are listed on the bill.
AWAIT RESPONSE

5. Camarero Say you would like to offer them a complimentary drink to compensate for the error.

5. Tú Thank him/her. Say your friend will have a brandy, you'll have a chilled orange. Explain why you don't want an alcoholic drink. Ask if it's all right to smoke.

6. Camarero Say yes, this is a smoking area. Ask another question <u>clearly relevant to the situation</u>.
.... ?

RESPOND APPROPRIATELY

6. Tú..

Van Gogh - Terasa Cafenelei noaptea

3L

1. En el restaurante

You are in a restaurant in Spain with a friend. You are about to finish your meal. You call the waiter or waitress.

The Examiner is the waiter/waitress. <u>Examiner begins</u>:

1. Camarero ¿Bueno, señores, ya han terminado o quieren pedir otra cosa?

1. Tú Sí, por favor. Y para terminar **un café solo** y **un café con leche**. Y **haga el favor de** traernos también la cuenta.

2. Camarero Aquí tienen el café. Y he traído también la cuenta. Espero que les haya gustado la comida.

2. Tú Bueno, pues. El primer plato y los postres **estaban** (Use IMPERFECT TENSE for description) deliciosos y la merluza que yo pedí **estaba** muy **jugosa**. Pero **a mi amigo no le gustó nada** el bistec. Me dijo que **estaba demasiado duro** (OR **estaba muy poco hecho**).

3. Camarero ¡Ay! Lo siento mucho. ¿Y qué tal el vino que les recomendé? ¿Les gustó?

3. Tú **Claro que sí**. Ese vino que **nos recomendó** tenía **un sabor muy fino**. Pero, perdone, **sólo pedimos media botella** y veo aquí en la cuenta que **nos ha cobrado** una botella entera.

4. Camarero Tiene que haber un error. Quizás haya traído la cuenta equivocada.

4. Tú Si, en efecto. Tiene usted razón. **Ya veo que** ésta no es nuestra cuenta. Nosotros pedimos gazpacho **de primer plato** y aquí pone sopa de pescado. **De segundo**, comimos el bistec y la merluza. **Sin embargo**, aquí dice pollo asado.

5. Camarero Sí, sí, es verdad. Lo siento. ¿Les puedo ofrecer alguna bebida a cuenta de la casa?

5. Tú Ah gracias. **Es usted muy amable**. Para mi amigo, un coñac y para mí, un zumo de naranja sin hielo, pero frío. Esta noche **tengo que conducir** y prefiero por eso no tomar más alcohol. Otra cosa, ¿se puede fumar aquí?

6. Camarero Sí. Aquí se puede fumar.
¿ .... ?

6. Tú..

un café solo	black coffee	**sólo pedimos media botella**	we only asked for half a bottle
un café con leche	white coffee	**nos ha cobrado**	you charged us
haga el favor de + INFINITIVE	please +VERB	**Ya veo que**	Now I see that
estaban/estaba	they were/it was	**de primer plato**	for first course
Use IMPERFECT TENSE for description of what something **was** like.		**De segundo**	For second course
jugosa	tasty	**Sin embargo**	However
a mi amigo no le gustó nada	my friend didn't like – NOTE **a** mi amigo	**Es usted muy amable**	You are very kind
estaba demasiado duro	it was too tough (meat)	**tengo que conducir**	I have to drive
estaba muy poco hecho	it wasn't done well enough		
Claro que sí	Of course		
nos recomendó	you recommended us		
un sabor muy fino	a very nice taste (wine)		

2. En el hotel

You have a summer job as a receptionist in a hotel in Madrid. A guest arrives.

The Examiner is the guest.

1. Tú   Greet and welcome guest.
       AWAIT RESPONSE

1. Huésped   Return greeting and say you have accommodation reserved in this hotel.

2. Tú   Ask guest his/her name, when the reservation was made and if it was made by phone, letter or fax.
       AWAIT RESPONSE

2. Huésped   Give name, date on which reservation was made and means used.

3. Tú   Say you're just checking the register. Ask if the reservation was for three nights, Tuesday to Thursday, single room with bath, breakfast and dinner.
       AWAIT RESPONSE

3. Huésped   Say that's correct. Ask what time breakfast is served.

4. Tú   Tell the guest when and where breakfast is served and ask what time he/she wants to be called tomorrow.
       AWAIT RESPONSE

4. Huésped   Say that tomorrow you want a 5.30 call as you must meet someone in the airport at 7.00.

5. Tú   Say there's no problem. Say you won't be on duty yourself in the morning and tell the guest your normal weekly schedule. Tell him/her what's on the breakfast menu and ask if he/she wants to order a taxi for the morning.
       AWAIT RESPONSE

5. Huésped   Say all you want for breakfast is white coffee and toast. Order a taxi for 6.15.

6. Tú   Say you've made a note of all that for the receptionist who will be on duty tomorrow morning. Wish guest a pleasant stay.

6. Huésped   Thank receptionist and say you judge by the accent that he/she isn't Spanish. Ask another question <u>clearly relevant to the situation</u>.
       .... ?

....

       RESPOND APPROPRIATELY

7. Tú ....

2. En el hotel

You have a summer job as a receptionist in a hotel in Madrid. A guest arrives.

The Examiner is the guest. <u>You begin:</u>

1. Tú Hola. Buenas tardes y bienvenido al hotel.

1. Huésped Hola. Buenas tardes. Acabo de llegar a Madrid y **tengo una reserva hecha** en este hotel.

2. Tú Bueno. ¿Su nombre por favor? **¿Y me puede decir** cuando hizo usted la reserva? **¿Y la hizo por teléfono**, por carta o por fax?

2. Huésped Me llamo Maria/Peter Conway. Hace dos semanas hice la reserva por fax. Creo que era el día dos.

3. Tú Espere un momento, por favor. **Tengo que verlo** en el registro. Ah sí. La reserva **era para tres noches**, **¿verdad? Desde** el martes **hasta** el jueves. Es **una habitación individual** con cuarto de baño y con desayuno y cena incluídos.

3. Huésped Sí, eso es. ¿A qué hora se sirve el desayuno?

4. Tú El desayuno **se sirve** entre las siete y las nueve en el restaurante **de aquí al lado**. ¿A qué hora **quiere que le llamen** mañana?
(SUBJUNCTIVE)

4. Huésped ¿Me pueden llamar muy temprano mañana, a las cinco y media? Es que tengo que estar en el aeropuerto a las siete para encontrarme con alguien.

5. Tú Está bien. No hay problema. Yo **no estaré de servicio** por la mañana. Sólo trabajo por la tarde, desde las cinco hasta las once. Para el desayuno tenemos café, zumo natural, tostadas con mantequilla y mermelada, yogur y fruta fresca. Como **usted saldrá tan temprano**, ¿quiere que le llamemos un taxi para mañana a primera hora?
(SUBJUNCTIVE)

5. Huésped Sí. Voy a necesitar un taxi para las seis y cuarto. No voy a desayunar mucho. Sólo café con leche y tostadas.

6. Tú **Vale. Lo he apuntado todo** para la recepcionista que estará aquí **mañana por la mañana. Que lo pase muy bien** aquí en nuestro hotel.

6. Huésped Gracias. Veo que usted no es español/a.
¿ .... ?

7. Tú ....

tengo una reserve hecha	*I've booked a room*	**de aquí al lado**	*here beside us*
¿Y me puede decir?	*And can you tell me?*	**¿quiere que le llamen?**	*do you want to be called?*
¿Y la hizo por teléfono?	*And was it by telephone?*	**no estaré de servicio**	*I'll not be on duty*
Tengo que verlo	*I have to check it*	**zumo natural**	*fresh juice*
era para tres noches	*it was for three nights*	**usted saldrá tan temprano**	*you will leave so early*
¿verdad?	*wasn't it?*	**Vale. Lo he apuntado todo**	*Fine. I've noted it down*
Desde ... hasta	*from the ... until the*	**mañana por la mañana**	*tomorrow morning*
una habitación individual	*a single room*	**Que lo pase muy bien**	*Have a very good time*
se sirve	*is served*		

3. En el supermercado

You are in a supermarket in Spain and cannot find some of the items you require. You seek the assistance of a supervisor.

The Examiner is the supervisor.

1. Tú Greet the supervisor.
AWAIT RESPONSE

1. Empleado/a Return greeting and ask if you can help.

2. Tú Say you have got most of the items on your list but there are some you cannot locate.
AWAIT RESPONSE

2. Empleado/a Ask which items he/she cannot find.

3. Tú Mention tea and any other two items. Ask which brands of tea they have.
AWAIT RESPONSE

3. Empleado/a Indicate where these items can be found and say that you only stock one brand of tea, as demand is limited.

4. Tú Say you're from Ireland and, like many Irish people you prefer tea to coffee.
AWAIT RESPONSE

4. Empleado/a Ask what youth thinks of Spanish food in general.

5. Tú Mention one dish you particularly like and one you dislike. Say you like Spanish wine and you think it's much better value than French wine.
AWAIT RESPONSE

5. Empleado/a Enquire about the differences between the cost of living in Ireland and Spain.

6. Tú Give two examples.

6. Empleado/a Comment on what youth has said. Ask another question <u>clearly relevant to the situation</u>.
.... ?

RESPOND APPROPRIATELY

7. Tú..

3. En el supermercado

You are in a supermarket in Spain and cannot find some of the items you require. You seek the assistance of a supervisor.

The Examiner is the supervisor. <u>You begin</u>:

1. Tú   Buenos días. ¿Trabaja usted aquí?

1. Empleado/a Hola. Buenos días. ¿En qué puedo ayudarte?

2. Tú   Pues, tengo **la mayoría de las cosas** en mi lista pero hay algunas cosas que **no puedo encontrar**.

2. Empleado/a ¿Qué es lo que buscas?

3. Tú   **Me faltan todavía** el té, el azúcar y la leche. ¿Qué **marcas** de té tienen aquí?

3. Empleado/a Encontrarás la leche en la nevera allí al fondo. El té y el azúcar están en el segundo pasillo. Pero sólo tenemos un tipo de té. Nosotros los españoles bebemos muy poco té.

4. Tú   Ah, sí. Yo soy de Irlanda, y como muchos irlandeses prefiero el té **más que** el café.

4. Empleado/a ¿Te gusta la comida española?

5. Tú   Por lo general, creo que **es muy rica** y hay platos que me gustan, **sobre todo** la paella. Sin embargo, **esa sopa fría**, ¿cómo se llama? Ah, sí, el gazpacho, **no me gusta nada**. **También** me gusta el vino español, el Rioja. **Tiene un sabor muy rico** y **es de mejor calidad que** el vino francés.

5. Empleado/a ¿Has notado muchas diferencias entre la vida aquí en España y la de Irlanda?

6. Tú   **El coste de la vida** en Irlanda es mucho más alto. Por ejemplo, esta botella de vino cuesta aquí seiscientas pesetas pero en Irlanda **yo tendría que pagar tres veces más**. También **el medio de transporte público** es muy caro. **He visto que** los billetes de tren y de autobús son mucho mas baratos en España.

6. Empleado/a Ah. Es muy interesante. No lo sabía.
¿ .... ?

7. Tú ....

la mayoría de las cosas	*the majority of the things*	**no me gusta nada**	*I don't like it at all*
no puedo encontrar	*I can't find*	**También**	*Also*
Me faltan todavía	*I 'm still missing*	**Tiene un sabor muy rico**	*It has a very nice taste*
marcas	*brands*	**es de mejor calidad que**	*it's better value to buy it than*
más que	*rather than*	**El coste de la vida**	*The cost of living*
es muy rica (la comida)	*it's very tasty*	**yo tendría que pagar tres veces más**	<u>*I would have*</u> *to pay three times more*
sobre todo	*above all*	**el medio de transporte público**	*the means of public transport*
esa sopa fría	*that cold soup*	**He visto que**	*I've seen that*

4. En el club juvenil

While on a three-month visit to a town in Spain you decide to join the local Youth Club.

The Examiner is the club secretary.

AWAIT GREETING

1. Secretaria   Greet youth and say you haven't met him/her before.

1. Tú   Return greeting and say you've only been here for the past week.
AWAIT RESPONSE

2. Secretaria   Ask where youth is from and if you can help him/her in any way.

2. Tú   Say you're Irish and you'll be here for three months; you'd like to join the Youth Club.
AWAIT RESPONSE

3. Secretaria   Say you're the secretary of the Club and the youth will be very welcome. Ask what his/her interests are.

3. Tú   Mention two sports in which you are interested and ask if they have facilities for these. Ask what the membership fee is.
AWAIT RESPONSE

4. Secretaria   Say facilities are available; it's 4.000 pesetas to join and 1.000 a month after that.

4. Tú   Ask on which days and at what times the facilities are available.
AWAIT RESPONSE

5. Secretaria   Say the club has the use of the local Sports Complex from 19.00 to 23.00 on Tuesdays and Thursdays.

5. Tú   Say Tuesday is fine but you can only come for an hour on Thursdays. Explain why.
AWAIT RESPONSE

6. Secretaria   Say there are other activities besides sport. Ask about youth's pastimes/hobbies, other than sport.

6. Tú   Mention two (non-sport) pastimes or hobbies and say why you are interested in them.

7. Secretaria   Say there are people with similar interests in the club so youth should make lots of friends. Ask another question <u>clearly relevant to the situation</u>.
.... ?

RESPOND APPROPRIATELY

7. Tú ....

4. En el club juvenil

While on a three-month visit to a town in Spain you decide to join the local Youth Club.

The Examiner is the club secretary. <u>Examiner begins</u>:

1. Secretaria   Hola. Buenos días. No te he visto por aquí antes.

1. Tú   Hola. Sí, es verdad. **Hace sólo una semana que llegué**.

2. Secretaria   ¿En qué te puedo ayudar? No eres de aquí, ¿verdad?

2. Tú   Soy irlandés y **pienso estar** tres meses en este pueblo. **Por eso**, si es posible, creo que **vale la pena hacerme socio** del club juvenil.

3. Secretaria   Yo soy la secretaria del club y nos gustaría mucho que vinieras aquí. ¿Cuáles son tus aficiones?

3. Tú   **Soy muy aficionado al** tenis y al baloncesto. ¿Tienen **instalaciones** para estos deportes? Y, otra cosa, ¿cuál es **la cuota de socio**?

4. Secretaria   Tenemos ocho pistas de tenis. Además, hay un gimnasio donde se practican el baloncesto y muchos otros deportes. Son cuatro mil pesetas la inscripción y mil pesetas al mes después.

4. Tú   **Vale. También quisiera saber** qué días de la semana **está abierto el club**. ¿Y **a partir de qué hora** se puede llegar para utilizar las instalaciones?

5. Secretaria   Todos los martes podemos utilizar el polideportivo del barrio y los jueves a partir de las siete de la tarde hasta las once de la noche.

5. Tú   Ah, bueno. **Los martes** me parecen muy bien pero **sólo podré estar** aquí una hora los jueves. **Es que** tengo clase de español **por la tarde**, de siete y media a nueve.

6. Secretaria   Aquí se pueden hacer muchas otras cosas aparte del deporte. ¿Qué otros hobbys tienes además del deporte?

6. Tú   También me gusta la música. Tengo una guitarra y **me relajo mucho tocándola**. Tengo una radio y **la escucho bastante**, sobre todo, por la noche, **antes de acostarme**. **De esa manera** puedo dormir pensando en otras cosas que no son del colegio y los deberes!

7. Secretaria   Bueno. Verás que en el club hay muchos jóvenes que son aficionados a las mismas cosas. Vas a hacer muchos amigos aquí.

¿ .... ?

7.Tú..

Hace sólo una semana que llegué	I arrived here only a weekago	¿a partir de qué hora?	from what time?
pienso estar	I intend being	**Los martes**	On Tuesdays
Por eso	Because of that	**sólo podré estar**	I can only be
vale la pena hacerme socio	it's worth becoming a member	**Es que**	It's because
Soy muy aficionado al	I'm very keen on	**por la tarde**	in the evening
instalaciones	facilities	**me relajo mucho tocándola**	I can really relax by playing it
la cuota de socio	the membership fee	**la escucho bastante**	I listen to it quite a lot
Vale	O.K.	**antes de acostarme**	before I go to bed
También quisiera saber	I'd also like to know	**De esa manera**	In that way
está abierto el club	is the club open?		

5. En la oficina de objetos perdidos

You have a holiday job in an office in Madrid. One morning, while travelling to work you leave your brief-case on a seat in a "Metro" station. Later you go to the lost-property office.

The Examiner is the employee.

WAIT FOR THE EMPLOYEE TO SPEAK

1. Empleado/a Greet youth and ask if you can help.

1. Tú Return greeting and say you lost your brief-case and you think you left it on a seat in this station.
AWAIT RESPONSE

2. Empleado/a Ask youth to describe the case and to say about what time it was lost.

2. Tú Mention the size and colour of the case and say what time you lost it.
AWAIT RESPONSE

3. Empleado/a Say you have several cases that fit that description. Ask what was in the case.

3. Tú Say it contained some documents, three or four letters, a small Spanish dictionary and two sandwiches.
AWAIT RESPONSE

4. Empleado/a Express surprise about the sandwiches and ask what type they were.

4. Tú Say what type of sandwiches they were and explain why you had them in the brief-case.
AWAIT RESPONSE

5. Empleado/a Say you have that brief-case alright.

5. Tú Say you're relieved to recover the brief-case as one document was very important and you had no copy of it.

6. Empleado/a Advise youth to be more careful and say he/she was lucky to get the brief-case back. Ask another question <u>clearly relevant to the situation</u>.
.... ?

RESPOND APROPRIATELY

6. Tú ....

5. En la oficina de objetos perdidos

You have a holiday job in an office in Madrid. One morning while travelling to work you leave your brief-case on a seat in a metro station. Later you go to the lost-property office.

The Examiner is the employee. <u>Examiner begins</u>:

1. Empleado/a Hola. Buenos días. ¿En qué puedo ayudarle?

1. Tú Hola. Buenos días. He perdido **mi maletín**. Creo que **lo dejé** en **un asiento** en esta estación de metro.

2. Empleado/a ¿Me lo puede describir? ¿Y a qué hora más o menos lo perdió?

2. Tú **Es de piel negra** y bastante grande con **una cerradura metálica** en el centro. **A lo mejor**, lo dejé aquí esta mañana **a eso de las siete y media** un poco **antes de subir al tren**.

3. Empleado/a Bueno. La verdad es que tenemos varios maletines así. ¿Qué cosas tenía en el maletín?

3. Tú Bueno. **Vamos a ver. Había** (Use IMPERFECT TENSE for description) algunos documentos, tres o cuatro cartas, un pequeño diccionario de español y, a ver ¿qué más? Ah, sí, dos bocadillos. Otra cosa, el maletín **no estaba cerrado con llave**.

4. Empleado/a ¡Ay! ¡Qué raro es juntar bocadillos con papeles! ¿Y de qué eran los bocadillos?

4. Tú **Eran bocadillos de jamón y queso. Los tenía** en mi maletín porque los había comprado unos minutos antes **en el quiosco del andén**.

5. Empleado/a ¡Ah sí! ¡Ya me acuerdo! Esta mañana alguien nos entregó ese maletín.

5. Tú ¡Ay! ¡**Qué alivio**! Estoy muy contento de que **haya encontrado** mi maletín. **Me preocupaba mucho** porque uno de los documentos es muy importante y **no tenía copia**.

6. Empleado/a ¡Qué suerte tiene! Hay que tener más cuidado porque hay muchos rateros por aquí. ¿ .... ?

6.Tú...

mi maletín	my brief-case	no estaba cerrada con llave	it wasn't locked
lo dejé	I left it	Eran bocadillos de jamón y queso	They were ham and cheese sandwiches
un asiento	a seat	Los tenía	I had them
Es de piel negra	It's black leather	en el quiosco del andén	at the kiosk on the platform
una cerradura metálica	a metal lock		
A lo mejor	probably	¡Qué alivio!	What a relief!
a eso de las siete y media	about half past seven	haya encontrado (SUBJUNCTIVE)	you have found
antes de subir al tren	before I got on the train		
Vamos a ver	Let's see	Me preocupaba mucho	I was very worried
Había	There were	no tenía copia	I didn't have a copy

6. En el hospital

While on holiday in Spain you borrow a friend's bike to go to the beach. You have an accident on the way and injure your arm. You go to the local hospital.

The Examiner is the doctor.

WAIT FOR THE DOCTOR TO SPEAK

1. Doctor   Greet youth and ask how he/she is.

1. Tú   Say you have just had an accident and you don't feel too well: your left arm is very sore.
AWAIT RESPONSE

2. Doctor   Ask when and how the accident happened.

2. Tú   Say about two hours ago; you fell from your bicycle when you were cycling to the beach: you can move your arm so you don't think it's broken.
AWAIT RESPONSE

3. Doctor   Say no, it's not broken; just a nasty sprain.

3. Tú   Say that's a relief and ask if the doctor can give you something for the pain.
AWAIT RESPONSE

4. Doctor   Say you'll write a prescription and the nurse will put his/her arm in a sling.

4. Tú   Ask for more information about the injury and the treatment.
AWAIT RESPONSE

5. Doctor   Give information and ask why nobody came with youth to hospital.

5. Tú   Explain why you are on your own. Say you like swimming and ask when you will be fit again.
AWAIT RESPONSE

6. Doctor   "Three weeks at least."

6. Tú   Say that's disappointing.

7. Doctor   Say it would be foolish to exercise the arm sooner. Ask another question <u>clearly relevant to the situation</u>.

.... ?

RESPOND APPROPRIATELY

7. Tú ....

6. En el hospital

While on holiday in Spain you borrow a friend's bike to go to the beach. You have an accident on the way and injure your arm. You go to the local hospital.

The Examiner is the doctor. <u>Examiner begins</u>:

1. Doctor	Hola. Buenos días. ¿Qué problema tienes?
1. Tú	**Acabo de** tener un accidente y **no me siento muy bien**. **Me duele** mucho **el brazo izquierdo**.
2. Doctor	¿Cómo y cuándo ocurrió el accidente?
2. Tú	**Hace dos horas** más o menos. **Me caí** de la bicicleta cuando **iba a la playa**. Por suerte **puedo mover el brazo**. Así que **no creo que esté roto**. (SUBJUNCTIVE after **no creo que**)
3. Doctor	No. No te lo has roto. Sólo te lo has torcido.
3. Tú	¡Ay! ¡Qué bien! ¿Puede usted darme algo **para aliviar el dolor** tan fuerte que tengo.
4. Doctor	Te daré una receta y la enfermera te pondrá el brazo en cabestrillo.
4. Tú	Gracias. ¿Cuánto tiempo **me va a doler**? ¿Y cuánto tiempo **tendré que llevar el brazo en cabestrillo**?
5. Doctor	Las pastillas te van a quitar el dolor muy pronto, pero vas a llevar el brazo en cabestrillo unos quince días. ¿Cómo es que nadie te ha acompañado a Urgencias?
5. Tú	Es que **no había nadie** en casa esta tarde. **Como sabía que** el hospital estaba muy cerca **por eso** vine sola. Otra cosa, como me gusta mucho la natación, voy a la piscina todos los días. ¿**Cuándo podré volver a nadar**?
6. Doctor	Tres semanas por lo menos.
6. Tú	¡No me diga! ¡**Qué malapata**!
7. Doctor	No es aconsejable que muevas mucho el brazo. ¿...?
7.Tú	....

Acabo de	*I have just*	**para aliviar el dolor**	*to relieve the pain*
no me siento muy bien	*I don't feel very well*	**me va a doler**	*it's going to hurt*
Me duele	*It hurts*	**tendré que llevar el brazo en cabestrillo**	*I'll have to keep my arm in a sling*
el brazo izquierdo	*my left arm*	**no había nadie**	*there was nobody*
Hace dos horas	*Two hours ago*	**Como sabía que …**	*As I knew that …*
Me caí	*I fell*	**por eso**	*because of that*
iba a la playa	*I was going to the beach*	**¿Cuándo podré?**	*When will I be able?*
puedo mover el brazo	*I can move my arm*	**volver a nadar**	*to swim again*
no creo que esté roto	*I don't think it's broken*	**!Qué malapata!**	*What a nuisance!*

7. En la oficina de turismo

You are travelling in Spain, by car with your family. On arriving in a town, in the late afternoon, you go to the Information Office.

The Examiner is the clerk.

WAIT FOR THE CLERK TO SPEAK

1. Empleado/a   Greet and welcome tourist.

1. Tú   Return greeting, say you've just arrived in the town and you'd like some information about the place.
                      AWAIT RESPONSE

2. Empleado/a   Ask what kind of information and say you have a variety of brochures.

2. Tú   Say you'd like to know something of the history of the town and the surrounding area, places worth visiting. Ask if there is a list of hotels.
                      AWAIT RESPONSE

3. Empleado/a   "Here's a booklet with all that information." Ask how he/she is travelling, who is with him/her and how long he/she intends to stay.

3. Tú   Tell him/her you are travelling by car, say who's with you and how long you intend to stay in this area and in Spain.
                      AWAIT RESPONSE

4. Empleado/a   Ask where tourist is from and whether he/she is driving.

4. Tú   Tell clerk where you are from and how long you've been travelling. Say your parents are sharing the driving and explain why you yourself are not driving.
                      AWAIT RESPONSE

5. Empleado/a   Say they must be fairly tired by now.

5. Tú   Say that your parents are exhausted but you're not so tired; still, you think you'll have an early night. Ask if the clerk can recommend a hotel.
                      AWAIT RESPONSE

6. Empleado/a   Say you can recommend the "Conde de Avila"; it's good and not expensive. Ask where the car is parked.

6. Tú   Tell him/her where the car is parked.

7. Empleado/a   Tell him/her how to get to the hotel. Ask another question <u>clearly relevant to the situation</u>.

.... ?

RESPOND APPROPRIATELY

7. Tú.. .

7. En la oficina de turismo

You are travelling in Spain, by car with your family. On arriving in a town, in the late afternoon, you go to the Information Office.

The Examiner is the clerk. <u>Examiner begins</u>:

1. Empleado/a   Hola. Buenas tardes. ¿Te puedo ayudar en algo?

1. Tú   Hola. Buenas tardes. **Acabo de llegar** y quisiera tener alguna información **sobre la ciudad**.

2. Empleado/a   Tenemos un montón de folletos. ¿Qué tipo de información buscas?

2. Tú   Bueno, **lo que más me interesa** es la historia de la ciudad y **sus alrededores**. Por ejemplo, ¿qué lugares de interés **vale la pena visitar**? También **quisiera ver** una lista de hoteles.

3. Empleado/a   Bueno. En este folleto encontrarás todo lo que necesitas. ¿En qué viajas y has venido con alguien? ¿Piensas quedarte mucho tiempo?

3. Tú   **Viajo en coche** con mis padres y **pensamos quedarnos** tres días aquí. Después, **vamos a seguir hacia** Alicante y **estaremos** en total **dos semanas** en España.

4. Empleado/a   Veo que no eres de aquí. ¿De dónde eres? ¿Eres tú el conductor del coche?

4. Tú   Somos de Irlanda. Esta mañana **salimos** muy temprano **de Burdeos**, en Francia. **Así que llevamos ocho horas viajando**. Son mis padres los que **conducen** porque todavía no tengo **el carné de conducir**.

5. Empleado/a   ¡Ay! ¡Cuántas horas de viaje! Debéis de estar muy cansados.

5. Tú   Es verdad. Mis padres **están hechos polvo** pero yo no tanto. Sin embargo, creo que **me voy a acostar bastante temprano**. ¿Podría usted recomendarnos un buen hotel que no esté muy lejos de aquí?

6. Empleado/a   Sí. Por supuesto. El hotel "Conde de Avila" se encuentra muy cerca de aquí. Es muy bueno y no es muy caro. ¿Dónde está aparcado el coche?

6. Tú   Tenemos el coche en el aparcamiento de **la esquina**.

7. Empleado/a   Después de ese semáforo es la segunda calle a la derecha.
¿ .... ?

7. Tú..

Acabo de llegar	*I have just arrived*	**estaremos dos semanas**	*we will be two weeks*
sobre la ciudad	*about the town*	**salimos de Burdeos**	*We left Bordeaux*
lo que más me interesa	*what I'm most interested in*	**Así que llevamos ocho horas viajando**	*So, we've been travelling for 8 hours*
sus alrededores	*the surrounding area*	**conducen**	*they're driving*
vale la pena visitar?	*is it worth visiting?*	**el carné de conducir**	*my driving licence*
quisiera ver	*I'd like to see*	**están hechos polvo**	*they are completely exhausted*
Viajo en coche	*I'm travelling by car*	**me voy bastante temprano**	*I'm going to go to bed early*
pensamos quedarnos	*we are planning to stay*	**la esquina**	*the corner*
vamos a seguir hacia	*we are going to continue towards*		

8. En el aeropuerto de Málaga

You have arrived at Málaga airport. You wait for your luggage and when it does not arrive you approach an official.

The Examiner is the official.

1. Tú Greet the official and say you have a problem.
AWAIT RESPONSE

1. Empleado/a Return greeting and ask what the problem is.

2. Tú Say you can't find your luggage and you think it may not have arrived on your flight.
AWAIT RESPONSE

2. Empleado/a Ask youth which flight he/she arrived on.

3. Tú Say where you have come from, give the number of the flight and say it landed an hour ago.
AWAIT RESPONSE

3. Empleado/a Say all the luggage should reach the "Arrivals" hall within half an hour of landing.

4. Tú Say all the other passengers who were on your flight seem to have collected their luggage; at least you don't see any of them here now.
AWAIT RESPONSE

4. Empleado/a Ask youth to describe luggage.

5. Tú Say you had two items of luggage and describe them.
AWAIT RESPONSE

5. Empleado/a Ask youth if he/she has a baggage receipt.

6. Tú Say yes. It's here with your passport.
AWAIT RESPONSE

6. Empleado/a Ask youth who's meeting him/her.

7. Tú Say who's meeting you and ask if it would be possible to let them know that you have arrived safely.

7. Empleado/a Say yes, we can do that immediately and then we'll go to the unclaimed baggage office. Ask another question <u>clearly relevant to the situation</u>.
.... ?

RESPOND APPROPRIATELY

8. Tú ....

correos
1988
4

Vuelos Transatlánticos

8. En el aeropuerto de Málaga

You have arrived at Málaga airport. You wait for your luggage and when it does not arrive you approach an official.

The Examiner is the official. <u>You begin</u>:

1. Tú   Hola. Perdone, señor. Tengo un problema. Quizás **usted podría ayudarme**.

1. Empleado/a Buenas tardes. ¿Cuál es el problema?

2. Tú   Es que no puedo encontrar **mi equipaje**. Creo que no ha llegado en mi vuelo.

2. Empleado/a ¿En qué vuelo llegaste?

3. Tú   Acabo de llegar de Londres en el vuelo IB 5657. Ya hace una hora que **aterrizó el avión**.

3. Empleado/a ¡Qué raro! Todas las maletas deberían llegar a la Sala de Recogida de Equipajes media hora después del aterrizaje.

4. Tú   Me parece que todos **los otros pasajeros** que estaban **conmigo** en ese vuelo ya **han recogido** sus maletas. **Por lo menos**, no veo a **ninguno de ellos** por aquí ahora.

4. Empleado/a ¿Me puedes describir tu equipaje?

5. Tú   Sí. Tenía dos maletas, una pequeña **de piel negra** con **una franja azul**. **La otra era** más grande, **del mismo estilo** pero **con ruedas**.

5. Empleado/a ¿Tienes el ticket de equipaje?

6. Tú   Sí aquí está, con mi billete y pasaporte.

6. Empleado/a ¿Quién te viene a buscar?

7. Tú   Bueno. **Hago un intercambio** con un chico de Málaga. Me dijeron sus padres que **iban a estar** aquí. **¿Me hace el favor de** informarles que **ya he llegado bien**?

8. Empleado/a Sí. Lo haremos en seguida y luego vamos a buscar tus maletas a consigna.
¿ .... ?

8. Tú..

usted podría ayudarme	*you could help me*	**La otra era**	*The other one was*
mi equipaje	*my luggage*	(IMPERFECT TENSE for description)	
aterrizó el avión	*the plane landed*	**del mismo estilo**	*the same style*
los otros pasajeros	*the other passengers*	**con ruedas**	*with wheels*
conmigo	*with me*	**Hago un intercambio**	*I'm doing an exchange*
han recogido	*they have collected*	**iban a estar**	*they were going to be*
Por lo menos	*At least*	**¿Me hace el favor de** (+ INFINITIVE)**?**	
ninguno de ellos	*none of them*		*Will you please* (+ VERB)?
de piel negra	*black leather*	**ya he llegado bien**	*I've arrived safely*
una franja azul	*a blue stripe*		

9. Un intercambio en España

You are sent on a student exchange to a school in Spain. On the morning of the first day you meet a teacher at the school door.

The Examiner is the teacher.

WAIT FOR TEACHER TO SPEAK

1. Profesor/a Greet student and say you haven't seen him/her before.

1. Tú Return greeting. Say you're on a student exchange and this is your first day.
AWAIT RESPONSE

2. Profesor/a Say you didn't know there was an exchange student in the school and ask where he/she is from.

2. Tú Tell teacher your name, your age, where you are from, which year you are in and how long you'll be in the school.
AWAIT RESPONSE

3. Profesor/a Say student is very welcome and ask what he/she was asked to do on arrival.

3. Tú Tell teacher what you were asked to do when you arrived at the school. Say you're twenty minutes late and explain the delay.
AWAIT RESPONSE

4. Profesor/a Enquire about student's leisure activities.

4. Tú Say you play basketball but you're not very good, you walk a lot, you watch sport on the television and you read best-sellers.
AWAIT RESPONSE

5. Profesor/a Ask what student hopes to do when finished school.

5. Tú Tell teacher which career you hope to pursue and why.

6. Profesor/a Comment on what student has said. Ask another question <u>clearly relevant to the situation</u>.
.... ?

RESPOND APPROPRIATELY

6. Tú ....

Track 50

9. Un intercambio en España

You are sent on a student exchange to a school in Spain. On the morning of the first day you meet a teacher at the school door.

The Examiner is the teacher. <u>Examiner begins</u>:

1. Profesor/a Hola. Buenos días. No te he visto por aquí antes. ¿Eres un nuevo alumno?

1. Tú Buenos días, señora. Sí. **Hago un intercambio** con un chico español y **hoy es mi primer día**.

2. Profesor/a Ah. Pues, no sabía que había un estudiante aquí ahora haciendo intercambio. ¿De dónde eres?

2. Tú **Soy de Irlanda**. Me llamo Peter y tengo dieciocho años. Estoy **en el último año** de colegio en Irlanda. **Sólo voy a estar** aquí durante tres semanas.

3. Profesor/a Pues, estamos muy contentos de que estés con nosotros. ¿Te ha dicho alguien lo que tienes que hacer cuando llegues al colegio?

3. Tú Bueno. **Me pidieron que fuera** a la oficina del director, **en cuanto llegara** al colegio. El problema es que he llegado **con veinte minutos de retraso**. **Me equivoqué de** autobús y **había mucha circulación**.

4. Profesor/a No te preocupes. ¿Quieres decirme qué te gusta hacer durante tus ratos libres?

4. Tú **Juego al baloncesto** aunque no juego muy bien. **Me gusta mucho salir de paseo**. En la televisión me gusta ver **los programas deportivos**. También **leo bastante**, sobre todo **los éxitos de más venta**.

5. Profesor/a ¿Y ya sabes qué vas a hacer cuando termines el colegio?

5. Tú Quisiera ir a la universidad para estudiar economía e idiomas. **Me encanta la idea** de vivir y trabajar **en otro país** y **quizás**, más tarde, **vendré a trabajar** a España.

6. Profesor/a ¡Ay! ¡Qué bien!
¿.. ?

6. Tú..

Hago un intercambio	*I'm on an exchange*	**Juego al baloncesto**	*I play basketball*
hoy es mi primer día	*today is my first day*	**Me gusta mucho salir de paseo**	*I like to walk a lot*
Soy de Irlanda	*I'm from Ireland*	**los programas deportivos**	*sports programmes*
en el último año	*in the last year*	**leo bastante**	*I read a lot*
Sólo voy a estar	*I'm only going to be*	**los éxitos de más venta**	*best-sellers*
Me pidieron que fuera	*I was asked to go*	**Me encanta la idea**	*I love the idea*
en cuanto llegara	*as soon as I arrived*	**en otro país**	*in another country*
con veinte minutos de retraso	*twenty minutes late*	**quizás**	*perhaps*
Me equivoqué de	*I got the wrong*	**vendré a trabajar**	*I'll come and work*
había mucha circulación	*there was a lot of traffic*		

10. Un encuentro con un compañero/a de clase

In October you meet a former class-mate whom you haven't seen since you both did the Leaving Certificate in June.

The Examiner is the class-mate.

1. Tú   Say hello and ask how he/she is.
AWAIT RESPONSE

1. Amigo/a "Fine, and you?"

2. Tú   Say you're fairly well now; you had an accident during the summer and spent three weeks in hospital.
AWAIT RESPONSE

2. Amigo/a Ask how accident occurred.

3. Tú   Say you were cycling to the beach with your sister when …
AWAIT RESPONSE

3. Amigo/a Ask what injury he/she suffered and if the sister was hurt.

4. Tú   Say your sister was cycling on the inside and wasn't hurt. Describe your injury.
AWAIT RESPONSE

4. Amigo/a Ask what he/she is doing now.

5. Tú   Say you are repeating the Leaving Certificate. Your results were fairly good but you didn't get enough points for … Ask what he/she is doing.
AWAIT RESPONSE

5. Amigo/a Say you are working in an Insurance Office in London; you're home for a few days.

6. Tú   Say you were in London once and give one reason why you didn't like it.
AWAIT RESPONSE

6. Amigo/a Say you're meeting some friends in McDonald's in five minutes. Invite him/her to join you.

7. Tú   Thank him/her and explain why you can't go along.

7. Amigo/a Say that's a pity. Ask another question clearly relevant to the situation.
.... ?

RESPOND APPROPRIATELY

8. Tú ....

Track 51

10. Un encuentro con un compañero/a de clase

In October you meet a former class-mate whom you haven't seen since you both did the Leaving Certificate in June.

The Examiner is the class-mate. <u>You begin</u>:

1. Tú   **Hola Pedro. ¿Qué tal estás?**

1. Amigo/a Muy bien. ¿Y tú?

2. Tú   Ahora **me encuentro muy bien**. Pero durante el verano **tuve un accidente** y pasé tres semanas en **el** hospital.

2. Amigo/a ¡No me digas! ¿Pero, cómo ocurrió el accidente?

3. Tú   Bueno, iba a la playa en bicicleta con mi hermana cuando, **de repente**, salió un coche **de una bocacalle**. **Me golpeó** y caí **al suelo**.

3. Amigo/a ¿Te hiciste mucho daño? ¿Y tu hermana, qué le pasó a ella?

4. Tú   **Perdí el conocimiento** y, al despertar, me encontré en el hospital. **Tenía el brazo roto** y **la cabeza vendada**. Como mi hermana iba en bicicleta, a mi derecha, **no le pasó nada**.

4. Amigo/a ¿Y ahora qué estás haciendo?

5. Tú   **Vuelvo a hacer** el Leaving. **Saqué una nota bastante buena** pero no lo suficiente como para **entrar en la universidad**. Y tú, ¿qué estás haciendo ahora?

5. Amigo/a Estoy trabajando en una oficina de seguros en Londres; he venido a pasar unos días con mi familia.

6. Tú   !Qué bien! Sólo estuve en Londres una vez pero no me gustó mucho. La gente **me parecía muy antipática**.

6. Amigo/a ¿Sabes qué? De aquí a cinco minutos vamos a reunirnos con un grupo de amigos en McDonald. ¿Por qué no nos acompañas?

7. Tú   Gracias. Lo siento, pero hoy no puedo. Mi madre sale **dentro de media hora** y **quiere que vuelva a casa** en seguida para cuidar a mis hermanos pequeños.

7. Amigo/a ¡Ay! ¡Qué lástima!

¿ .... ?

8. Tú...

me encuentro muy bien	*I feel alright*	**la cabeza vendada**	*my head bandaged*
tuve un accidente	*I had an accident*	**no le pasó nada**	*nothing happened to her*
de repente	*suddenly*	**Vuelvo a hacer**	*I'm repeating*
de una bocacalle	*from a side street*	**una nota bastante buena**	*My results were quite good*
Me golpeó	*It hit me*	**entrar en la universidad**	*to go to university*
al suelo	*to the ground*	**me parecía muy antipática**	*seemed very unpleasant*
Perdí el conocimiento	*I lost consciousness*	**dentro de media hora**	*in half an hour*
Tenía el brazo roto	*I had a broken arm*	**quiere que vuelva a casa**	*wants me to return home*

GW00492684

CONTENTS

INTRODUCTION

God's House Tower has a history spanning nearly 800 years and its latest incarnation is as an arts & heritage venue, providing a new contemporary art gallery space which will support up-and-coming artists in the city, as well as showcasing some of the incredible works of art from Southampton's Designated collections.

The tower, built around 1400, will fulfil the heritage brief focusing on the building's two main functions over past centuries, as a gun tower and as a gaol.

The tower and its inhabitants have many more stories to tell and this book aims to expand on the two main exhibition themes but also to fill in the gaps in the long history of God's House Tower. God's House Tower has done duty as a hospital, mortuary, storage warehouse, archaeology museum and has been an inspiration to artists old and new. It is also about story-telling 'if the walls could talk', whether that is the Dutch accent of gunner Peter Breme, the singing and dancing of Keeper Truss and Mary his wife, the groans of prisoners working the mill, or sobs of children about to be transported to Australia.

POWDER:

The Medieval Town:
Normans,
Gunners &
Defence of the Realm

POWDER: The Medieval Town: Normans, Gunners & Defence of the Realm

Although there had been settlements in Southampton in the Roman and Anglo-Saxon periods, the medieval town can almost be styled a Norman new town. The street outline had been set out towards the end of the Anglo-Saxon era but it was the Norman conquerors who built the walled town which is still the centre of the city of Southampton. 1066 saw a period of military occupation in England, the victorious Normans, descendants of the Vikings who had raided and colonised the old Saxon kingdoms, stamped their authority on Southampton. This alien culture became the dominant force in the development of Southampton as a town and a port. This was visible in their first construction projects, a motte and bailey castle atop a towering mound right inside the precincts of the town, and the church of St Michael built in thanks for victory and dedicated, in 1070, to the patron saint of Normandy, St Michael the Archangel.

Streets were renamed. The two main streets running north to south, down to the town quays, were now called French Street and English Street, reflecting the two communities in the town. Indeed so key was the control of Southampton to the Normans that thirty French families were planted in the town. It was Southampton as a safe harbour which was important to the Normans, to ease their passage back and forth to France and to facilitate trade between the two dominions. To ensure customs duties could be levied and trade controlled the town needed gates.

The Normans built in stone, quickly replacing the initial wooden palisades thrown up post-Conquest. Stone however was in short supply, as there was no quarry around Southampton, a town built on brickearth and gravel. The nearest quarry was at Bembridge on the Isle of Wight, convenient as a stopping off point for ships visiting the port to pick up limestone. In addition the Normans had access to finer stone quarried at Caen which could be used to finish and decorate their buildings, around doorways, windows and arches. Lime pits were dug and the nearby oyster beds provided shells to make the mortar that would join the stones together. Masons would shape the stone into blocks to make walls that would stretch up to ten metres high and three metres thick. It was a massive building project, and work needed to be prioritised – gates first, then corner towers and finally walls to join up these structures. The walls to the north and the east of the town were built first, the Normans being more concerned with attacks from the land by disgruntled Saxons than invasions from the sea. In addition

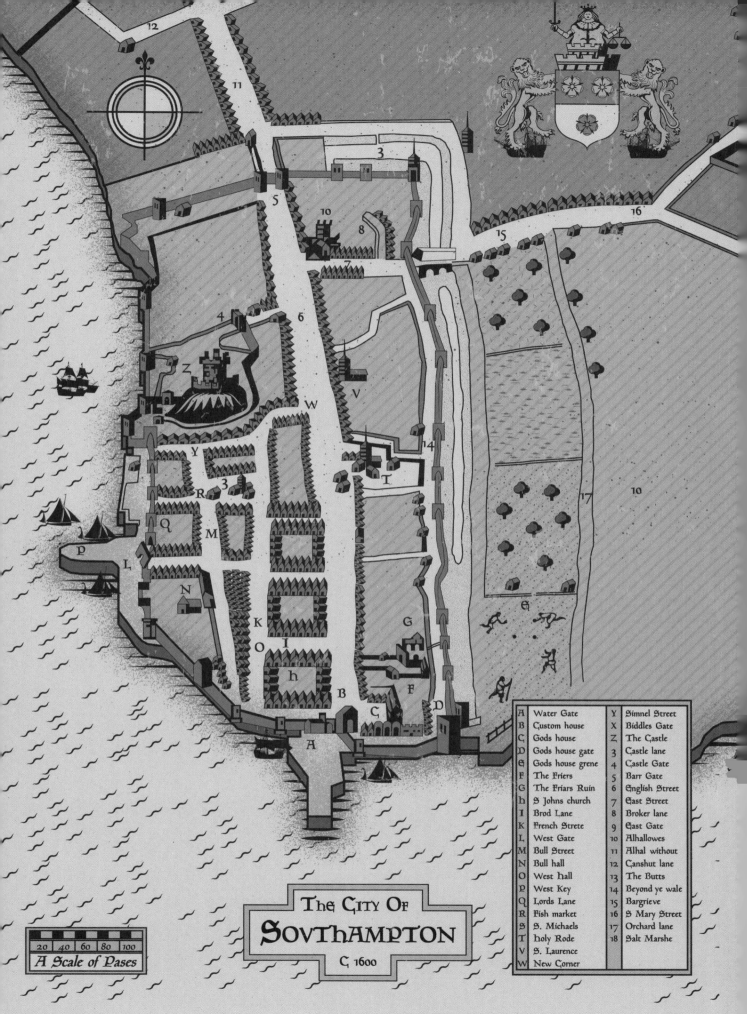

THE CITY OF SOVThAMPTON

C. 1600

A	Water Gate	Y	Simnel Street
B	Custom house	X	Biddles Gate
C	Gods house	Z	The Castle
D	Gods house gate	3	Castle lane
E	Gods house grene	4	Castle Gate
F	The Friers	5	Barr Gate
G	The Friars Ruin	6	English Street
h	S Johns church	7	East Street
I	Brod Lane	8	Broker lane
K	French Strete	9	East Gate
L	West Gate	10	Alhallowes
M	Bull Street	11	Alhal without
N	Bull hall	12	Canshut lane
O	West hall	13	The Butts
P	West Key	14	Beyond ye wale
Q	Lords Lane	15	Bargrieve
R	Fish market	16	S Mary Street
S	S. Michaels	17	Orchard lane
T	holy Rode	18	Salt Marshe
V	S. Laurence		
W	New Corner		

A Scale of Pases
20 40 60 80 100

Guy Stauber's re-imagining of John Speed's map of 1611

6

the Norman merchants who migrated to the town wanted to live on the shore side, building tall stone tenements with large warehouses facing onto the quays to facilitate ease of trade and movement of cargoes. This trade was based on wine. French wine flowed into the port of Southampton before being distributed around the country. It came in such amounts that beneath the town buildings dozens of vaults were constructed, mostly barrel shaped to accommodate the barrels of wine as well as other goods. With trade came money which enabled more buildings to be built in stone: churches, houses, trade halls, as well as the growing defences.

Southampton Old Town Walls

As the Normans became more integrated into England, tensions began to grow between the English king and the king of France. The English kings as Dukes of Normandy owed allegiance and fealty to their French counterpart which did not sit easily with men who were also crowned monarchs in their own right. The situation became even more strained when Henry II inherited the throne of

Castle Vault

England. He was also Count of Anjou, as well as Duke of Normandy and by his advantageous marriage to the French heiress Eleanor of Aquitaine, now had that duchy as well as Maine, Nantes, Therouanne, and Gascony, so in fact controlled of more of France than the king of France himself. This led to almost continual warfare throughout the medieval period. Initially the French king gained all the success regaining nearly all the territory which was formerly part of Henry II's Angevin Empire. In the fourteenth century, however, the English king Edward III decided to try and reclaim his heritage, and so began a conflict known as 'The Hundred Years War'. Southampton found itself in the front line of the conflict and the first blood went to the French.

"The old town of Hampton was brent in tyme of warre, spoyled and rasyd by French pyrates". John Leyland

In October 1338 a French fleet, supported by Genoese mercenaries, sailed up Southampton Water and landed on the undefended shore of Southampton near the bottom of Bugle Street. They set fire to buildings in the town, slaughtered the local population, broke into cellars and warehouses and looted their contents. After two days they were eventually ejected from the town by the county militias. The town now faced the fury of Edward III, who was even suspicious that it was the townspeople themselves who had looted his wine vault. He ordered the town to build seaward defences on the west and south of the town, to complete the encirclement of Southampton by stone walls. They were not traditional medieval walls but walls that could accommodate and make use of the latest weapons: guns.

Building work was interrupted by the arrival of the Black Death in 1348, a pandemic which reduced the population of the known world by at least a third. The chronicler Henry Knighton wrote that the plague had entered England through the gates of the town of Southampton.

Illustration - Martin Davey

"THE DREADFUL PESTILENCE PENETRATED THE SEA COAST BY SOUTHAMPTON" Henry Knighton

The town was devastated. A population of 4000, which was quite modest for a medieval town, fell to just 1800. It took nearly two hundred years before the population recovered. However the tragedy also created opportunities for those that survived. Southampton entered a new period of economic prosperity, this time built on the export of wool and the import of luxury goods brought into the town by the Italian merchants of Florence, Genoa, Lucca and Venice.

War however remained a constant threat. The Hundred Years War dragged on, followed by the Wars of the Roses and then fresh conflicts as the Tudors under Henry VIII renewed the dream of re-conquest in France. New enemies appeared during the reign of Henry's daughter Elizabeth I when England faced the might of Spain and once more Southampton was in the front line. God's House Tower was crucial in the defence of the realm.

GOD'S HOUSE GATE & TOWER: Defence of the realm

The gate and tower that were built in the south east corner of the town defences have had a variety of names over the centuries. The gate led onto the Platform Quay and looked over the town saltmarsh, so was often called Saltmarsh Gate, but it was also called Lambcote Tower and sometimes the Mill Tower. The name by which it is now known is God's House Gate taking that name from the nearby God's House Hospital. The gate in fact had probably been built on land originally owned by the hospital which had been established c1189. The hospital had also been given the responsibility of maintaining the gate and tower in the 1454 defence terrier. In medieval England there was no standing army so all the town towers and walls were divided up and attached to local guilds and institutions for their maintenance.

God's House Hospital was what was known as a Maison Dieu, a religious establishment which provided hospice and alms houses and also temporary accommodation to travellers and pilgrims. These establishments were always built next to gates and entrance ways, so that the hospital inmates could easily come out and beg alms from travellers entering the town. As Southampton was the starting point for the 'Old Way' a well-established pilgrim route to Canterbury, there would be a steady flow of pilgrims passing this way.

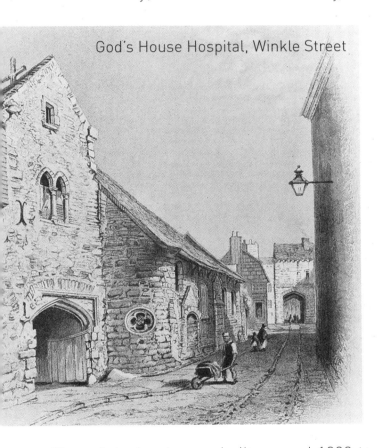
God's House Hospital, Winkle Street

There was a particular feel to the culture of the town around God's House Gate. As well as the Maison Dieu, there was a Franciscan Friary next to that complex. The main street which led from God's House Gate came out onto the main high street, English Street, near to the Water Gate and Town Quay. To the south of the street were stables, lofts and cellars leased to prominent merchants. The gate looked out over marshes and oyster beds with views down to the river Itchen. There was also a bowling green, an area for archery practice, orchards and grazing for horses.

The original gate was built around 1280 to give access to the Platform Quay. The wooden gate was protected by a portcullis that could be pulled up inside the vaulted roof of the gate and into the tower above. The defences to protect the gate were strengthened in around 1320 when an angled tower was added to the south of the gate. The gateway passage was also extended which enabled the room above the gate to be enlarged. The gate gave access to the walls on the east at a high level, useful for any patrols or at times of attack. There are also references to the gatehouse being used as a temporary prison, probably because it was sturdily built and was a guarded structure. Running along the eastern walls was a double ditched moat which was fed by sea water at the Platform Quay. During excavations of Southampton these ditches were shown to be 38 ft, and 40 ft wide.

Winkle Street with a view of God's House Gate

The ditches were important not only for defence but also because they provided water power for one of the town's main mills which was built adjacent to God's House Tower. The ditches also served as a sewer system for toilets. In the middle ages people did not have toilets in their houses. Some would have cesspits built in their gardens, or the alternative was to empty the contents of chamber pots out into the street. If lucky, passers-by were alerted by the cry of 'Gardez L'eau' from the French for 'watch the water'. The shout was soon corrupted to 'Gardez Loo'. The Corporation did build public toilets, usually near to the town gates because of how crowded the gates would be with people coming in and out, and because

God's House Garderobe

of access to water which would to some degree cleanse the latrines. These toilets had names like 'The Jakes', which were at the Bargate, the 'Wedraft House' at West Gate, 'The Little House of Sighs' and the 'Little House of Easement'. The closest toilets to God's House were the 'Friars Benches' originally built as the reredorter within the Friary complex. It was a stone building which jutted out over the ditches, the waste flowing southwards under God's House Tower. The Friary reredorter still survives. The ditches were a source of food, with fishing and herbage (the right to grow certain crops) rights, and so were rented out to prominent citizens. As an important corporate building God's House had an internal toilet or garderobe, from the French for 'protect your clothes' incorporated into the fabric of the building and built over the town ditches.

God's House Gate in the fourteenth century was solely a defensive structure. It had several upper levels but these also appear to have focused on the military needs of the town. The chamber above the Gate was not designed for domestic use as it lacked any amenities such as a latrine or a fireplace. The level directly above the Gate was where a springald, a large-scale crossbow, would have been located while the highest level probably served as some type of lookout. This highest level no longer exists as it seems to have been removed when God's House Tower was built. It would have been the highest point in the south east of the town and would have commanded a strong viewpoint; a valuable feature for the first fortification of the town's seaward approach.

As the possibility of further war with France heightened at the beginning of the fifteenth century, additional defences were put in place. Around 1400 a freestanding tower was built east of the Gate, straddling the moat or ditches as they were now known. The tower was designed to protect the sluices which regulated the flow of water in and out of the ditches. The tower was built for the use of guns, it had gun ports on three sides in the keyhole style for the use of smaller artillery, a very early example of this type of gunport. On the roof large gun embrasures were built for the siting of big cannon.

Keyhole Gunport

When Henry V came to the throne in 1413 war with France became imminent, prompting the final medieval building works which took place at God's House Tower. A long gallery was constructed joining the new tower to the existing gatehouse. This was a purpose-built gun battery, designed to defend the Platform Quay and the harbour of Southampton, and probably the earliest example of such a construction in England.

The accounts of the mayor John Benet record the sum of £100 which was to be received from the collectors of the King's Subsidy John Foxholes and William Soper for the repair and improvement of the new tower near the gate called 'Goddeshous Gate'. By a writ patent granted on 11th July 1417 by Henry V, the king had stated that customs dues could be used to fund the building by a levy of 3s on a tun of wine and 12d on every pound in the port. John Benet claimed costs for 64 ½ tons of stone called 'Rageston', a hard limestone, at 10d the ton, '150 stone called Freston', a finer stone that was easier to cut, priced 5s a ton, and 32 pieces of timber bought wholesale for £4 16d. Other materials included two hundred new boards at a cost of 30s, 11 fother of lead which cost 106s 8d, a fother and 8s quarters of burnt lime, at 10d the quarter with carriage, and eighty cartloads of sand at 3d a cartload. Those receiving wages included Bartholemew the mason and ten other stone cutters working 54 days; John Shadyington and eight other stone cutters for 35 days work; eight labourers for 24 days; John Chamberlyen, John Weytteney and five other carpenters for 20 days, all at 4d a day; and the Romsey plumbers John Plommer and John Cok.

> "The south gate stondith not even ful south but south est: and ther is ioinyd to it a castelet welle ordinauncid to bete that quarter of the haven" John Leyland

GUNS & GUNPOWDER

The town started to buy guns after the French raid of 1338. Guns were an expensive item and initially the town bought only small guns but their armaments were enhanced by gifts of guns from the king. Guns needed storing and they were useless without supplies of gun-stones and gunpowder. God's House Tower and gun battery became the main venue for keeping the town's growing arsenal. By the 1430s there are known to have been six guns in the town, by the 1460s this had risen to twenty-five. The biggest guns were given names such as 'Thomas with the Beard' and 'Maid Meg'. The array of guns was eclectic, in a survey of 1468 they included a muzzle-loading brass gun, two breech-loading pieces, another with three chambers, a great gun on its own wheeled carriage, a serpentine and a number of broken guns and a raft of gun chambers.

Fifteenth century cannon and carriage
Illustration - Martin Davey

Tudor Gunners - image with thanks to the Suffolk Free Company

The design of guns improved rapidly from the temperamental fourteenth century constructions. Sir John Dawtrey, owner of Tudor House, was appointed to strengthen the defences of Southampton in the early years of the reign of Henry VIII. Dawtrey bought four guns from John Fortuna Catalynage at a cost of £22 10s 0d, but later sold them onto the king ... for £40 2s 4d. By the sixteenth century the town owned large cannon that needed great wheeled carriages to support and move them, these guns were called demi-culverin and full culverin. They also owned smaller, lighter pieces such as the falcon and the falconet.

WEAPONS HELD IN STORE 1468

One broken gun

2 whole guns and one serpentine

Spruce chest with 19 chambers to organ gun after specified

¾ of a barrel of powder

Diverse sorts of gun-stones

Broken iron pondery

In the cheney two chains of iron and the hangers of iron pondery

2 iron great stakes and 3 ladders

Chamber of the great gun

IN THE MILLHOUSE

[Mill tower was the name given to God's House Tower in 1434]

2 cart guns

1 peys organs in a cart

9 guns

1 great gun

1 gun upon trestles chambered of himself

2 windows of the same house with 2 guns

6 gun chambers

1 great broken chamber for the cannon 'Thomas with the Beard'

2 whole chambers for them with 8 guns-tones and 8 tampons

1 little Rondelet with gunpowder

Jack

Breast plate

WEAPONS HELD IN STORE 1601

One fowler and a chamber
one sling and two chambers
3 fowlers serviceable 2 lacking stocks
one minion serviceable
one falcon serviceable
one falcon without carriage
one robinet of brass
one falcon of brass broken
one fowler
25 bills
90 demi culverin shot
150 saker shot
24 whole culverin shot
16 minyon cross bar shot
17 saker cross bar shot
180 minion shot
89 falcon shot
11 bows and some sheaf arrows
2 langcon shott
2 Cat shot of iron
5 saker ladles
one whole culverin ladle
one demi culverin ladle
one dry vat almost full of gun match
one falcon of iron with carriage
2 minion ladles
2 falcon Ladles
one robinet ladle
3 sponges
2 falcons of brass
one bastard minion of brass
3 old pikes not serviceable
in the powder howse
9 barrels of powder filled
one brass culverin
one demi culverin of iron
one saker of brass crased
one new carriage for the culverin
5 pair of new wheels with carriage for ordinance
4 saker carriages
one demi culverin carriage

Pike

Brigandine

Demi culverin

16

Glossary of terms for guns & armaments used in the town of Southampton in the sixteenth century with thanks to the Royal Armouries

Morian

Dagger

Cross Bow

Almain Rivets – armour breastplate and simple arm defences, mass produced in Germany for common soldiers

Bandoliers – belt worn across the shoulder for holding cartridges

Basis – type of small-bore cannon or breach-loading gun

Bills – staff weapon based on agricultural bill hook

Biskeniers – musketeers

Bows – longbows

Brass Bassler – type of gun

Breast Plate – metal defence for the front of the torso

Brigandines – type of flexible armour for the torso, made of metal plates riveted between layers of fabric

Brown Shot – type of munition

Calliver – handgun, light musket

Chain Shot – artillery projectile consisting of a chain between two balls, used for fouling rigging and masts of ships

Chamber – removable piece of a breech-loading cannon into which gunpowder was placed

Corn Powder – gun powder formed into large pieces like peppercorns

Corselette – half-armour comprising breast, back and gorget (neck defence), helmet, tassets (upper thigh pieces) and arm defences

Crossbow Shot – expanding bullets or cannon balls

Culverin – heavy artillery piece

Dagger – double edged knife

Demi-Cannon – heavy siege gun

Demi-Culverin – slightly lighter than culverin

Falcon – either type of gun or instrument for bending a crossbow

Falcon Shot – shot for small-bore artillery piece

Forlocks – general term for a matchlock gun, fired by piece of burning match cord

Fowlers – firearm, longer barrelled for greater accuracy and used for hunting

Gabions – wicket baskets filled with earth used as a defensive shield

Gorget – metal defence for the throat and collar area

Gun-stones – stone shot for artillery pieces

17

Halberd – similar to a bill, but purpose built

Half Hake – short pike

Handguns – hand-held firearm

Harquebus – early heavy musket

Harness – armour

Heltes – helmet

Hoyndarde – measure of shot Iron Shot – miscellaneous cannon shot made from cast iron

Jacks – thick padded fabric armour for the body, could also have jacks which were small metal plates

Javelin – light spear

Knapp Scull – type of helmet

Last – measure of gunpowder 2400lbs

Linstock – staff with a piece of match cord at one end, used to ignite powder

Mail Coats – mail garment with or without sleeves

Minions – cast iron gun

Murrain Heads – type of helmet

Musket – matchlock

Partisan – bladed spear

Pike – long spear

Pole Axe – staff weapon with a variety of heads

Privy Coat – light coat of defensive mail worn under ordinary clothes

Rammer – rod used to push cannon ball down the barrel of the gun

Rapier – sword with light, long blade for thrusting

Robinet – engine used for throwing darts or stones

Rutters – mercenary horsemen

Sacar Shot – shot for saker which was a cast iron gun

Saker – artillery piece

Serpentine – trigger lever on a gun

Serpentine Power – fine powder

Skaverer – Scourer for the barrel of the gun

Staves – staff weapon

Sword – double edged and straight bladed

Touch Boys – ignition device

Visors – removable face-protection on a helmet

Cannon implements

Caliver

Poleaxe

18

GUNPOWDER

Gunpowder was probably first used for military purposes in Europe early in the fourteenth century. Many of the early weapons were made of wrought iron, of tubes built up from iron strips or bars forged together and strengthened. Such guns were typically loaded at the breech end and provided with a detachable chamber for the powder.

Gunstones and iron shot

The town mayors spent substantial sums on the acquisition of shot and the provision of gunpowder. In the mayoral accounts the first mention of gunpowder is in 1506-7 when the merchant and burgess Mr Fleming provided a barrel of powder at a cost of 51s. Iron shot, gunpowder, saltpetre, and brimstone were purchased in London where they were transported to the Swan at Holborn to be picked up by the town officers. Mark Dingley provided 22 hundred weight of serpentine powder and two hundred weight of corn powder, a huge amount of powder which all needed to be stored somewhere.

The cellar of God's House Tower was designated as the gunpowder store, this was a groin vault with a newel staircase at the west end to communicate with the floor above. To make gunpowder you needed coal, saltpetre and sulphur but the secret ingredients were dung and urine. Dung was collected from hen houses, pigsties, sheep pens, stables and public toilets. Pigeon cotes, such as the one at the nearby Friary, had droppings that were rich in nitre. A trench was dug, and filled with quicklime and straw. Manure and urine were added daily for three weeks to turn the mixture into nitrate. This was then dug up, and boiled in lead or copper vats to evaporate the liquid, and make crystalized saltpetre.

The town sometimes employed outside specialists like Parson William Levit, a former canon of the collegiate church of South Malling, and the King's gun-stone maker. He made iron shot and ordnance and oversaw the iron mines in Sussex. Sussex had become an important centre in the gun-founding industry, improving the process by which cannon were cast in one piece and then bored. The town did however need to appoint its own official town gunners who had the skill and responsibility for making gun-stones and gunpowder as part of their duties.

"FOR THE ACCOUNT OF ALL SUCHE BILLS AS WERE GEVEN OUT FOR THE LONNE OF POWDERE FOR THE PROVIZONS OF HYR MAJESTIE AND THE TOWNE AS FOLLOWEITH THE 16 OF FEBRUARY 1589"

Tudor Gun Crew - image with thanks to the Suffolk Free Company

THE GUNNERS

Initially the appointment of town gunners was a casual affair, as and when needed. In 1454 a gunner would have been paid by the day receiving 6d for making gunpowder, handling and repairing guns. However after a serious incident in 1475 involving a threat from French ships which had seized a Portuguese trading vessel, it became clear there needed to be a more organised response to the town's artillery defence. This event showed the town guns not to be in good shape and it was only the luck of Lord Audley's gunners being in the town which enabled the town to respond. When guns were used they could get damaged, so repairs were needed both during the action, as well as afterward. In 1475 the cord which was the safeguard on the stock of the gun, 'Thomas with the Beard', broke when the gun was fired, showing that it was important in such situations to have professional men on hand who could make running repairs.

Henry VIII's cannon
Tudor House garden

When Sir John Dawtrey was appointed by Henry VIII to be in charge of the maintenance of the defences of Southampton he brought in specialist German gunners to oversee the town armaments. In this same period Balfer Lynne, another foreign worker, agreed to serve as town gunner in 1512, for a yearly fee of 26s 8d plus a gown worth 10s. Lynne was given the exclusive contract to make every gun-stone both great and small, for which he would receive 2d a time. In one instance he worked with the smith Inglebard to make gun pellets using nineteen and a half pounds of iron and 40lb of lead as part of the process. When he made gunpowder he would receive 7d a day for himself and 4d a day for every man who worked with him. In the same year the town steward Richard Heckley was employed in organising a range of activities around the town guns and he used casual workers like the Fleming Deryk Berebrewer to help move the guns around, the smith Thomas Byrd to make running repairs, William Wheller to clear gun barrels and Hugh Carpenter who was occupied unstocking and stocking the great gun. The great gun was so large it took twelve men to move it into the town. The town was also happy to use visiting trained labour such as the crew from Italian galleys or even Frenchmen to maintain the guns and make the gun-stones.

Throughout the first half of the sixteenth century the town continued to employ gunners from the Low Countries and Germany because of their specialist skills, skills that were not available amongst the local workforce. The Breme family, from the Low Countries, were typical of these economic migrants. Peter Breme was employed as the Corporation's master gunner along with his two sons Peter and Thomas. Unlike their predecessors, the Bremes and the other town gunners of this period, up to six in number, were now on annual retainers and often served for years. As official servants of the town they were entitled to wear the town livery, which was provided annually in the form of red kersey and white cotton cloth which the men would have had made up to fit. Clothes were a valuable commodity in the sixteenth century and many people would just have one set of clothes that they kept fresh by changing the linen they wore underneath. If you had a little more money you could buy new sleeves to change the look of your outfit. To have quality uniforms was an important bonus as well as giving status to their wearers. The hazards of being a gunner included getting your clothes burned when sparks flew from the firing of the guns. One gunner was paid 12d in 'reward' for the damage done to his clothes, so the gunners were no doubt pleased to be provided with a livery to preserve their own outfits.

As is the case of the Bremes, the gunners' positions were not full-time so gunners also employed in other trades such as beer brewers, blacksmiths, glaziers, and plumbers. Some combined their gunnery position with other corporate appointments such as that of Town Sergeant. Town Sergeants were officers of the court under the aegis of the mayor and were four in number. By a charter of Henry VI the Sergeants as well as attending the mayor and Corporation were sworn officers 'to execute all attachments, arrests etc within the town and its precincts'. They had to look after the debtors' and felons' prison and collect the tolls for the poultry and vegetable market. They were known as the four Sergeants at Mace, the mace being a ceremonial staff that had originally been a weapon, a heavy duty truncheon.

The master gunner would lead the team and he would be responsible for the firing of the large cannon. This had to be practiced as all the men needed to fulfil their part. The master gunner was also responsible for training other townsmen in the firing of the guns in order to support the regular gunners in times of attack. With the various guns that the town held the gunners had to be able to use the muzzle-loading guns, cast from bronze, as well as the older wrought-iron artillery. There was a range of ammunition, consisting of iron shot as well as stone balls and chain shot used for disabling the rigging of enemy ships. The men needed to learn the routines for priming and firing a gun and how to decide the line and path of a shot. Professional treatises on ballistics began to be written at this time.

FIRING THE GUNS

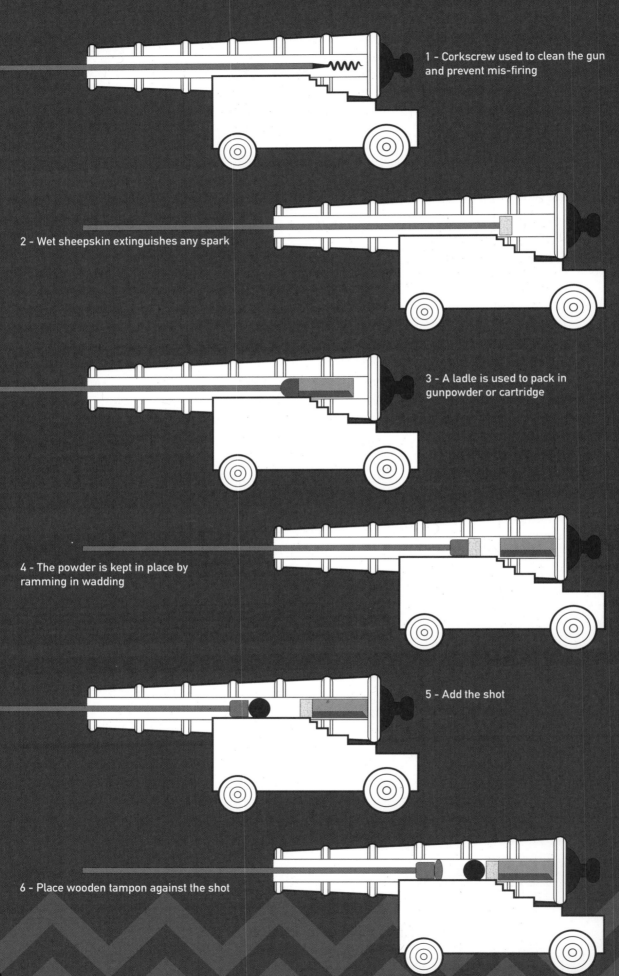

1 - Corkscrew used to clean the gun and prevent mis-firing

2 - Wet sheepskin extinguishes any spark

3 - A ladle is used to pack in gunpowder or cartridge

4 - The powder is kept in place by ramming in wadding

5 - Add the shot

6 - Place wooden tampon against the shot

23

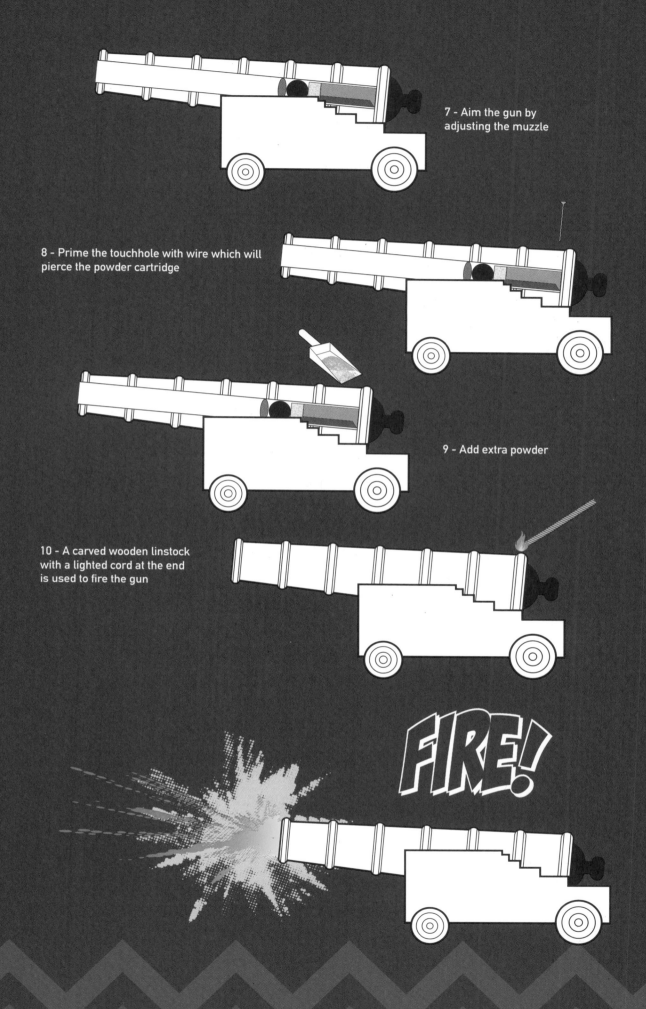

7 - Aim the gun by adjusting the muzzle

8 - Prime the touchhole with wire which will pierce the powder cartridge

9 - Add extra powder

10 - A carved wooden linstock with a lighted cord at the end is used to fire the gun

FIRE!

THE DANGERS

To protect the gunners and the guns during a battle, wooden hoardings and shutters were built around gun placements to guard against fire coming their way. Gabions, also known as 'basketts', were provided. These were made of wicker and cylindrical or conical in shape, filled with earth and placed on the parapets of the town wall to give extra cover.

Unfortunately at the end of Henry VIII's reign when the king again turned his attention to war against France, this led to an accident in Southampton where at least one of the town gunners was killed. Six French ships appeared off the Isle of Wight in 1542 and in the ensuing gun battle one of the town ordnance exploded. John Ynglette's arm was so badly broken that a specialist bonesetter was called in from Nutbourne as was a surgeon from Portsmouth. The gunner Harmon (Herman) Smith was killed outright and the town in recompense paid for his shroud, his pit maker, bedesman and cleric. The town mayor's own chaplain, Sir Ector, said Mass for Ynglette but there is no record of his burial, so perhaps the Mass was in thanksgiving for his survival. As well as the loss of life there was a great deal of damage done to the guns and their supporting stages and carriages.

A merchant ship owned by Mistress Bory, also had its mast hit by mistake. The defence of the town was successful and some of the French force was captured. Ironically seven French prisoners of war were employed as labourers, helping with the repairs to the defences, and they were paid 4d for their trouble.

The widow of Harmon Smith meanwhile found herself in straitened circumstances after his death and appealed for financial support from the Corporation. She received 24s 7d because of the poverty she found herself in and because her husband had died in service to the 'Lord King and town'.

"BECAUSE hER hUSBAND WAS KILLED WITh ONE OF ThE GUNS IN SERVICE OF ThE LORD KING AND ThE TOWN"

Gabions

THE LIVES OF THE GUNNERS

In telling the story of the God's House Tower as a gun battery, the stories of seven gunners have been chosen and given below to illustrate the lives of the men charged with defending the town. We know so much about them because of the survival of many sixteenth-century town documents which are held in the Southampton Archives. A free-to-use database has been created giving details of over 19,000 individuals who appears in the records of the town between 1485 and 1603 www.tudorrevels.co.uk

DERYK BEREBREWER 1483-1524

Brewhouse

Deryk Berebrewer was an 'alien' the name given to people who were not born in England. We do not know precisely where he was born but looking at his name and his profession as a brewer he is very likely to have been from the Low Countries. The English did not take to making and drinking beer until the fifteenth century when the process finally arrived in the country, thanks to immigrants from the area we know as the Netherlands. Deryk was probably one of that number, and was certainly living in Southampton in the 1480s as he turns up twice in the mayor's court as a perpetrator and victim of two affrays and bloodsheds in 1483 and 1489. The Flemish/Dutch were not only prized for their skills at brewing but also for their knowledge about gunnery, and that made Deryk very useful to the town when Henry VIII ascended the throne. Henry was only eighteen when he became king. Physically he was what was expected of a medieval monarch, handsome, athletic, educated, rich and ambitious. That ambition included the desire to reclaim lands in France once ruled by his ancestors. He saw himself as the heir of the victor of Agincourt, Henry V, so it was no surprise that he soon made plans to invade France. Southampton was one of the country's premier military ports and was central to the king's plans.

To that end men like Deryk were needed to get the town's guns into good working order and make sure there was enough ammunition. In 1512 Deryk can be found moving the town guns into new positions and was paid regularly every eight to fourteen weeks throughout the year for working on the town ordnance. In January and February 1513 he took delivery of lead, iron and match, all materials that were needed to fire the guns. Guns were moved back and forth between the 'store house', which was probably God's House Tower, and the castle. The castle was the personal property of the king and was where he would stay when he visited the town. When Henry arrived to inspect the preparations for war Deryk, with the support of two other gunners, was asked to fire volleys to entertain the king. Henry's ambitions for the war came to nothing but he never gave up on that dream and throughout his reign was often in Southampton. Henry also made foreign alliances in the furtherance of his aims. In 1522 the most important person in Europe was in Southampton, following a state visit to the English Court: The Holy Roman Emperor, Charles V. He had been in England for six weeks, and travelled with many encumbrances.

In a letter to Cardinal Wolsey, Henry VIII's chief advisor, the Emperor whilst making preparations for the trip complained:

After we wrote you, we went over the list of the persons of our household who are accompanying us to England in an effort to cut down the number of horses to 500. We have done evrything we could, but we shall have so many notable persons in our company that we cannot reduce the number to less than 700 horses, without counting mules and pack horses which will, however, be only about 400, as you may see by the new list we are sending you. Give Wolsey this list, and tell him it is the best we can do. Say also that when we sent the first list, which came to eleven hundred horses, we thought we were going all the way by land to Falmouth. For this long journey Wolsey advised the restriction to 500 horses, but he also wished us to come with a suite befitting a great prince. Now that we are only going to Southampton, we cannot believe that Wolsey would wish us to curtail our suite so severely, for if we reduce the number to 500 horses, we shall have to leave behind our council, and some of our gentlemen and other officers of state, as you may see by the marked list. We have already deleted from the list our great chaplain and several of our gentlemen, and we have allowed to most of the rest only two horses apiece and to many only three horses.

Charles was not only Holy Roman Emperor, with sway over most of central Europe, but also King of Spain and Duke of Burgundy ruling over the Low Countries and parts of France. In addition as a result of the voyages of exploration supported by his grandparents Ferdinand of Aragon and Isabella of Castille, he was also in possession of swathes of South America. He was the nephew of Henry VIII's consort, Catherine of Aragon. To welcome such an august personage Deryk was again employed as a gunner, shooting the guns to welcome the Emperor to the town.

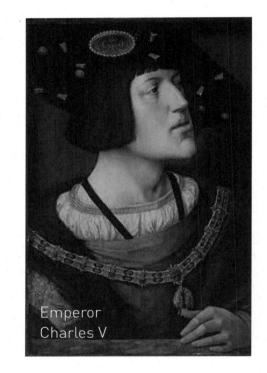

Emperor Charles V

The town spent 42s, the equivalent of three months' pay for an ordinary craftsman, on over a hundred weight of gunpowder for the salute. By 1524 Deryk was dead, leaving behind a widow Maude, who was herself registered as an alien and had probably moved to England with Deryk half a century before. Maude's wealth was assessed at 20s in the tax records for that year. A tax that would go towards financing Henry VIII's next war with France.

BALTHAZAR LYNNE 1511-14

Balthazar Lynne was probably a compatriot of Deryk Berebrewer. He undoubtedly worked alongside Deryk during the period of Henry VIII's first French war but unlike Deryk he seems to have been a professional gunner. He first appears in the records of Southampton in 1509, when it was likely he was a newcomer, and as a foreigner as he needed someone established in the town to act on his behalf to enable him to sell a cargo of fish. The fish included red herring, a fish very popular with Dutch fishermen, mackerel and stockfish. Stockfish is dried fish, a method used to preserve fish, usually cod, to extend the period it can be used as food. It became very popular after the discovery of 'Newfoundland' in North America where cod was plentiful, and from the early 1500s was being brought back from there to the port of Southampton. The fish

Stockfish

was dried on racks usually for about three months and then matured for another couple of months so that about 80% of the water had evaporated. Once sold at fish markets, like the one adjacent to St Michael's church in Southampton, it could be re-hydrated by being soaked or added to stews. The man who acted for Balthazar was Herman Johnson who lived near St Michael's and was also probably an immigrant from the Low Countries or Westphalia in the Rhineland. Unlike Deryk, Balthazar was paid an annual wage of 26s 8d and given a town livery gown worth 10s and the title of town gunner. He had taken up that post mid-1511-12 accounting year when he received a half-year's wages, so probably had started work in March. By the summer he was busy making gun-stones, producing four in August receiving 2d for each stone. Later that year he was stocking up on gunpowder, 234lb of it, worth £3 18s. The gunpowder was kept in the 'storehouse'. Balthazar produced an additional 100lbs of gunpowder which was kept in wooden barrels. The second batch was valued at 33s 4d and the barrel valued at 12d. In January 1513 the town was strengthening its walled defences, due to concern over possible French attack and Balthazar assisted in this work. He also was employed making improvements to the guns acquiring 15 fathoms of hawser rope, a thick cable for binding guns to their carriages, as well as making 43 more gun-stones. In April he was making another 22 gun-stones, and also casting lead pellets for use in smaller guns. He disappears from the records after 1514, his appointment probably being only for the duration of the war which came to an end that year.

PETER BREME 1515-1572

Tudor Windows

Peter Breme was born around 1515 and was also an 'alien', an economic immigrant who first appears in the Southampton records working on a private house as a glazier in 1539-40. He married a woman called Joan who was born in 1519, his son Peter was born in 1548, there were two more children, Thomas and Catherine. He had probably moved to the town to maximise the opportunities he had as a trained glazier. Glass was an expensive commodity and had rarely been seen outside of churches and palaces, but by the sixteenth century improved methods of manufacture had brought glass within the purchasing power of wealthy burgesses. Southampton was having something of an economic boom and the Corporation wanted to invest in public buildings to illustrate the town's wealth and their growing independence from the Crown. Peter was employed on glazing the windows of one of the town's most important buildings, the Audit House. This was a place where the town council met, where town books were kept, and where banquets were held to honour important men. Traditionally the wealthiest of the foreign merchants leased West Hall, they had the money to make improvements. In the 1560s it was the Portuguese woad merchants who occupied the property. In 1570 Peter was paid £135 0s 5d for the work he carried out there.

The property even had glazed windows in the kitchen and buttery. He also glazed three windows in the town's new almshouses which contained 26 ft of glass. The town had a new school paid for by bequests from William Capon the last precentor of St Mary's Chantry and the wealthy merchant John Capelyn. The school was in a converted loft but it did have glass windows, which unfortunately proved too much of a temptation to the boisterous school boys, learning Latin within. After they broke the windows in 1565 Peter was brought in to undertake repairs. Peter's skills did not end there, he was also a painter, so he painted the casements around windows, and the bars that protected them and also worked on the statues of lions which stood outside of the north entrance to the town, the Bargate.

He lived in Holy Rood parish on French Street in a well-appointed house which had a central hall, parlour, kitchen, buttery with an upstairs fore chamber and a back chamber. At the front there was a shop, and the property would have been similar to the surviving 58 French Street. As might be expected the house was glazed and had removable wainscoting. Windows and wooden wainscot were considered valuable

assets and part of a property's fixtures and fittings along with pieces of furniture. The house was decorated with painted cloths which would have hung on the walls, more affordable than the tapestries in the houses of the wealthy. Peter did own beds, a sign of wealth, some silver, linen, and plenty of kettles, pots, knives, ladles, platters, stools and a chair. Again the family's relative prosperity is illustrated by ownership of spice plates and a salt cellar with a cover. He also owned more than one set of clothes, he had three gowns, three pairs of hose, a cloak and two capes in his wardrobe, all of which were recorded in his inventory made at the time of his death in 1572.

58 French Street

The family were musical: Peter could play the drum and flute, skills he passed onto his sons. He was so proficient that he was given the privilege of playing to welcome Elizabeth I when she visited the town in 1568. He was even paid a 5s fee, a week's wage for most people. These musical talents were also employed when he attended the town musters, where all able-bodied men between the ages of 16 and 60 had to turn out for military training. He played for the town watch, again another duty that townsmen had to undertake on yearly rotas, patrolling between the hours of dusk and dawn. In the muster of 1555-6 he was listed as an able-bodied gunner, who personally owned two handguns. By this time he was also on retainer as one of the town's official gunners. He had been recruited half-way through the year and received a partial retainer of 17s 8d plus two yards of red kersey and three quarters of red cotton and two and a half of white cotton to make his livery. Like his predecessors he had to make or procure gunpowder, including the 14lb of saltpetre and similar amount of brimstone for the gun salute planned for the Queen. It is not surprising therefore that in the inventory of his property in 1572 he had 13 casks and four containers containing dry powder, and sieves for sifting gunpowder stored in his stable. In his fore chamber he had a hearth on which to dry the powder and in his shop was a soldering iron, with flasks, charges, moulds and lots of pewter. His personal arsenal included a shooting target, an early type of musket called a calliver, plus a rapier and four bow staves.

His son Peter took over the glazing business and was appointed the official town glazier with Peter Foxe, which gave them the monopoly for work in Southampton. He and his brother both followed their father as town gunners, and Peter junior also played the fife at musters. Another duty was to assist the mayor in the town court when there were foreign witnesses who needed to be deposed, and he was official translator for the Flemish. He was still a town gunner in 1607 but not long afterwards lost his position, and his livery was taken from him because of his 'contemptuous behaviour'. He was keeping an unlicenced ale house, but he ignored orders to close it down. His last mention in the records is in 1611. Brother Thomas was employed as a gunner in 1566 so must have been born before 1550 at the latest. He was a drummer, and kept the town drum which he was paid to 're-trim' in 1586. He followed the family trade of glazier and ran a victualling house in the town, for which he, unlike his brother, had obtained the correct licence. He seems to have been a supplier or retailer of weapons, supplying the ship *Requital of Hampton* with a dozen bandoliers and cartridges for muskets, three callivers, six deal boards and 41lb of powder in 1599. He disappears from the records in 1600.

RICHARD NETLEY c1528 -1575

Drum and flute player

Richard Netley was born before 1528 and by 1549 had joined the Corporation in a junior capacity as Town Sergeant and keeper of the town gaol at the Bargate. His duties included the delivery of messages, and the escorting of prisoners to the county gaol in Winchester or even up to London. He had to see the Trinity Fair ran smoothly and collect fees from visiting traders. His position as gaoler gave him the opportunity to earn extra money from prisoners who would have to pay for their meals, 2d for a bed and even 2d if they were clapped in irons. He had come to the notice of the town whilst serving Henry VIII's son the young king Edward VI, as a gunner in his French war in 1549. On his return from the conflict he was appointed town gunner and asked to supervise the town ordnance. It might have been expected that gunners had some musical ability, as he performed on the drum and flute. His duties did not prevent him from dabbling in other ventures, including in trading some woad with the Portuguese. In 1558 he, with eighteen others, was appointed one of the town's official horse hirers. They were allowed to charge 8d for the first day's hire and 6d for each following day. For those travelling further afield to London or to Bristol, it was estimated the journeys to be 7 days for which 6s was to be paid for horse hire, and any extra day was 6d. A two day trip to Salisbury would cost 16d. The horse hirers had to have horses or geldings prepared and available for the post, the couriers who carried important messages around the country. Having horses meant Richard needed a stable, which he rented in Holy Rood parish at an annual rent of 16s.

The Bargate

Richard got into trouble on a couple of occasions for digging on the Bargate ramparts, which ran from the Bargate down to the East Gate, which had caused them to fall down. He had to repair them or pay a 10s fine. He was also investigated with regard to the ownership of some white kersey cloth and accused of not paying his debts. Not paying your bills was common practice and Richard was owed money himself by other merchants. At some point he had also set up a weaving enterprise. This had become an important industry in the town in the 1570s and 80s instigated by the French Protestant Huguenot refugees, so he may have had some connection with the French Church. He lived in All Saints parish, and was married to a woman called Agnes and had six sons: Adrian, Christopher, John, Michael, Thomas and William. He also had another young relative living in his household called Jane Netley. Their property included a hall, shop, kitchen, fore chamber inner chamber, and outer chamber. His house was well furnished with painted cloths, glass windows, chairs, beds, linen, cutlery and dishes including porridge dishes.

He died in 1575, outlived by his widow and five of his sons. Christopher who predeceased his father had been a joiner, Adrian, John and Thomas worked as weavers, and William worked in a linked trade as a hosier. Michael operated as Bargate Broker, taking tolls from traders going in and out of the town and he operated a mill down near the old Trinity Chapel. In his will Richard Netley left 20s to the poor of the town at his burial. In the inventory of his property, his clothes included three gowns, two coats and an old doublet. His personal arms were a halberd, a pair of Almain rivets and a handgun with furnishings. He owned a gelding, a nag and a cow.

WILLIAM BOTTERELL 1505-1566

William Botterell was a practical man, a craftsperson who could turn his hand to many things. In his early days he worked on building projects, making the cream and timber-framed houses so familiar in Tudor England. He was a dauber making the wattle and daub infill that went between the oak timber framing of houses and he hewed the slates for the roofs. He was given the task of overseeing the Italian galleymen the town employed to work on the large warehouse at West Quay called the Ronceval – which may suggest he had some understanding of their language. He worked on the bulwarks, the defences that encircled the town, and even decorated the town gates in preparation for the arrival of the Emperor Charles V. He helped the town mason, the

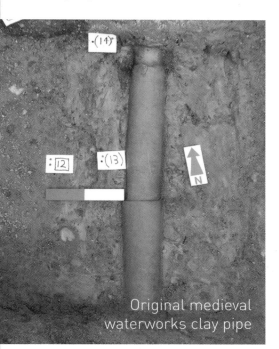

Original medieval waterworks clay pipe

town plumber, the roof slaters, known as helliers, and the carpenters on large building projects such as work on the West Quay and on the Wool Loft. In his later years he appears to have decided to focus on plumbing projects. The town had a piped water supply that had originally been laid by the monks of the Friary back in the thirteenth century. By the fifteenth century the maintenance of the water supply had been taken over by the Corporation. Southampton was the first town in the country to have a municipal water supply. The spring was situated off Hill Lane and the water was piped down to the Conduit House, which still survives on Water Lane, and from there to the Friary and then to public cisterns outside Holy Rood

and St Michael's Churches. Some of the wealthier merchants had spurs – not always legal ones – which took water to their houses. William worked on gutters which took rainwater off the roofs of houses, cleaning and soldering those that were leaking. He maintained the cistern in Goswell Lane, Holy Rood and the one at the Friary and even the conduit at Lady Dawtrey's property, now the museum of Tudor House. He dug trenches to lay new pipework and to find leaks in the system. As well as lead for solder, he used resin and tallow to make sere cloths to bind the pipes, and made wooden planks to lay underneath the cisterns. He seems never to have stopped working to make sure that the water kept flowing. He was eventually appointed the town's official plumber and given a livery gown. His proficiency in making pipes and working in lead was probably the reason he became one of the town gunners. His busy schedule may have led to him being ordered to take more practice in gunnery, and to train others, letting the Corporation know who attended the sessions. In 1557 he was paid to mend the lead which had been blown up in God's House Tower. He continued to work until he eventually disappears from the records in 1566 when he was probably in his late sixties.

GILBERT CLEMENT 1550-1620

Gilbert Clement first appears in the records as a servant, an occupation which usually equates as an apprentice although he could have been a skilled worker, in the household of Nicholas Capelyn one of the wealthiest men from probably the most important burgess family in Southampton. The career Gilbert pursued was as a blacksmith and clockmaker. As a blacksmith he would not just be employed in shoeing horses but more as a craftsman smith working in metal and making items such as the metal flags which were held in the paws of the lions which stood outside the Bargate. He made the iron hand that was raised when the Admiralty Court met at sessions under the jurisdiction of the Southampton mayor. He knew how to use a gun as he supplied his own calliver, a type of early musket, when he turned out for the town musters. By the 1590s he was appointed as town gunner and was given the additional appointment as the maintainer of the clock and chimes in St Michael's Church. These public clocks were important to the local population. People did not have watches, a few might have had sundials, but it was the town clocks that divided the day for them. He earned 54s 4d for his maintenance work and 26s 8d as a gunner, plus of course his livery which included a coat. By the beginning of the seventeenth century Gilbert had diversified further.

Hand that was raised at fairs and courts to show they were in operation

He took in lodgers like the incomers William Ravenscroft and his wife who had to supply sureties if they wanted to stay in the town. The guild of Cutlers and Smiths complained against him accusing him of buying and selling knives, swords and daggers rather than sticking to his own trade of dressing guns, clocks and jacks. He may have been the person who created the quarter jacks that can still be seen in the tower of Holy Rood Church, styled in the images of Sir Bevis of Hamtun and his squire Ascupart. Gilbert described himself both as a gun maker and smith, and the armourers and cutlers complained again in 1613 for his meddling in things belonging to the trade of armourers and cutlers. In 1613 he had risen in his position within the town to being admitted as a free commoner. These were Freemen, also known as commoners in Southampton, who were those persons who paid a fine to be allowed the freedom to set up a craft or trade in the town and to be admitted to a guild or corporation (if one existed for their occupation). Gilbert died in 1620.

HENRY PEACH 1600-15

Henry Peach was by profession a sailor, and in common with many sailors when not at sea ran a tippling house, a small ale house in part of his house in Holy Rood parish. Often these houses would offer lodgings to the large transient population visiting the port. It was a family business, and Henry had to rely on his wife Constantia to keep things going when he was at sea. Constantia seems to have been a fiery character who was bound over to keep the peace following an altercation with Alice James, the wife of another tippler John James. Her husband along with a family friend Walter Feverell, the local butcher, had each to pledge £10 surety for Constantia to behave herself. This was a large sum of money, equating to over six months' wages for an ordinary person. Their drinking den was popular with visiting sailors and in 1602 Henry had to give a witness statement following a fatal knife fight. Peter John from

Henry Peach -
License to travel used
for escaping the plague

Emden in East Friesland testified he and another Fleming, William Yobson, had been drinking in a cellar near the custom house. William had been trying to find work, hoping to get a position as a gunner on the ship *Margaret & John*. According to Peter an argument had broken out and the two men got into a knife fight. The coroners John Friar and Roger Pedley, questioned another mariner, John Hyer of Bergen in Norway, whose testimony was translated by Thomas Foster a Flemish merchant. Hyer said the two men had in fact been quarrelling about the theft of a petticoat and in the course of the quarrel Yobson had taken a knife from another Fleming who was asleep. Whatever the cause Yobson was fatally wounded and his body was found near the Watergate. The incident did not affect Henry Peach who continued to operate a tippling house, but in 1604 he temporarily abandoned his property. A severe bout of plague had broken out in the town, probably brought there by members of the court of King James I who had left London to escape the outbreak there. Before it took hold people were still allowed to travel if they could offer some proof of good health and obtain a certificate of health. This is what Peach did and transported himself, Constantia and their two children to Hamble. The family survived and were back in Southampton by 1610 when they were in trouble for offering lodgings to newcomers to the town, Richard Hamon and his pregnant wife. The couple were ordered to move on so as not to be a financial burden to the town.

God's House Gate, landward side

Peach had previously been in trouble for selling ale in unsealed pots, and not to the correct measure. It may have been a further inspection which caused an incident with the town constable James Capelyn. Peach beat and abused Capelyn and as a result found himself locked up in the Bargate. It appears that Henry might have been dead by 1615 as Constantia was involved in negotiations with James Frier over the apprenticeship of Walter Stephens. Walter Stephens was apprenticed to James Frier a cooper who received 30s as part of the contract. Something must have gone wrong as Frier agreed to repay 20s and hand over the indentures of apprenticeship to Constantia. It appears Walter Stephens was her son, and was born around the time of the death of his father Walter Stephen senior a tippler, the first husband of Constantia. Constantia would have been widowed around 1596 and married Henry Peach soon after, quick remarriages were not uncommon in this period. It may have been therefore that the tippling house was Constantia's and Henry had come into possession of it by marriage. As Constantia was negotiating with James Frier herself it is likely that by 1615 she was again a widow and having to look after the interests of her children.

Henry's role as a gunner was probably also his position on a ship. All the merchant ships carried guns and had to protect themselves against pirates and privateers. Often in times of war the town would bring guns off the ships of local merchants to boost the fire power in the town, and could call upon the trained ships' gunners to assist in manning guns when necessary. The town musters recorded the military skills of all the men of the town, for example whether they were a knight and had horse and armour, if they were an able-bodied gunner or archer, what personal weapons they owned which could be put into the town service. If men had no skills and no weapons they would be given other tasks as pioneers, to lay waste to crops and drive out animals to prevent any invaders getting hold of them.

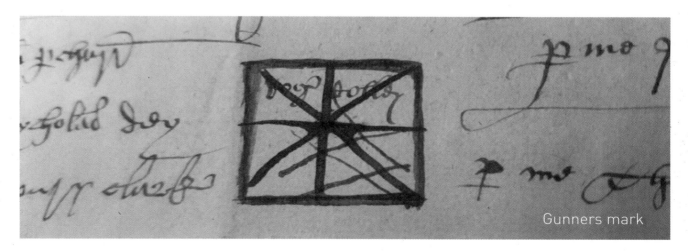

Gunners mark

GUNNERS FOUND IN THE SOUTHAMPTON RECORDS

DATE	GUNNERS NAME	ADDITIONAL INFORMATION
1508-1512	Peter Gonner	Paid 13s 4d for his work 1512 - Shoots guns for the king Alien worker
1509-1514	Balfer (Balthasar) Lynne	Paid 6s 8d for four gun-stones 1512 - Paid 26s 8d April 1512 - Paid £13 8s for 234lbs of gunpowder Alien worker
1512	Mark Stroyborow	German gunner employed by Sir John Dawtrey for 2 months on the defences 7s, plus worked for a further 3 weeks 4s 8d.
1512	Gaurede Smith	German gunner employed by Sir John Dawtrey for 2 months on the defences 7s, plus worked for a further 3 weeks 4s 8d.
1512	Christopher Wingate	German gunner employed by Sir John Dawtrey for 2 months on the defences 7s.
1512-1513	Master Perowe	1512 - Works 5 ½ months and is paid 20s per month. "His man" Michæl is paid 39s for his work with Perowe
1512-1513	Michæl	26th March - paid for 2 months work 7th May - paid 20s for 2 months work as Perowe's man 12th June - paid 15s for one and half months' work Mr Perowe's man
1512-1513	George Pootton	1512 - Works a month as a gunner for 8s and made 30 stones for the guns 5s

DATE	GUNNERS NAME	ADDITIONAL INFORMATION
1512 - 1521	Derek Berebrewer	1512 - Paid 42s for shooting the guns for Emperor Charles V Alien worker
1523-68	John Norton	Brewer and gunner 1557-8 gunners wage for half a year and nine weeks 17s 8d Alien Worker
1524-1549	James Cooper	1524 - Registered as an alien 1549 - Ordered to take more practice in the gunnery
1526-1547	Richard Cobley	1528 - Paid 20s for his work 1542 - Claims money for poverty
1528-1529	Roger	1528 – Salary 20s pa but only paid 5s for his work
1537-43	John Ynglette	Packer and gunner
1542	Harmon Smith	1542 - Dies when the gun he is manning explodes Alien Worker
1545-49	John Netley	1549 ordered to take more practice in gunnery and note names of those who attend
1528-75	Richard Netley	1549 - Fights in the war with France 1550 - Appointed Sergeant and Keeper of the Gaol Weaver and horse hirer
1555-62	John Donnenge	1555-6 able-bodied gunner, servant of Peter Breme 1561-2 drum player and gunner wages 13s 4d Possibly Alien worker
1547-55	James Florry	1555 - Paid 33s 4d for his work 1555 - Paid 9d for mending the tubs and hoops

DATE	GUNNERS NAME	ADDITIONAL INFORMATION
11541-1563	Edward Bogley	1557 - Paid 27s for his working for nine and a half weeks as a gunner 1562 - Works as town gunner 40s pa and Mayor's Sergeant
1557-1584	Richard Elkins	Paid 26s 8d annually for his work as a gunner
1557-1566	William Boterell	1557 - Paid 18d to repair the lead blown up
1561-1567	John Norton	Paid a yearly rate of 26s 8d
1539-1572	Peter Breme	Paid a yearly rate of 53s 4d Employs a servant named John Donnenage Glazier Flemish
1548-1611	Peter Breme	Glazier and ale house keeper son of Peter Breme senior Parents Flemish
1566-1590	Thomas Breme	Son of Peter Breme senior 1566 - Paid 13s 4d Glazier Parents Flemish
1565-1577	John Robinson	Mariner Appointed one of the town gunners, and not to depart the town without the mayor's permission in 1575
1567-1629	Gilbert Clement	1594 - Paid 26s 8d for his work Maintained the clock and chimes at St Michæl's Church Maintained the calliver in Audit House Clockmaker and blacksmith
1545-1610	Henry Foster aka Hellier	Town plumber and appointed master gunner in 1575
1590-1615	Henry Peach	Sailor and Gunner

THE GUNS FALL SILENT

In the second half of the sixteenth century there were rapid changes happening in England prompted by Henry VIII's religious reforms known as the English Reformation. After the Reformation the area around God's House Tower had changed. The Friary was defunct and a new grammar school was situated over the Winkle Street stables, known as the King Edward VI Free Grammar School. In the second half of the sixteenth century the street would have rung out again with French voices, as Protestant religious refugees from France and the Low Countries flooded into the town. They had been given the chapel of St Julien's at the God's House Hospital as their place of worship. By 1600 ideas about defence had moved on. Henry VIII had begun the process by building a series of forts further down the coast, designed to repel invaders long before they reached Southampton. From the 1590s God's House Tower no longer held a key role in the defence of the town and there were many complaints made at Court Leet about the state of decay in and around the tower.

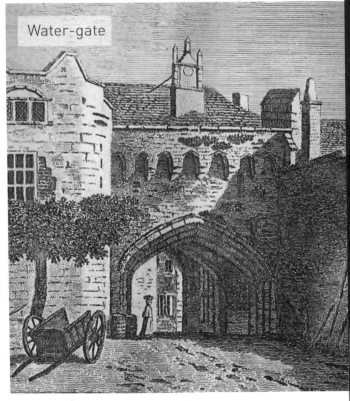

Water-gate

"The TOWN WALLS FROM GOD'S HOUSE TOWER TO The WATER GATE ARE IN DECAY"

Even when work was carried out it was often of poor quality. Henry Foster who was a gunner himself and lived not far from the tower on Winkle Street, had been given a contract to undertake repairs, but people complained it was 'cheape'.

By 1602 a hole had appeared in God's House Tower, through which witnesses said they had seen a big boy pass in and out, and they thought it big enough for a man to do the same. The hole was still there three years later. Whenever God's House Tower is mentioned, it is said to be decayed or in extreme decay.

ITEM WEE PRESENT THE TOWER OF GODES HOWSE AND THE HOUSE AND PLATTFORMES THEREOF TO BE VERIE MUCHE DECAYED AND NOTWITHSTANDINGE THE SUNDRIE PRESENTEMENTS FORMERLIE MADE WEE FYNDE NOE AMENDMENT THEREOF MADE. BUT RATHER A CONTYNEWALL DECAYE WHICH BEINGE LIGHK TO GROWE WEE DESIER THAT YOUR WORSHIPPS WILL HAVE DUE CONSIDERACONS THEREOF

Weapons were being stolen as early as 1602 when eighteen pikes were reported as being missing. By 1619 the guns could not be moved because their carriages were un-useable. Even if the guns were still capable of being fired there was no powder and shot. In 1623 the gate was so dangerous that it was thought that if children crawled under it there might be a terrible accident. By 1624 water was getting into the tower as the lead had been stolen off the roof, and the doors were broken. The timber in the roof was rotting, and the iron ordnance was eaten with rust. In 1698 it was reported that the town was in a poor way and in decline.

"IT IS A PLACE OF NO STRENGTH NOW BY REASON OF THE CASTLE BEING RUINED AND THE FORTIFICATIONS NEGLECTED AND THE GUNS TAKEN THENCE" Celia Fiennes

PRISONERS:
Southampton Town Gaol:
Keepers, Debtors, Felons &
House of Correction

PRISONERS - Southampton Town Gaol:
Keepers, Debtors, Felons & House of Correction

By the end of the seventeenth century it was necessary to find a new use for God's House Tower and calls were made for the building to be used as a Bridewell or House of Correction. In 1697 repairs were undertaken to the roof of the building and in 1707 the Bridewell was established in the room above the gate. The rest of the building was let out to various townspeople for many different uses. George Rowcliffe used it as a workroom for his job as a shipwright. In the first half of the eighteenth century John Grove and his daughter Ann appear to have used the tower as a hospital or lodging for sick or wounded soldiers and sailors. England was again at war with France, but the campaigns were happening in faraway lands as England, now formally united with Wales, Ireland and Scotland, was busy building what was to become the British Empire. Southampton was still a major military port, and where there were large numbers of soldiers, disease often followed. With limited hospital provision entrepreneurs like the Groves saw an opportunity. However when John Grove died the authorities stepped in to prevent Ann from carrying on the enterprise alone and shortly after the tower passed into the possession of Mark Noble, who styled himself a gentleman.

"UNDER THE POWER OF AN INSULTING TYRANICAL GAOLER"

Although the establishment of the Bridewell gave some relief to the town's main prison at the Bargate it was still overcrowded with felons and debtors. In 1736 the prisoners held in the Bargate complained about their conditions petitioning the House of Commons. The debtors John Heather, Samuel Day, Joseph Smith, John Debron and John Pond protested that they had been confined in a small narrow room not exceeding sixteen feet square under the power of an insulting "Tyranical" gaoler. Some debtors in this period even took the option of emigration to the new American colony of Georgia as an alternative to prison. The founder James Oglethorpe wanted his colonists to be given the opportunity for a new start, but was also aware that families had a more stabilising influence and insisted that any debtors taking up his offer be married. To that end in 1738 a series of mass weddings took place on the outskirts of Southampton at Peartree Church in Itchen Ferry village for colonists bound for Georgia.

Southampton Ward Apr. ye 10th 1736

To The Honble The House of Comons
In Parleamt Assembled

The Humble Petition of the Poor=Debtrs in this Ward
In and for the Town & County of Southampton

Sheweth—

That Yor Petitionrs for Years past has been and Still are
Close Confined Prisoners within the Borers & narow
Compass of One Small Roome not Exceeding Sixteen foot
Square Under the Power of an Insulling Tyranicle Goaler
And although Wee Long since have been Endevouring
for Liberty (That Precious darling) By Punctually Complying wth
the Rules of ye Late Act of Parleamt made In ye behalf of Debtrs
wth respect to ye Imprisonmt of their Persons, Yet this Corporation
Contrary to ye Sd Act & Amendmto dont think Proper to Summons
Cr nor Give Us a Hearing, Others are Rendr Judgemt Upon
Judgemt and then Stops proceedings without Carrying Us into Execucon
So That Yor Petitionrs are denyed the Benefitts of ye Acts, and by
Reason of our long Imprisonments are not able to pay for
Our Supereceeding ye Plantiffs Actions, whereby Yor Petitionrs &
Ffamilys are become the Reale Objects of all Mt Chariotys
Reduced to all the Hardshipps of Extream Want & Poverty

Wherefore Yor Petitionrs in the most Humblest
mann & Prayr the Concideration of This Honble House to Grant
Such Relief That Yor Poor Petitionrs may obtaine their Liberty to prevent
the Totale distruction of Themselves & ffamilys and As in duty Bound
Yor Humble Petitionrs Shale for Ever Pray
&co

John Hoather
Saml Day
Joseph Smith
John Nelson
Fr. Ford

Petiton of Debtors

It was several years before the Corporation responded to the overcrowding. At the Quarter Sessions held on 18th January 1760, the Grand Jury presented that it had been found in many instances that the gaols of the town were insecure and inconvenient and that a more convenient place be provided for the purpose of the public gaol, and they recommended God's House Tower. The Grand Jury inspected the plans delivered by Mr Joseph Taylor and approved one of them.

The scheme was for three floors at the east end and a house of correction at the west. In 1761 the town passed an order to sell the old iron guns and cannonballs in the tower and in 1762 William Lisle did work on the lead of the tower, Richard White provided brick and stonework and the chimneys were made good.

Bargate Courtroom

Plans still survive for the translation of God's House Tower into the town's new prison, however in reading the prison inspector reports it does not look as if the prison was built as the plans suggest. Although God's House Tower provided more room the situation of the new prison was always going to be insanitary. The tower particularly suffered as fetid, stagnant water was still lying in the ditches beneath the tower.

In addition the prison's new toilet block built in the dark and overshadowed court-yard to the north of the main building deposited its waste into the old town ditches, which were right next to the exercise yard. The pressure to move the debtors' prison from the Bargate was in the end driven by plans for pavement improvements needed to help in the promotion of Southampton as a genteel bathing resort. The plan was to insert a postern gate for foot passengers into the Bargate and going through the area of the debtors' prison. Finally in 1775 the main tower at God's House Tower was turned into the debtors' prison, and in 1786 the Bargate prison was closed (to enable a second postern on the west side) and the felons were moved from there into the former gun battery. This final move was probably prompted after a visit to the old prison in 1784 by the prison reformer John Howard. He was the author of *The State of Prisons* in 1777. He had discovered during his visits to prisons across the country that some prisoners who had been acquitted were still in gaol as they could not pay the gaoler's fees. The prison reform charity, the Howard League for Penal Reform, was named after him.

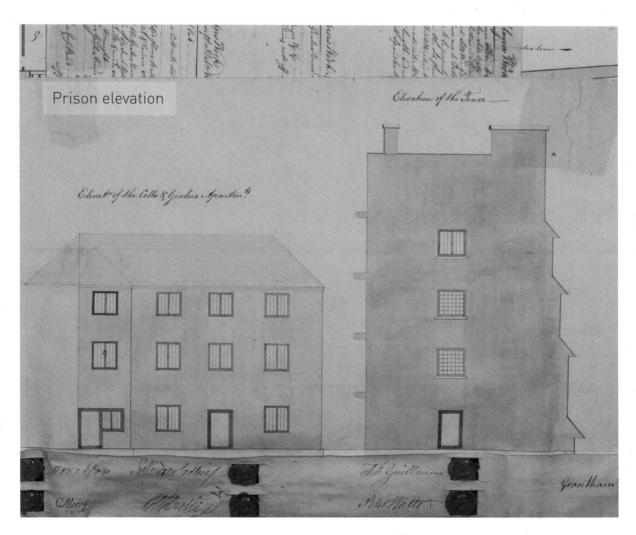

Prison elevation

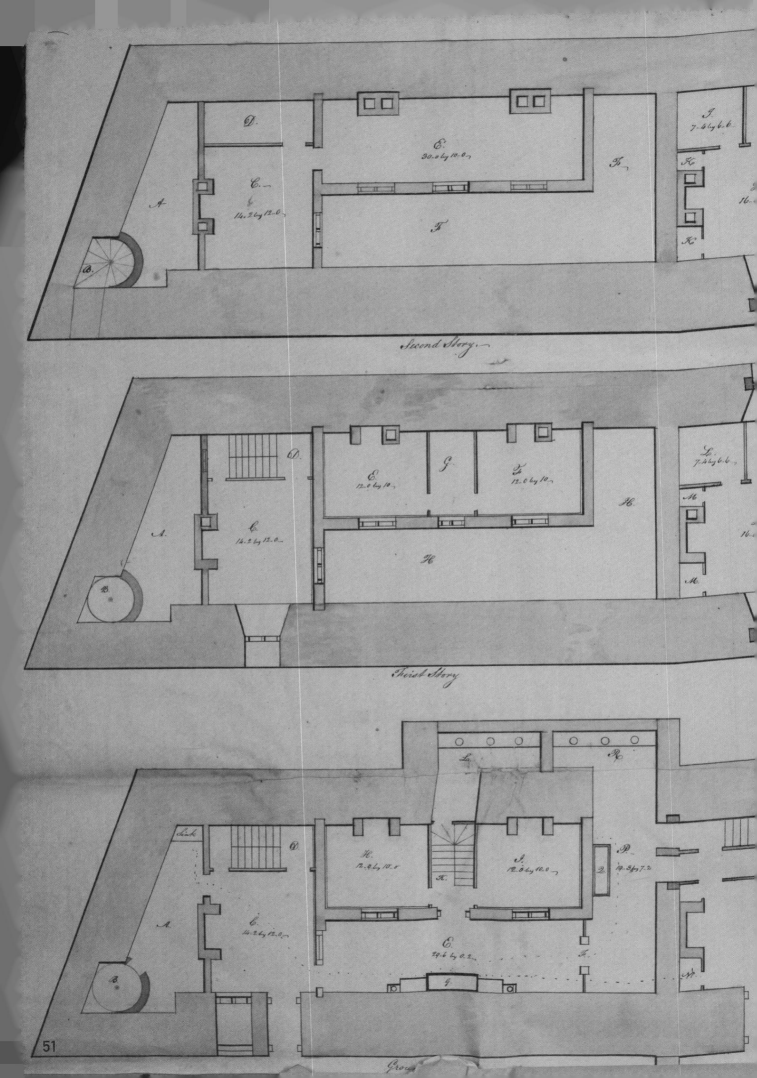

Second Story.

First Story

Grou

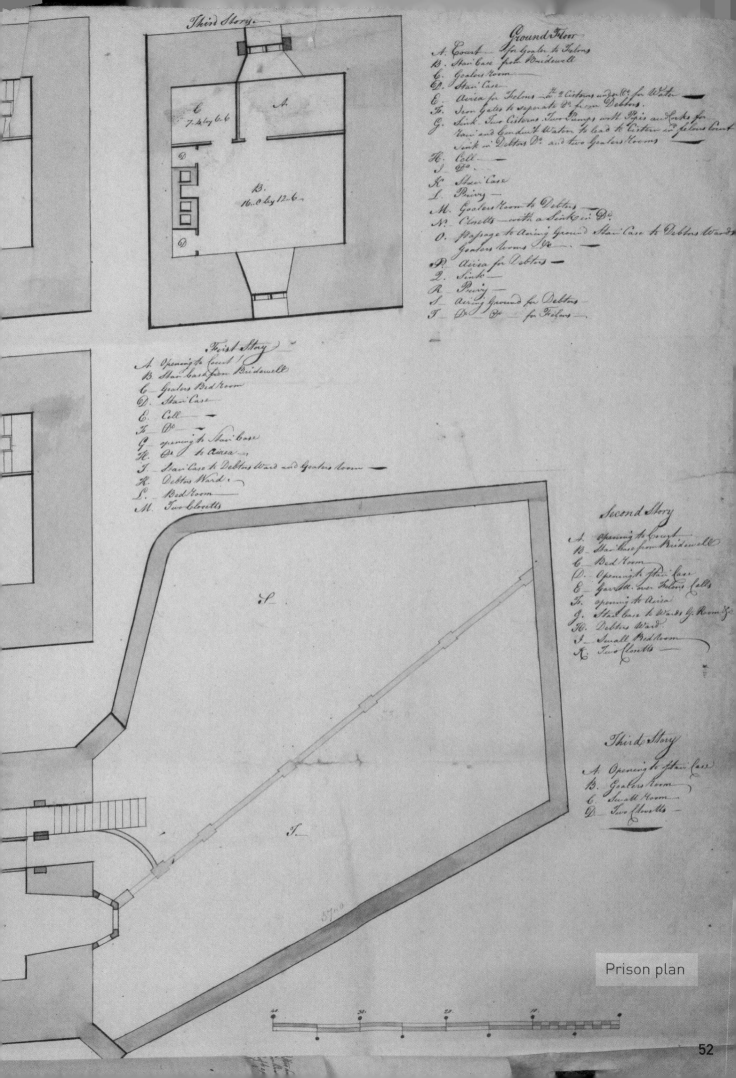

Third Story.

C
7.4 by 6.6

A.

B.
16.0 by 12.6

Ground Floor
A. Court for Goaler to Felons
B. Staircase from Bridewell
C. Goalers Room
D. Staircase
E. Airea for Felons w. 2 Cisterns under D. for Water
F. Iron Gates to seperate D. from Debtors.
G. Sink. Two Cisterns. Two Pumps with Pipes and Corks for Rain and Conduit Water to lead to Cistern in Felons Court Sink in Debtors D. and two Goalers Rooms
H. Cell
I. D.
K. Staircase
L. Privy
M. Goalers Room to Debtors
N. Closetts with a Sink in D.
O. Passage to Airing Ground Staircase to Debtors Wards Goalers Rooms &c.
P. Airea for Debtors
Q. Sink
R. Privy
S. Airing Ground for Debtors
T. D. D. for Felons

First Story
A. Opening to Court
B. Staircase from Bridewell
C. Goalers Bed Room
D. Staircase
E. Cell
F. D.
G. opening to Staircase
H. D. to Airea
I. Staircase to Debtors Ward and Goalers Room
K. Debtors Ward
L. Bed Room
M. Two Closetts

Second Story
A. Opening to Court
B. Staircase from Bridewell
C. Bed Room
D. Opening to Staircase
E. Garret over Felons Cells
F. opening to Airea
G. Staircase to Wards G. Room &c
H. Debtors Ward
I. Small Bed Room
K. Two Closetts

Third Story
A. Opening to Staircase
B. Goalers Room
C. Small Room
D. Two Closetts

S.

T.

Prison plan

52

As well as the prisoners being moved to the new premises some of the Corporation staff were also transferred there. The Town Sergeants were traditionally the men with the responsibility for day-to- day law and order in the town, and amongst their various duties had been looking after the prison at the Bargate. It was these men therefore who first took on the custody of the new gaol and retained that responsibility until 1835. We know that the Bridewell was in the care of John Lambert in 1757, with the support of Isaac Cropp another Town Sergeant. Lambert was still there in 1772 when he was given permission to erect a shed – at his own expense – in the garden which was attached to the Bridewell, as well as inserting a doorway into the wall to give access onto the street. Not all the officials were as upstanding as they might have been and in 1778 William Stratton, Sergeant at Mace, behaved so badly that he found himself suspended and the junior Sergeant Richard Moody was appointed to take over the Bridewell until further notice. The Corporation did try to bring in warders from outside of the town who had prison experience, such as Joseph Becket who had been storekeeper at Cold Bath Fields prison in London. He moved to Southampton in 1819 to become keeper of the House of Correction.

The prison was not quite as secure as the authorities might have liked however, and the first prison 'break-out' took place in 1788 in the wake of the Bonfire Night Riots. The local population had become disgruntled because the mayor had been trying to forbid bonfires within the town. The demonstration turned into a riot. When the disturbance was brought under control three ringleaders were sent to God's House prison with sentences of between twelve and eighteen months. Two of the offenders escaped when confederates threw a rope over the prison wall. Having iron-barred windows did not prevent prisoners from making an attempt for freedom. In 1758 Harry James, a prisoner of the House of Correction in the custody of John Lambert, had been imprisoned on 'a violent suspicion of stealing a parcel of shirts'. He was found trying to escape by removing an iron bolt out of one of the prison windows and cutting away part of the stone.

"A VIOLENT SUSPICION OF STEALING A PARCEL OF SHIRTS"

Barred prison windows

PRISON REPORTS

Nationally, concern was growing over the regulation and operation of prisons and this led to a system of regular prison inspections, although the reports seem seldom to have been acted upon. Among the surviving documentation in the records of the town clerk Thomas Ridding are three early reports on the Southampton gaols dating from 1802, 1803 and 1807 which give an overview of the three prisons which made up the town gaol at the start of the nineteenth century.

The debtors' gaol was overseen by the Sergeant at Mace Jeffery Truss who received £15 a year Sergeant's salary as well as being in receipt of the 4s the debtors had to pay on entering prison, and the 20s that they paid on discharge. Other charges could also be levied if prisoners could afford better food or conditions. For those who were classed as paupers the town did make an allowance of 6d a day plus a weekly bushel of coals.

> Southon Gaol May 9th 1814
>
> Sir
>
> A person calling on me this morning and stating he had been liberated from the fleet Prison under an act call'd Ricell's improved for the relief of Insolvent Debtors, and at the same time telling me I was intituled to the ~~same~~ above being confined three calender months) I should therefore be glad to know if this is the case or not, by the bearer, and you will oblige Sir
>
> your obt Hble Servt
>
> T. G. Willington

Letter from the debtor Willington

The debtors' gaol was situated in the first floor of the tower, but with access to a small courtyard measuring 46ft by 36ft. The yard was not paved and the prisoners had to share it with ducks, fowl and other creatures that were kept there. The debtors occupied two rooms which had glazed windows and fireplaces but were only 16ft by 12ft in size. For their comfort the Corporation provided each prisoner with a wooden bedstead, woollen mattress, two blankets and a rug. If the debtor still had some resources, or family and friends on whom they could call, they could rent a room at the top of the tower which had been furnished by the Keeper for a rent of 2s 6d a week. There was no surgeon appointed to look after the debtors but the mayor would supply one if required. This part of the prison was not over-full. In 1802 there were four prisoners recorded but in 1803 and 1807 only one.

In this early period the debtors were often gentlemen who for various reasons had amassed debts they could not pay. George Byles was an educated man with a family but had a debt of £33 which saw him imprisoned in the debtor's ward in 1804. He had suffered an accident which had led to him losing a leg, and this may have contributed to his distressed state. His confinement caused him to write a lengthy poem entitled *Reveries in Confinement*. He must have had good connections as his poem was printed locally by Thomas Skelton the bookseller priced at 2s 6d and was presumably a method of helping him clear his debts, as well as being a warning to others. In addition to the public sales 165 copies had been presold to subscribers which included the mayor and other worthies of the town. Extract from Reveries in Confinement -

Here barr'd secure within these massy walls,
Whose creeking doors the tender heart appals,
Huge iron bolts, and locks of triple force,
The dim apartment, and the gloomy course;
The hollow winds low 'rustling thro' the mound,
And more than echos seem to talk around
Too oft by the blue taper's glimm'ring light,
I pass the solitary hours of night;
Stranger to rest, my thoughts perpetual roam,
And heave a sigh from prison to my home.

The felons' gaol, for serious offenders, was under the eye of William Dymott, by profession a tailor, and like Truss a Town Sergeant for which he received his £15 Sergeant's salary. In addition he was paid £20 per annum for his work as a gaoler, but there were no additional fees from prisoners attached to his position. He was supported in his work by a surgeon, Mr Keele, who was paid according to the work he undertook. This suggests that prisoners in the Common Gaol were likely to be in poorer health than those in the debtors' gaol. The felons' gaol was also part of the old tower, on the ground level, with access to a court-yard measuring 34ft by 7ft which contained a pump and stone sink. Unfortunately the pump was frequently without water, especially in hot weather. The prison area was divided up into four small rooms of about 11ft square with iron-grated and glazed windows.

The prison was served by a fireplace and each prisoner had a wooden bedstead, straw-in-sacking bed, two blankets and a rug. Over the door of the entrance to the prison, which was through a small square door inserted in the south wall (to the left of the new entrance to the current building) was painted 'Pray remember the Poor Prisoners Box', in an attempt to extract alms from any visitors. The prisoners certainly needed extra support as they were only given an allowance of 6d a day and a bushel of coals per week for their subsistence. Again the numbers of prisoners was low at the time of the inspections: three in 1802, four in 1803 and just one in 1807.

"PRAY REMEMBER THE POOR PRISONERS BOX"

The third prison, the Bridewell, was overseen by Joseph Payne. The Bridewell prisoners had only committed minor offences and it was expected their stay would be relatively short. The Keeper had his Sergeant's salary of £15 a year augmented by £2 for his duties at the Bridewell. No additional fees were paid by the prisoners. Again Mr Keele was the surgeon on call. The prisoners here had 6d a day for their subsistence and the weekly bushel of coals. The prison had a day room of about 15ft square with two sleeping rooms of 12ft by 9ft. The rooms were furnished with a crib-bedstead, straw-in-sacking bed, two blankets and a rug each. Again the Keeper offered an alternative, for those who could afford it, of a room in his house, furnished, for 4s per week. The prisoner numbers in 1802 were one, in 1803, two and in 1807 one.

The inspector did not record the names or sex of the prisoners, but women as well as men would have been incarcerated. As the century progressed there was more and more concern about the females and males being able to converse together and that they were being held in close proximity.

Feb:y 2nd 1808

Town & County of Southampton

To J. J. Truss

	£	s	d
Dressing town hall	0	13	4
pens Ink & paper	0	4	0
Chips	0	4	0
Brooms	0	3	9
Charcoal	0	2	6
Sweeping prison Chimnies	0	3	0
hair broom 2/9 heath do 2/3	0	5	0
½ doz Moses	0	7	0
Oil	0	1	0
Sauce pan & mending do	0	5	6
Coals for the debtors one Bush: Br week from Sept. 22nd to Feb.y 2nd 19 Bush: 10 Bush: 13/h 9 do 15/9	1	9	1
Stamp	0	0	2½
	£3	18	4½

Audit House Southampton
Feb.y 2d 1808
ordered payment at an adjourned Session
Laws — Clerk of the Peace JB

Gaolers costs

Prisoner manacles

As well as a custodial sentence, prisoners were often given an additional punishment of hard labour. This happened to Jacob Duell in 1790 who was convicted of wilful and corrupt perjury and fined one shilling. He was to be imprisoned in the House of Correction for two years 'there to be kept to Hard Labour and until he pays the said Fine and then to be discharged'. Other punishments included being put in chains and fetters, as happened to the smuggler Cornelius Rose who was considered violent and needing to be fettered. Michael McDonald a deserter from the 13th Foot in 1800 was kept in handcuffs. He had been taken at Salisbury and was due to be returned to the military camp at Netley. He was twenty-two, of fresh complexion, 5ft 6ins tall with dark hair and grey eyes. The army covered the costs of his incarceration, including 4s 6d subsistence and 3s 6d for the aforementioned handcuffs.

As the century progressed the population of Southampton started to grow and in parallel the number of inmates in the gaol also grew. In 1818 sixteen persons were committed, in 1828 nineteen. The prison report of 1830 showed commitments during that year

SC9/4/580

1760 Mr William Stratton Dr. to Wm. Unwin decd

July. 14. To Fettering a man ——————— 1.S.0
       To a Large Chain & Staple ——————— 5.0
       To a pair hand Cuffs ——————— 1.6
Nov. 26. To Repairg a Lock ——————— 0.4
1761
Apr. 12. To an old ps. fetters & fetterg a man —— 4.0
    16. To a Large piece chain & 2 Rings —— 4.6
                £ 0.16.4

Bill for fetters

were ten to the gaol, eighty-three to the Bridewell and twelve to the debtors-ward. The rise in criminal activity and prisoner numbers led to the government considering what other punishments might be given to prisoners to further dissuade them from their life of crime. By 1823 a hand-crank mill was already in place in the airing ground of the Bridewell, an exercise area which land had been reclaimed from the sea. It was designed for four men to use working a pair of stones and with a dressing machine which was in an adjacent room. The men would work for six hours a day making a fair supply of corn which was produced for the public. The mill had cost £90.

A report survives from 1830 which discusses the merits of the mill and suggests that the authorities may have been correct in their thinking.

On entering the Southampton Bridewell, and requesting to see it as a stranger, 'Sir,' rejoined the Governor, 'we have now no prisoners; we have but three or four men, and one woman'. I enquired how this happened? 'I believe, Sir, it is owing to the Mill; they do not like the labour we have now; they used to do nothing, and they did not mind being sent to prison; but the case is altered.'

The prison visitor witnessed four men working the mill, and even tried it himself to better understand the nature of the punishment. He found the operation comparatively easy and thought it was not a particularly severe punishment; but then he was not put to work there for the entire day. Indeed the prisoners begged to differ saying that if he saw them at the end of the day he would find them 'worn out enough'.

"WORN OUT ENOUGH"

The writer felt it right and proper that the prisoners should be wearied and exhausted by the task, with the only relief being when they slept at night, after which they would rise the next morning temporarily refreshed only to find themselves trapped in the endless cycle of working the mill, sleep, and work again. This the writer felt would get them to appreciate the sentence of the law. The writer also believed this type of punishment would inspire useful industry and the formation of good habits in the prisoner as well as physical improvements to hands, arms and limbs. The prisoner's constitution he reasoned would become used to physical work and no longer find it irksome or indeed painful. Thus improved by the punishment the prisoner would be restored to society, be inspired to look for an honest day's work in the future and then the Bridewell would become redundant, its cells empty.

The hand mill at God's House Tower gaol did have the advantage of producing something useful, grain for making bread. The treadwheel which became the dominant tool for punishment was more soul-destroying as it produced nothing. The prison reform movement saw the treadwheel as being of no use as it did not mimic any type of work that a prisoner might undertake when released. The action the treadwheel required was the use of the ball of the foot alone which in the view of Dr Good negated the discipline of providing a useful skill.

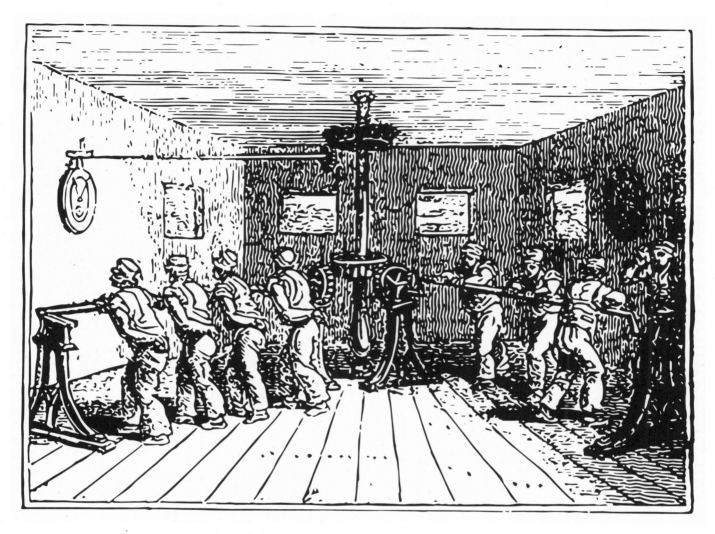

Hand crank mill for prison labour

The culprit just freed from the Tread-wheel, though he should have escaped the diseases and injuries to which he has been exposed while under its domination, has gained nothing to facilitate his progress in any useful employment: with a greater hatred of a prison life he will have no greater means, and, perhaps, may have fewer of avoiding it; while the hand-crank man will find that, under your improved machinery and regulations, he has been serving a most valuable apprenticeship, and has become initiated in the healthful and vigorous arts of thrusting, pulling, heaving, and bearing burdens; for the action of the cranks on the several muscular positions of the body, in effect, prepares it for the various relative duties of manual labour.

Women prisoners also used the hand mill but were more usually employed in the production of oakum. This was the process of cutting old rope into pieces, striking it with a hammer to get rid of the tar with which it had been coated, then unravelling it to turn it into recyclable fibres. The work was hard, monotonous and unpleasant, prisoners could develop blisters and sores on their fingers, and the air would be thick with brown dust. The recycled oakum did have a value and could be sold to caulk wooden ships and even to make string or stuff mattresses and led to the expression 'money for old rope'. With Southampton being a maritime port the output from oakum picking was 'in good demand in the town'.

Picking oakum

"MONEY FOR OLD ROPE"

In the new rules for the prison issued in 1855, rule 49 directed that no female prisoner or any boy under fourteen years of age, nor any prisoner not sentenced to hard labour, be under any circumstances, placed on the tread-wheel. Also no prisoner complaining of bodily ailments should be put to hard labour without the sanction of the medical officer. The maximum height which any one prisoner should ascend on any single day was set at 12,000 ft, and in addition measures were to be taken to prevent the exposure of prisoners to cold on leaving the tread-wheel.

For some prisoners their stay in God's House Tower was not followed by release, as it was just the first stage in their sentence. For some prisoners that meant transportation to the other side of the world to spend their time in penal colonies which had the dual purpose of punishment and of helping to advance colonization.

TRANSPORTATION

In 1764 Thomas Cooper the younger, a saddler from Southampton was accused of stealing a book, a volume of magazines from 1762, belonging to Thomas Scard and a cheese from George Whitmarsh. Despite his father putting up a bond for his good behaviour he was convicted and was transported by William Rice on his ship *Matthew* to the island of Nevis and into the custody of Horatio Herbert on 25th May 1764.

In 1765 the servant of the sometime mayor and town doctor John Monkton was sentenced to transportation to America for seven years. He had been accused of stealing his master's rum, wine and brandy along with two glasses and purloining a dead hare which was being transported to London. William Stow was convicted alongside his brother Joseph, who had been suspected of stealing rum from a previous employer, William Yeats. Joseph claimed that the rum came from a smuggler, but there were too many witnesses against him and his brother. Peter Thorn's evidence was particularly damning as he saw Joseph undo a padlock to John Monkton's store and come out with something concealed under his arm. They were convicted and ordered to be sent to the colonies and plantations in America. Thomas Dormer the younger was bonded to transport the men in his ship *St George Snow* which was moored at the Water Gate quay. Should the men escape he would have lost the £100 bond he had agreed for undertaking the job. America was at this time still a British colony and prisoners were routinely sent there as punishment and to help the development of the colony through their labour.

Australian penal colony

In 1783 God's House Tower prisoner James Lawrence was convicted and sentenced to be transported to America for seven years. The date of Lawrence's sentence is significant as it falls at the time when the American War of Independence was coming to a close, which it did in the September. After that time prisoners could not be transported there, but fortunately for the justice system, Australia had been discovered by Captain Cook in 1770. In 1787 the First Fleet of eleven convict ships left Portsmouth with nearly 1500 men, women and children on board. They were led by Captain Arthur Phillip who lived at Lyndhurst in the New Forest. In 1826 two God's House prisoners were sentenced to be transported to Australia, Frederick Head aged just twelve and a half and George Jennings Ball aged 20. Frederick had been working as a labourer when convicted of Grand Larceny, and he was reported as being of good behaviour. George was a carpenter, who had already been in trouble in Jersey and been transported to Southampton, his behaviour was considered very bad as he had 'endeavoured to break prison since his trial'. George was one of 192 convicts transported on the *Albion* on 21st September 1826, arriving in New South Wales on 14th February 1827. Prior to transportation prisoners were sent to the prison hulks, old ships that were moored at Portsmouth and Gosport. This had happened to another prisoner in 1819 when Joseph Wilkinson had been sent to the *Laurel*, a hulk at Portsmouth.

Prison Hulk, Portsmouth

18 April 1820.

Order for removing
Henry Butler &
Wm White alias
Burridge Convicts
Confined in Southampton
Gaol to the Hulks
at Gosport. & ......
Receipt for Convicts

Order for prisoners to be sent to the hulks

The *Laurel* was originally the Dutch sloop *Sireene* captured in 1796, opened as a prison hunk in 1802, and used as such until 1820. It could take up to 389 prisoners. In 1820 Henry Butler and William White were delivered from God's House gaol to Captain Alan Lamb who was responsible for the Gosport hulks. In 1821 Robert Burbidge was also sent to the hulks. Burbidge, a nineteen year old, had been found guilty of stealing and sentenced to seven years. He also was of very good behaviour but his bodily state was said to be much debilitated, this may have been why he was not immediately transported. In fact the only Robert Burbidge who did arrive in Australia, did not do so until 1832 with a fourteen year sentence. Henry Butler arrived in Van Diemen's Land (now Tasmania) to begin his seven year sentence on 12th January 1821, along with 183 other convicts. In 1825 another child prisoner, Joseph Parker, aged thirteen was sentenced to seven years' transportation for a felony and sent first to *Bellerophon* at Sheerness where his behaviour was said to be improving and his bodily state was good. He sailed on the *Albion* in 1826 and arrived in New South Wales on 14th February 1827. In 1829 Dan Boshier was sent further afield to Woolwich, where the *Captivity*, *Ganymede* and *Discovery* hulks were moored. His crime was stealing beams and boards and he had been sentenced to fourteen years on 28th April. He was transported on the *Claudine* on 15th August and arrived in Australia in December. Hulks provided a place to gather and hold prisoners until there were sufficient to fill a prison transport vessel to the colonies. These decommissioned naval ships once stripped of their masts, rigging and sails, provided cheaper accommodation than building prison barracks. This temporary solution lasted for eighty years. Convicts being transported via Portsmouth and Gosport would have been marched to the hulks and it has been suggested that they were held in barns on the way, one such place is thought to be an area of Sholing. The place came to be known as 'Botany Bay Farm' and there is still Botany Bay Road in Sholing today.

"HE HAD ENDEAVOURED TO BREAK PRISON SINCE HIS TRIAL"

The year 1831 saw the biggest influx of prisoners into Southampton in the wake of the 'Swing Riots' uprisings against the depredations of the agricultural depression and the introduction of mechanised farming. Dozens of men found themselves in Southampton for a 'special gaol delivery' charged with machine breaking, rioting, and other linked crimes. Several men were sentenced to hang though most had their sentences commuted to transportation. Three ships the *Eleanor*, *Eliza* and *Proteus* took 116 men from the Southampton trials to Australia with sentences ranging from seven and fourteen years to life. These were not hardened criminals, they were ploughmen, blacksmiths, stonemasons, farmers and many had witnesses who testified on their behalf of their good characters. The majority of the men came from the villages surrounding Southampton. One group was charged with stealing a sovereign from Harris Bigg Withers. At the trial Bigg Withers offered to 'willingly pay whatever charge might be paid' to provide the accused with legal counsel. The men were all found guilty and Bigg Withers recommended mercy be extended to them. They were transferred down to the hulk *Hardy* but were only there for a matter of days before they boarded the convict ship *Eleanor*. Harris Bigg Wither is generally remembered for being a suitor of Jane Austen. The majority of the Swing Rioters were granted a pardon in 1836, but most appear to have remained in Australia. Those that were married often requested and were granted permission for their families to join them there. Transportation finally ceased in 1857.

THE DEATH PENALTY

For some prisoners the destination was final. In the eighteenth century any theft over the value of 1s was considered to be Grand Larceny and carried the heaviest penalties. There were those who paid the ultimate price, at the public gibbet which was situated on Southampton Common, near the Burgess Road crossroads, and the Cutthorn ancient town meeting place. This had been a site of justice and punishment since the Anglo-Saxon period. It was usual for execution sites to be near these meeting places and close to crossroads where victims would be buried in unmarked and unsanctified ground. Luck and who was appointed as Judge at the assizes could be the difference between life and death. In March 1783 there were four prisoners being held in God's House charged with crimes that could have resulted in the death penalty. David Williams and John Iago were acquitted and discharged. James Lawrence was transported and Thomas Michell was found guilty of forgery and condemned to be hanged. Michell was given a reprieve until the 15th May, and there is no evidence the sentence was carried out. The last three public hangings were John Marchant hanged for the murder of his wife Elizabeth in 1760, Daniel Moreto who met the same fate in 1766 for forgery and, finally, on 27th July 1785, the Southampton gallows claimed its last victim when William Shawyer was publicly executed.

Illustration of the hanging of
William Shawyer -
Martin Davey

Shawyer had been committed by the mayor John Monkton and Thomas Guillaume in their roles as Justices of the Peace on the 28th February 1785. He was charged with 'Feloniously and burglarously entering the dwelling house occupied by Maria the wife of Beauchamp Bagenal Esquire and stealing divers plate.' Bagenal was the second richest man in Southampton after the Earl of Peterborough. Charles Stuart was also committed around the same time, on 24th May, and was charged with two other anonymous 'Persons' as having fraudulently cheated Robert Dobbs, a sailor from St Mary's, out of his silver watch. The verdicts for both cases were handed down on 9th July but with very different outcomes. Shawyer was convicted and sentenced to be hanged and Stuart was acquitted. It might be supposed that the social status of the theft victims may had influenced the outcome. Moreover Shawyer had been in a position of trust, as a servant, in the Bagenal household. He was not a very adept thief burying his haul of plate in the garden of his lodgings where it was easily discovered in a cucumber bed. There was a petition to the Secretary of State and to the king, raised by Shawyer's brother in an attempt to have the execution sentence commuted but without success.

This execution was unusual as despite there being 160 capital offences judges would often use their discretion in sentencing not to levy a capital punishment. However there were some members of the judiciary, like Judge Eyre, who campaigned that all people who had been sentenced to be executed, should see that sentence carried out. He felt it was more of a deterrent with no opportunity to re-offend. His campaign was at its height in 1785.

Shawyer was executed on the 27th July. His last journey began around 10am, and the Hampshire Chronicle reported that he had been very low after his conviction and those who saw him emerge from the gaol were doubtful that he would live to reach the gallows. He was placed in a cart covered with black cloth and had a handkerchief over his face to avoid seeing the 'unusual concourse of spectators who surrounded him'. Six sergeants on horseback were on duty that day. It took just over an hour to reach the Common. Shawyer spent an hour in prayer and devotion, he was comforted on the gallows by the Reverend Mant of All Saints Church who was an acquaintance of Jane Austen and her family. After the hanging Shawyer's body was removed from the gallows and taken, by his relatives, in a hearse to his home village of Bishops Waltham for burial.

CHILD PRISONERS

The age of criminal responsibility in the eighteenth century was seven, so it was not at all unusual to find children locked up. Even today the age of criminal responsibility is only ten. Some of the offences resulting in time in prison seem harsh. Robert Hill was apprenticed to James Newlyn to learn how to make women's shoes. His chosen profession obviously did not agree with him because he ran away to join the army. A warrant was raised for his arrest and incarceration in the House of Correction. Today many of the crimes would be seen as petty, and many of the young miscreants imprisoned in God's House gaol were recorded as being illiterate. In 1819, James Arnold, 15, George Kennedy, 12, and Richard Rider, 15, stole knives and other articles from the shop of Mr Davids. They were lucky to escape transportation and in the end were sentenced to one year's imprisonment.

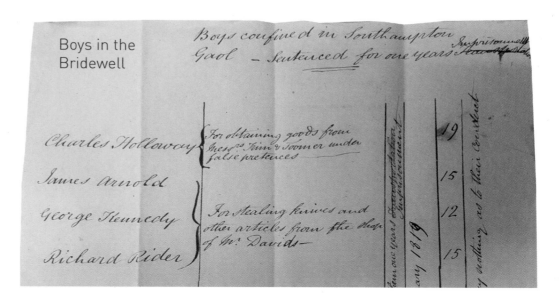

In 1837 George Powell, 14, Charles Newman, 15, and John Veal, 14, stole half a pound of tea. Tea in this period was a valuable commodity not least because of its transportation costs, being brought from India and China in clipper ships. Those who could afford to buy tea would keep it under lock and key in specially-made tea caddies. Francis Kendall was only eleven when he was committed for an assault on Edward Biles the elder, he could not pay his fine and so was sent to prison for two months. Edward Witt, 13, Edward Stubbs, 13, William Towney, 13, Isaac Wilkins, 13, Henry Edwards, 11, and James Stubbs, 12, were all involved in the theft of peas. Witt and Stubbs were sentenced to one month's imprisonment with hard labour. Towney, Wilkins, Edwards and Stubbs each received a fourteen-day sentence. It was not till the middle of the nineteenth century that punishments and imprisonment for children were separated from those of adults with the introduction of the Juvenile Offences Act of 1847 and the establishment of Reformatory Schools in 1857.

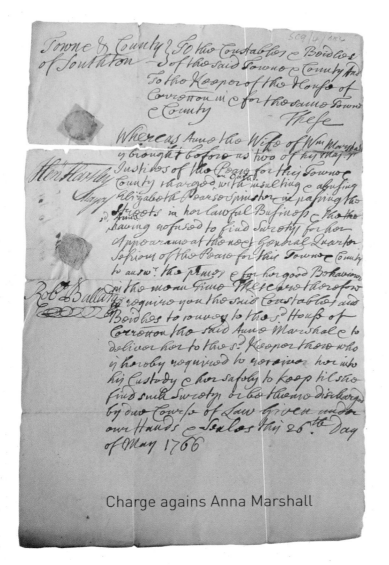

Charge agains Anna Marshall

FEMALE PRISONERS

Women, as well as men, were kept in the God's House gaol often for offences that were specific to their sex, ranging from verbal abuse and vagrancy to having an illegitimate child or being convicted of murder. In 1766 Anne Marshall was committed to the House of Correction for insulting and abusing Elizabeth Pearse whilst she was about her lawful business in the street. Anne refused to find surety for her appearance at the sessions and so was imprisoned pending the hearing. Since the medieval period women were subjected to punishment for being scolds or having 'venomous tongues'. Having a child out of wedlock could also result in spending time in the House of Correction.

In 1830 Sarah Robinson of All Saints parish had had an illegitimate child but had refused to tell the authorities the father's name. The Corporation would want to know the man involved so that he could take on any financial responsibility for the child rather than this falling on the town. In the event they discovered the man in question was James Fox of King Street, a brazier, and he joined Sarah in the Bridewell. Some women took drastic methods when having illegitimate children. Harriet Mansbridge was placed in the Common Gaol for the murder of her newborn child, as was Mary Rowsell, charged with the 'wilful murder of her newborn baby girl' in 1787. In July 1822 Louisa Crouch of St Michael's parish brought an indictment against Elizabeth Sheppard, currently confined in the Common Gaol, for murdering her female 'bastard child' in the previous March. Neighbours Henry Butler, a carrier, William Wallis, a bricklayer, Charles Maul esquire and Sophia Sheldon, the wife of William Sheldon, whitesmith, were all called as witnesses. Women were also imprisoned for prostitution such as Elizabeth Oliver and Harriot Mundy, both twenty, in 1847.

However they were fortunate as things became harder for women in 1864 when the Contagious Diseases Act was passed. Women suspected of immoral behaviour could be arrested and suffer compulsory checks for venereal disease and find themselves incarcerated in 'Lock hospitals' which specialized in treating sexually transmitted disease. The Act was introduced to protect soldiers. There was no similar action against men.

Women did threaten to commit capital crimes as well. James Davis, a gardener, took an oath that he heard Jane Newland, the wife of John Newland, hearth maker, swear that she would be the death of Anne Fuller a servant to the informant the next time that she came that way. Some women did commit and attempt murder. At the summer assize of 1790 Christian Lisle was tried for murder, along with Jacob Duel, who had been arrested for perjury, and been committed since the Lent Assizes.

Eliza Harding was incarcerated on 5th August 1831 on the 'strong suspicion' of administering or causing to be administered a poisonous nut called Nux Vomica to Edward Boyland. The nut was commonly called the 'vomiting nut' or the 'poison nut tree'. The seeds contain strychnine and brucine both of which are toxic in large doses. Eliza Harding was just fourteen and had been a servant of Boyland, a Southampton tailor, for about seven weeks when she went to the chemist looking for something to kill mice. Shortly before breakfast on 5th August Eliza

Accusation against Jane Newland

was in the kitchen and had a tin cup containing five brown beans which she put on the fire. When Boyland enquired what it was for she said she was going to take it herself. Boyland went out and returned a little later making a cup of tea which was also drank by his wife, a child and his lodger. Mrs Boyland thought the tea tasted bitter and on examining the kettle found two beans in the water. Her husband, who had drunk more of the tea, then began to be ill, his throat and stomach on fire, he was overcome with thirst and then he started frothing at the mouth. The local surgeon was sent for and on examination of the patient ordered him to take an emetic as he had been poisoned. Suspicion fell on Eliza and her mysterious beans. The girl panicked first saying she knew nothing, then that the beans had fallen in the kettle by accident and finally saying that she had drunk a pint of the liquid and would be dead within the hour. Two more of the beans were found in her pocket. Eliza was imprisoned for attempted murder. Described by her employers as being of a 'sullen and morose disposition' she confessed to nothing. After seven months in God's House Tower gaol she came before the Assizes. The judge Mr Justice Gaselee found there to be some difficulty with the evidence and ordered Eliza's acquittal.

"SULLEN AND MOROSE DISPOSITION"

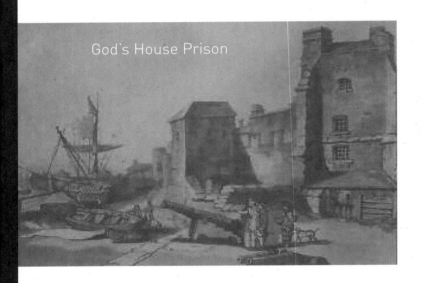
God's House Prison

An Elizabeth Harding, possibly a relative of Eliza's, had previously been sentenced to seven years' transportation in 1802 but was granted a Free Pardon. Another letter dated 1805 also gives her a Free Pardon, but it is not clear if this is a confirmation of the earlier pardon or an additional pardon for further offences.

Often women found themselves in gaol for theft, of items which were quite small, or were items of clothing or food. For example, Fanny Whitehorn of Lyndhurst, a single woman, was imprisoned for the theft of two loaves of bread from John Lisle in 1837, or like Hannah Fry, in shades of Oliver Twist, who had stolen a handkerchief from Anne Whitehorn in the same year. Abigail Sullivan, wife of the labourer John Sullivan of St Mary's parish, stole port and bacon from Edward Thompson of All Saints. Charlotte Mist, another single woman, stole clothing from Benjamin Mills and Maria Knight stole money from William Davis. Girls as young as thirteen were remanded such as Eliza Watts and Anne Steele who took a piece of bacon valued at a shilling, and a pair of shoes worth one shilling and sixpence. Eliza Moody a twenty four year old woman, who the court noted could read and write well, was committed in 1837 for stealing a 'French Thibet shawl' valued at 10s. Along with Caroline Lane she was also accused of stealing a small green silk shawl, one imitation dahlia flower valued at 3s and one imitation acorn flower worth 1s.

There is only one surviving record of a woman being in the gaol for debt. Charlotte Braxton a spinster from Newport on the Isle of Wight was in trouble in 1795, but did manage to raise enough money to pay off her creditors. £3 13s was repaid to Mr John Arnold, a hairdresser and perfumer, and to Mr Jonathan Wavell, a mercer and draper, both from the Isle of Wight and ten guineas to Alexander Leeth. Wavell and Arnold dropped their charges and asked that she be released. For the destitute there was little support and one Martha Pope was imprisoned for a month with hard labour in 1837 for vagrancy.

Women were always in the minority in the prison and were more likely to find themselves as victims, as happened to Louisa Blank in 1835 and Maria Small in 1836. In 1835 Joseph Culley of All Saints was the prosecutor on an indictment against John Blake, labourer, for 'feloniously stabbing, cutting and wounding' one Louisa Culley otherwise called Louisa Blake with 'intent to kill and murder the said Louisa on the 13th of June at the parish of All Saints'. It appears Louisa was the common law wife of Blake, and probably Joseph was a relative of hers, but there is nothing in the indictment to explain why she was attacked. In 1836 Thomas Venables, a labourer living in the parish of St Mary, assaulted Maria Small, beating, wounding her and ill-treating her with the intent to violently and feloniously 'ravish and carnally know and do other wrongs to her'. As the indictment concluded the assault did great damage to Maria Small.

MALE PRISONERS

The men imprisoned were confined for a wide range of crimes, examples of which are contained in the records of the Town Clerk. These records do not feature all the prisoners or all the crimes but give a sense of what offences landed people in prison. Theft was common, of course, and the items taken were usually of more value than those taken by the female prisoners. In 1786 the accounting house of one of the town's most important industrialists was broken into by Charles Petty. The Taylors were major contractors for the Royal Navy for whom they designed wooden blocks and pulleys needed for raising sails and moving guns. Their business premises were in St Michael's parish and their accounting house was part of the building in Westgate Street. In the same year Robert Coward stole five and a half guineas from a coffer of James Fray, tapster, at the Coach and Horses Inn in All Saints parish and William Chaplin broke into the bricklayer Samuel Chamber's house in St Mary's parish intending to commit burglary. Chaplin was thwarted however, as Chamber's wife Elizabeth was there and disturbed him, but she was much terrified by the experience.

In 1820 John Hope was committed into the Common Gaol for breaking into Mrs Gilbert Ricketts' house and stealing clothing and a silver watch. In 1837 George Hood, aged 21, was caught stealing a fustian jacket, one linen waistcoat, one cotton handkerchief, and one silk handkerchief, valued at 5s, all the property of one John Bishop. In 1837 Edward Simmonds was charged with having feloniously stolen one copper metal bucket valued at 3s, the property, for the time being, of John Brewer, the gaoler of God's House prison. Robert Raines was arrested for attempting to pick pockets in Above Bar, also in 1837.

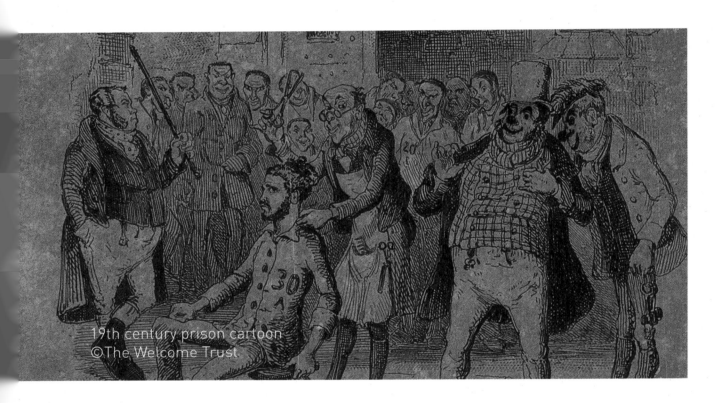

19th century prison cartoon
©The Welcome Trust.

The prison report for 1837 includes information on sentencing. George Warren a young man of 22, with imperfect reading and writing, was found guilty of stealing a brass lock, the property of his master. His sentence was six months in prison with the first and last fortnight in solitary confinement. When James Giffard, also 22, stole a pair of boots from John Morris he received three months with hard labour and also spent his first and last week in solitary confinement.

There were a number of people who were charged with embezzlement, coining and forgery. Forgery became more prevalent with the introduction of paper bank notes. Francois Raison was gaoled for altering a Bank of England note from £1 to £5. He was sentenced to fourteen years' transportation in September 1818. He sailed on the *Globe* which arrived in New South Wales on

8th January 1819. On route he had an accident and fell from the boom of the ship and his leg went into the copper of boiling water. He was treated with cerat resin according to 'Dr Kentish's method' and was on the sick list on arrival between 10th and 15th January, but later discharged. In 1837 Thomas Lea, aged 34, and said to be of superior education, was convicted of embezzling certain monies, the property of his master. His sentence was six months' imprisonment with hard labour, and with the first and last fortnight of his sentence to be spent in solitary confinement. John Webb, aged 22 and illiterate, was found with a quantity of base coin, and was sentenced to the same punishment as Lea but without hard labour.

Selling goods outside the normal markets could also bring you to the attention of the authorities. In 1798 Antoine Legaldie a merchant from Lyon in France, where he had worked for thirty years, was detained. He had spent the previous six years in Jersey where he had offered goods such as umbrellas, handkerchiefs and other articles for sale about the town. He had however undercut the local shopkeepers who applied to the court to have him sent out of the Island. When he arrived in Southampton Legaldie had 25 guineas, plus shirts, stockings, two pairs of breeches and other articles with him which were currently held at the custom house. He said his reason for leaving France was 'trouble breaking out'. This would have been the time of the 'Terror' at the height of the French Revolution.

Assault charges in 1837 included James Saunders, 20, and George Todd, 18, for obstructing a constable in discharge of his duty, and Anthony Rider for assaulting a constable. Desertion both from the army and from your family was another offence. Charles Macquire alias Charles Write was sent to the House of Correction as a rogue, vagabond and deserter from the 90th Regiment of Foot in 1833. In 1837 Thomas Young, 31, was imprisoned for leaving his wife and family chargeable to his parish, as was George Hall, aged 34, whilst William Stewart, 18, was charged with vagrancy.

More serious crimes included rape. William Macdonald raped Harriet, the daughter of Anthony Summers, aged just six and three quarters. Charles Barrett committed a similar crime against Maria Saunders, daughter of Mrs Elizabeth Bay and aged just nine years and five months. The age of the girls was of legal significance as if they were aged ten or older they were considered to be responsible and therefore the sexual act would not be considered as rape.

Being homosexual in the eighteenth century could find the culprit committed to prison or worse. This was an offence only for men, as the concept of lesbianism was not recognised at the time. In 1786 John La Lacheur, a mariner, and William Greenaway, a labourer, were committed to the felons' gaol for having 'committed the detestable crime of Sodomy or Buggery'. A letter of 1772 survives giving the gossip around another case involving homosexuality in Southampton.

LETTER OF 1772

The vice that has so lately excited the talk in London, has made its appearance here. It seems as if the military had taken it intirely up. Mr B[ickerstaffe] celebrated in Mr K[endric]k's poem, being an officer on half-pay; Mr Jones [Capt Robert Jones], lately capitally convicted at the Old-Bailey, a Captain in the Artillery; and our hero at this place also an officer in the army. A report had circulated in a whisper to his discredit, and the Master of the Ceremonies, at the Long Rooms, told him of it, and at the same time hinted that he must clear his character, otherwise he could not possibly be continued any longer a member of that company; this was yesterday evening. He left the rooms, and went home, when the constables came to apprehend him. On being acquainted therewith, he endeavoured to escape by the garret window; but the casement being too small, he was taken with his body half out of the window, and committed to the Bridewell in this town. It appears, that he made the attempt on a journeyman shoe-maker, who works with Mr Day of this place, who, though offered money, manfully refused it, and insisted upon bringing the culprit to condign punishment. This being market-day, an effigy of him, dressed in scarlet, was set on the pillory, with its arms through, and on one side a roll, on the other a pint of beer; this afternoon it was carried about the town, and in the evening is to be burned in triumph. He has been at this place about three months, and is between forty and fifty years of age.

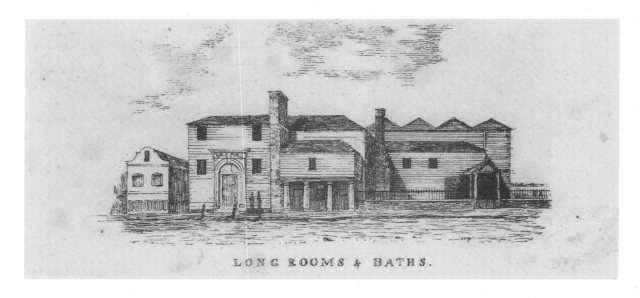

LONG ROOMS & BATHS.

The Long Rooms were the Assembly Rooms of the bathing resort, built on the site of Mr Martin's bathing establishment, originally to give a viewing area for those wanting to see the baths. It became, however, the centre of entertainment where balls were put on under the auspices of a professional Master of Ceremonies. Isaac Bickerstaffe was originally from Dublin, and in 1745 had joined the 5th Regiment of Foot, known as the Northumberland Fusiliers. He had ambitions to be a writer but had not been very successful so went back to the army joining the Marine Corps. He then began to collaborate with the composer Thomas Arne and the pair wrote successful plays and operettas. After the scandal of 1772 he fled to France and died in obscurity. In July 1772 Robert Jones was convicted for assaulting Francis Hay who was only thirteen, the age of consent for boys being fourteen. Jones was found guilty and sentenced to death, but was offered a pardon if he left the country. Jones is also credited with popularizing ice-skating and fireworks. Who the Southampton officer was who got stuck in the garret window has not yet been ascertained.

For most crimes we know very little about the reasons for the crimes, the impact on the victims or the wider biography of the prisoners in God's House gaol. However there are two cases for which we have additional material to the inspectors' reports, and prisoner transport information. One is a case of arson which drew the attention of an insurance company and the second about the experience of a debtor who left a cache of letters behind, both of which survived thanks to an archivist who rescued the solicitor's records from a skip.

PRISONERS TALES
A case of Arson: Hill & Kingsmill

On 5th February 1816 The Hampshire Chronicle reported the fire which took place in French Street.

On Wednesday night, about half-past eleven o'clock a fire was discovered in a dwelling-house at the upper part of French street, opposite St Michael square, formerly the Paymaster's office of the Military Depot, but now in the occupation of a man by the name of Hill, a straw bonnet manufacturer. The flames were first discerned issuing through the shop window shutters and bottom part of the door, but in a few minutes afterwards the upper part of the building was likewise perceived to be on fire. The alarm was instantly given by ringing the fire bells, and sounding of the bugle of the South Hants Militia; and in the space of a quarter of an hour nearly 200 persons were assemble on the spot; but by this time Hill's house was completely enveloped in flames from the roof to the ground floor, so that it was useless to attempt saving any of the premises furniture, there was none to be seen. Two engines arrived soon after, but owing to a defect in the pipes and water, some time elapsed, so that the conflagration threatened the most direful consequences; indeed, had it not been for the unremitting exertions of the officers and the privates of the South Hants, who nobly followed the example of a few gentlemen and respectable inhabitants of the town, God only knows where or when the calamity would have ended, as in the beginning of the business not a fireman was to be seen or any person from whom the smallest information could be obtained. About twelve o'clock the flames had communicated to an adjoining house, inhabited by ten individuals, six of them helpless infants, who were awakened by the bursting open of the street door and the cry of fire. At this moment the flames had spread to the upper chamber, where the children were sleeping, when, with a humanity which will ever render his memory dear to the good and virtuous, Mr Charles Ward instantly forced his way up the stairs, and happily succeeded in saving four of the little innocents; his exertions were nobly seconded by Lieut. J Watts of the 85th regiment, who was fortunate enough to rescue another of the children, and the six were safely conveyed out of the house in the arms of their distressed father, followed by the mother. Shortly after this, while Mr C Ward, Mr Gradige, Lieut Watts and Mr C Whittenooth, were saving the property of the sufferers, the whole front of the building gave way, and fell into the street, when; melancholy to relate, the frame of the bow-window struck Mr C Ward in the head, and killed him on the spot; the three gentlemen (whose exertions were conspicuous through the whole business) nearly shared the same fate; indeed they all received considerable contusions. This shocking catastrophe greatly increased the melancholy scene, and nothing but dejection was visible in every countenance. The flames still raged with unabated fury; nor was it till a plentiful supply of water was obtained from Mr Knight's, the tallow-chandler, contiguous to the spot, that any hopes were entertained of their being subdued; but thanks to the unwearied perseverance of the officers and soldiers, and the unceasing activity of Lieut Watts and Lieut Claribel RN together with that of Mr Gradige, and a few sailors, it was happily got under about four o'clock in the morning, and with the destruction only of four dwelling houses and a stable.

The paper however goes on to report that the calamity was shocking enough, but that there was a very strong suspicion that the premises had in fact been set on fire by the occupiers of the house which first caught fire. Two men, John Kingsmill and John Hills, were due to be examined by the local magistrates, and if suspicions still persisted they would be committed to the Bridewell.

Ward memorial

In addition two looters were already in prison for plundering what property had managed to be saved from the fire. Thomas Ridding, the town clerk, wrote to the insurers of the building, The Royal Exchange Assurance Company, alerting them to a possible fraud and that John Hills had rented the fired house 'with intent to injure and defraud your Corporation of £800'.

The insurance company investigated and the trail took them to another confederate of Hills and Kingsmill, a man called Wetherhilt who was living in Rochester. The company notified Ridding that they aimed to produce a watertight case with strong evidence 'as it would be most mortifying if two such notorious Culprits were to escape on a Question of mere Form'. They had traced a previous fraud which had been perpetrated against a Mr David James at Dartford. The suspects had made a claim for lost stock and furniture in the French Street fire and were claiming for hats that were lost to the value of £600. It also transpired that the French Street property had only been insured two days before the fire for £1000.

"IT WOULD BE MOST MORTIFYING IF TWO SUCH NOTORIOUS CULPRITS WERE TO ESCAPE ON A QUESTION OF MERE FORM"

TOWN AND COUNTY OF }
Southampton. }

To the Constables, Beidles, and other Officers of the Peace in and for the said Town and County of Southampton, and to the Keeper of the Bridewell *in and for the same Town and County.*

WHEREAS, *John Kingsmill*

is brought before me, one of his Majesty's Justices of the Peace in and for the said Town and County, charged upon Oath, with *strong suspicion of having on Wednesday the thirty first day of January last been aiding and assisting John Hills in wilfully maliciously and unlawfully setting Fire to a House belonging to Simon Craske at the Parish of Saint Michael in the said Town and County*

THESE are therefore to command you, the said Constables, Beidles, and other Officers of the Peace, to convey the said *John Kingsmill*

to the said *Bridewell* and to deliver *him* safely to the said Keeper thereof, and you the said Keeper are hereby required to receive into your Custody the said *John Kingsmill*

and *him* safely to keep till the next General ~~Quarter Seffions~~ *Gaol Delivery* of the Peace, to be holden for the said Town and County, or till *he*

be difcharged by due Courfe of Law. Given under my Hand and Seal the *sixth* Day of *February* in the Year of our Lord One Thoufand Eight Hundred and *sixteen*

Wm Lintott
Mayor (L S)

[T. Skelton, Printer, No. 12, High Street, Southampton.]

Charges against Hills & Kingsmill

The two accused were bought to trial, but unfortunately the trial appears to have collapsed fairly quickly, ironically due to the evidence from a representative of the insurance company. It was a technicality, the description of the property in the policy was wrong. It was described as being made from brick, timber and tiles but was in fact constructed of lath and plaster. The conclusion was that as the Royal Exchange Assurance Company could not be answerable to the assured (Hill) because of the error, the jury were, in consequence, bound to consider the prisoner uninsured. He therefore as a point of law could not be charged with any evil motive or intent. Hill was acquitted and that meant the other indictment against Kingsmill could not be supported.

The unfortunate victim Charles Ward, as a captain of the Yeomanry Cavalry, was given a military burial at the family church in Nursling and his friends and admirers commissioned a memorial to his 'perpetual memory, public spirit and private worth', which can still be seen in St Michael's Church.

A case of Debt: John Geagan

There is one prisoner about whose incarceration we know a great deal because of a surviving cache of letters that were exchanged between him and his lawyer, Thomas Ridding, between 1808 and 1811. John Geagon was imprisoned in the debtors' gaol at God's House sometime before January 1808. He was trying to get his case reviewed at the King's Bench and in the meantime wanted to get information on the rules of the prison where he was under the supervision of the gaoler Jeffery Truss. Ridding told him he might obtain a writ for less than three guineas but referred him to the gaoler for other information. It appears that it might have been possible for Geagan to live under licence on a payment of £10 if he agreed to keep certain prison rules. It seems that Geagan did not pursue the licence as he was still in gaol in March 1809 when his case came to the court of Common Pleas where he was defendant in a case of damages. Geagan must have been unsuccessful as he remained in prison trying to find a way of paying his debts. He had obtained a promise from an acquaintance who offered to advance him a sum of money and was requesting a list of his creditors, but again his hopes were dashed. Geagan was still in prison in January 1810 when there began a series of letters which complain about his treatment at the hands of Truss the gaoler, his wife who assisted him in his duties and some of their several children.

Southampton January 23ʳᵈ 1810

Dear Sir,

As Trusß has refused to give me any
explanation of the very infamous treatment I have
experienced from him. I must now beg you will
shew my letter to the Mayor. I am ready to bring
forward many charges persons, who have
witnessed every charge mentioned in that letter
Batten, the shoe-maker, who leaves this tomorrow
can prove the manner in which I have been
treated ever since he has been here.

In consideration of Trusß's advanced age and
numerous family I did not wish to write to the
Mayor. If you will have the goodness to
inform me when you intend seeing the Mayor
I will write to him at the same time.
If you could make it convenient to call on me
tomorrow morning I should be very happy
to see you —

I am,
Dear Sir,
Yours very truly
John F. Geagan

Example of John Geagan's letters

Geagan complained bitterly about the Trusses 'infamous manner' which he had tried to ignore, but having just heard that he was likely to spend at least another three months in prison, wanted to report the daily insults he had been subjected to. He had previously written to the Corporation about the Trusses who he described as being of advanced age, to request some kind of apology for Mr Truss's conduct and an undertaking not to repeat it. By this time Geagan reports he had been in prison for sixteen months and, as was usual in the case of debtors, had been in the habit of giving 'presents' to his gaolers to receive better treatment. However, when he was no longer in the position of being able to continue with the gifts his treatment from the Truss's deteriorated. He mentions specifically that visitors had been ordered from his room in an abusive manner, even though the Truss family kept him awake until midnight on numerous occasions. Geagan had been ill, no doubt due to the insanitary conditions of the prison, but while he languished in his sick bed Mrs Truss organised social gatherings - with dancing – inside the prison. Geagan felt it had been done with the express purpose of disturbing him. Their eldest daughter Mary, he accused of deliberately making horrid noises on the stairs, when his illness was so acute it was thought he would not recover.

The situation got even worse, with the other prisoners being constantly inebriated due to the liquor being brought into the prison. This resulted in disturbances in the early hours, quarrelling, and the crashing of doors. One of the worst culprits was Mrs Bone, whose husband, a tailor, was incarcerated in the prison. Mrs Bone brought rum in, and the Trusses and the other prisoners sat and drank together till they got drunk. Before the tailor Bone was discharged, Geagon accused the Truss family of encouraging Bone to send Geagan insolent messages, even though they were in 'no way acquainted'. In fact Geagan said 'had I even chosen to descend so low as to associate with a tailor, the very impertinent manner in which I was informed he spoke of the mayor, would have prevented my having anything to say to him'. Geagan was refused permission to continue to take exercise on top of the tower and was told that the family would no longer attend to his needs. Geagan believed his treatment stemmed from his refusal to pay for the education of one of Jeffery Truss's children.

Christmas had also been disrupted when the prison was left open after 11pm on Christmas Eve to facilitate Mrs Bone who had been spending the evening at the theatre, and not for the first time, whilst Geagan's visitor, Mr Temple, was ordered off the premises promptly at 9pm. The letter finally ends with a postscript expressing concern that the gaoler would no longer run errands or arrange for others to do so, including the calling of a porter to deliver letters to the solicitor's office. He re-iterates that the root cause for his ill-treatment is his refusal to educate the gaoler's daughter. He finishes by complaining that he had rewarded the family more than any other prisoner who had been in the gaol.

"TRUSS'S FAMILY HAVE BEEN FAR MORE AMPLY REWARDED BY ME THAN BY ANY PRISONER THAT WAS EVER HERE JFG"

A few days later Geagan is in better spirits, he is in correspondence with a Mr Woodley, a friend of his from the Island of St Kitts in the West Indies. It transpires that Geagan was not without financial resources, the problem was that they were tied up in a plantation on the island of St Kitts. The Trusses again seek to interfere, refusing to see letters delivered promptly, and continuing to be insolent. Geagan offers the testimony of Batten, a shoe-maker, who has been in prison with him, and is about to be released, who can corroborate the ill-treatment experienced from Truss and his family.

Geagan has however managed to contact his relatives in St Kitts and his mother has been involved in selling the estate to be able to send £1000 to her son.

The money promised back in June 1808 had still not appeared by January 1810. The solicitors for the buyer wanted to receive a Power of Attorney from Geagan giving up all claim on the estates. As well as continuing to write to Thomas Ridding about the Truss family, Geagan also asks to be informed about the proper hour for opening prisons in the morning, which he believes generally to be 7am. Mr Ridding, who one senses is getting a little exasperated by the continuing correspondence, replied:

Dear Sir

I am rather at a loss to answer your note as to the time the prison should be opened. It never having become a question since I have been Undersheriff whenever we are at any loss not having much Practise we generally apply to the Gaol at Winchester to know the Custom there. I should think seven was too early in the winter though perhaps not so now. I will write to Winchester and on hearing will let you know. I am Dear Sir your truly Tho.

Ridding

It turns out that in Winchester the prison was open at half past six from Lady Day (25th March) to Michaelmas (29th September) and in the winter from sun rising.

Geagan was still in prison in January 1811 when he wrote to complain that Mrs Truss had refused to 'dress' his dinner. The next letter was on March 1811 when Geagan asks his solicitor to call upon him but Mr Ridding was busy with a council meeting but promised to call as soon as he could. The story then takes a very different twist. Mr Ridding has interviewed the Trusses and reveals that their daughter Sarah has had a daughter, the father being John Geagan! In addition both Truss and his daughter made a complaint that Geagan had beaten them and pulled their ears. Ridding concludes 'I can't summon no wonder they don't come near you'.

"I CAN'T SUMMON NO WONDER THEY DON'T COME NEAR YOU"

Geagon's response to his solicitor's letter was to assure him that he wanted only to do everything in his power to secure 'the present and future happiness of his (Truss's) daughter and her child, for both of whom I certainly have the greatest regard, the former is indeed most justly dear to me'.

He believes that the fault and cause of the trouble sits with Mrs Truss, Sarah's stepmother. He paints Mrs Truss as 'brutal', the archetypal wicked stepmother suggesting that she would have no concern about expelling the unfortunate Sarah out of the family home: He reflects that in May last, when Sarah was in an advanced stage of pregnancy, he considered not seeing her, he dates that event as the time from when her father was ill-treating him but does not consider that the two events might be connected. When Mrs Truss threatened that unless Geagan continues to support the girl she would be put out of the house, he sees this as an expression of the stepmother's ill-treatment of Truss's 'second daughter', rather than perhaps the woman trying to get some redress from Sarah's seducer. Geagan however sees no fault in his own behaviour

In writing the petition and in every thing else that I have done it must be evident to every person that I can have no motive but the future welfare and happiness of my child and its mother, the latter not being able to prosecute her studies from being prevented coming to me is certainly a great disadvantage to her.

It seems, therefore, that Geagan had changed his mind about taking on the education of Trusses daughter, but took advantage of that situation.

A flurry of letters were then delivered to Mr Ridding, four on the same day of April 2nd 1811. Geagan pleads with the solicitor to meet with him, and repeats that anything that Mr or Mrs Truss has said is false. Not getting the response he wants, Geagan then petitions the mayor who did visit him, and spent some time listening to his complaints. However he was somewhat put out when the mayor also met separately with Mr and Mrs Truss, and again he attacks Mrs Truss

That unfortunate woman Trusses second daughter is completely under the control of a tyrannical mother-in-law she does not even know that she has any person to whom she can look up for protection and therefore it is more than probable she was compelled to say whatever her mother-in-law pleased.

Mr Ridding is very measured when he replies to the increasingly frantic Geagan, reminding him that he has spent a lot of time on his case, and also informing him that he had advised the mayor to speak to Sarah alone so that she would not be influenced by her parents. Sarah, they found to be 'truly satisfied with the conduct of her Family & quite at large, under no Restraint'. Furthermore she denied being in touch via letter with Geagan. She said she had not been ill-treated by her family, on the contrary she said it was Geagan who would not let her 'stir out' and she alleged he had struck her when she 'did not learn well'. The Justices recommended to Mr Truss that he find his daughter a situation with some comfortable family as a nurse or ladies' maid. Their judgement was that Geagan and Mr & Mrs Truss were equally to blame with regard to the situation, and that Sarah should on no account visit her former lover. They did conclude that they could have no objection to Geagan seeing his daughter but they could not force her mother to enable this to happen. They thought that as the child was at the present time 'out to nurse', that is being fed and looked after by a wet nurse, a common practice in the period, that the nurse could – upon some payment – bring the child to see her father.

Geagan wanted to challenge the outcome but Ridding advised him against again approaching the Justices who he felt would then prevent any contact between Geagan and Sarah, and as he succinctly put it 'if that was Mrs Truss's object you might be certain she would gain that'.

The final letters are all about Geagan finally selling property in the West Indies. He puts in place the Power of Attorney in July 1811 which had been drafted a year before. The draft still survives in Thomas Ridding's papers and shows that John Julius and the Hon John Woodley were to be appointed to act for Geagan, as the son and heir of John Geagan deceased. Geagan states he is now resident in Southampton, but not that he is in the town gaol. He asks his attorneys to sell the estate called Harris and Fabies situated in the parish of St John's Capestone, on the island of St Christoper with all its appurtences including the slaves and to assign the same to Henry and Richard Rawlins.

Geagan received a discharge from Mr Dennistown's solicitors in October 1811. In December the 'long expected deeds' were due to arrive. Geagan had two money drafts one for £350 and one for £490 3s 10d, and it is to be assumed that this finally procured his release.

POSTSCRIPT

In 1810 a report on the prison in which John Geagan had been incarcerated, recorded that there were four rooms in the Common Gaol that were locked at night, but were open during the day so that the prisoners could mingle. It took male and female prisoners and could hold up to twelve people. The Bridewell had three rooms and two sleeping rooms plus a common room, the rooms were locked at night, and the prison could hold up to ten people. The debtors' gaol had two rooms which could take ten prisoners. Ordinary prisoners received 6d a week for food and clothing if necessary, but the debtors only received subsistence money if they were in real distress. There were no particular written regulations in respect of any of the gaols.

John Geagan was son of John Geagan senior, who died in Trinidad in 1800. His father owned slave estates at Laurel Hill and Adelphi in the Arouca district, which were worked by thirteen slaves, who produced sugar. His estate on St Kitts was known as 'Geagan and Harris' in the parish of St Johns. John's mother, Maria Geagan, continued to trade in muscovado sugar after her husband's death. In 1804 she shipped five hogsheads of sugar to Messrs George and Robert Dennistown on the ship *Penelope*. Dennistown was presumably the same man mentioned in John Geagan's final letters. Maria Geagan was still living in Trinidad in 1814.

Jeffery Johnson Truss was born in 1748. He was of the parish of Holy Rood, and is described as having a large family including at least two daughters, Mary and Sarah, mentioned in John Geagan's letters. He married twice, the Mrs Truss mentioned in the letters being his second wife. He had married the thirty-two year old Mary Rogers on 9th January 1794. Previously in 1779 he had married Marianne Hewlett but she had died sometime before 1794. He had been gaoler of the Debtors' from at least 1785 and was still there in 1811. In 1785 he and another Town Sergeant Thomas Phillips purchased a property on East Street consisting of a tenement, stable and gardens from a Thomas Smith for £322. A Mary Truss of the debtor's prison is recorded as dying on 9th June 1815, presumably the daughter who had so annoyed John Geagan. Jeffery Truss may have been the son of the Geoffery Truss who ran the Half Moon Tavern on Butcher's Row in 1783-4, or this could have been Jeffery himself. He died on 8th April 1829 in Upham aged 81. The second Mrs Truss lived on until December 1833, she was then living at Preshaw Farm and aged 71.

Sarah Truss was born on 5th June 1789 to Jeffery Truss and his first wife Marianne Hewlett, she lost her mother whilst still a young child, no more than five years old. In checking the parish records the birth of Maria Eliza, daughter of Sarah Truss was recorded on 12th August 1810, so the child would have been conceived whilst Geagan was a prisoner in God's House Tower. When the birth was registered on 27th October 1810 John Fitzgerald Geagan was named as her father. On 12th November 1811, John Geagan and Sarah Truss were married in St Mary's Church, Southampton by special licence. As the formal date of his release from prison is not clear, it may have occurred prior to his solicitor's letters of December 1811 or he could still have been a prisoner at the time of the wedding.

THE BRAVERY OF A GAOLER

The story of the gaolers is scanty but one 'turnkey' has his name preserved for posterity on a plaque fixed to the exterior of Holy Rood Church on the High Street. On Tuesday 7th November 1837 just after 11pm smoke was noticed coming from King and Witt's counting house near to Gloucester Square, just around the corner from the God's House prison, and easily visible from its windows. The alarm was quickly raised, and a crowd collected, the fire bell was set ringing, and policemen's rattles 'sprung'. However it took an hour for the first fire engine to arrive and another twenty minutes before water was obtained. Up until this period there was no national fire service, with the fire engines being employed by insurance companies. Buildings would display fire plaques on the outside of their properties so the companies would know they were insured with the relevant company. The town had tried to bolster this arrangement by having some men specifically appointed by the town to fight fires and just before the events of 1837 had established a Fire Department under the control of the town waterworks commission.

Plan of King & Witt warehouse

The following ground plan of the building shows where the different bodies were found, the figures referring to their names

1. Harley
2. Rose
3. Brown, alias Henwood
4. George Diaper
5. Jones
6. Budden
7. The spot where the first six bodies, and that of Mr Sellwood, (since deceased) were taken.
8. Fire commenced.
9. Openings where a rocket case might have been thrown in.

Whilst waiting for help to arrive a few individuals started to empty the warehouse of ledgers and the other contents of the counting house and more dangerously some gunpowder. They then started to empty the ground floor and first storey, forming a human chain. It was now approaching 1am. The fire could have – if not contained – destroyed a quarter of the town. Disaster was looming as the flames reached stored oil, varnish, and turpentine. Many containers of turpentine were removed but one was dropped and the contents spread across the floor. When this caught fire the flash of flame burnt the faces and hands of many, whilst others had their shoes and lower part of their trousers burnt. The turpentine flowed over the floor burning the legs of the volunteers and then exploded driving the men against pillars and walls. Some who tried to escape were crushed by a falling wall. Things were made worse as the explosion caused the front doors to close, and then there was a second explosion and a third which caused the front of the building, at least sixty foot high with walls three or four bricks thick, to explode with a terrific crash, burying all between the store and the outer wall. From inside, it was reported later, could be heard shrieks of agony and wild despair. The flames then engulfed the building. It was estimated that around forty people were caught in the building from the near 150 helping to put out the fire and rescue the goods, and twenty-two men lost their lives.

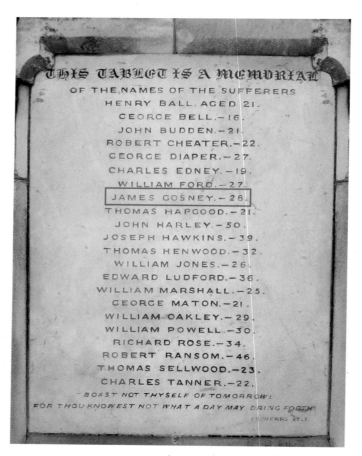

"22 BRAVE AND DISINTERESTED MEN"

Plaque to the 22 victims of the King & Witt fire at Holy Rood Church

The God's House Tower gaoler Mr John Brewer and the yardsman of the Bridewell, James Gosney, were two of the company who had tried to help extinguish the fire at King and Witt's warehouse. Brewer had seen the fire from his bedroom window. He went to assist along with Gosney a former marine employed as an assistant gaoler. In evidence he gave to the coroner's inquest, Brewer described how he had helped to take out packets of gunpowder and between forty and fifty carboys of turpentine. He had initially thought the fire could be put out by a few buckets of water but, unfortunately, there was no water supply readily available. He had first seen the fire at 11.15pm and on rushing to the site tried to knock down a shed to stop the spread of the flames but without success. He then went around the front of the building and this is when he saw a great quantity of gun powder on the ground floor. He got the powder into a tub and then carried it out of the building before he turned his attention to the turpentine. As the fire took hold he had to remove himself and was about five or six foot within the door when the first explosion took place. He thought that the fire had spread from an upper floor and met with explosive matter on the second floor. A second explosion followed immediately. He had heard an explosion once before he told the coroner – at a former period of his life – and thought the explosion at King and Witt's was similar, but more severe. He had dealt with gunpowder for six or seven years previously before becoming gaoler at God's House Tower. The second explosion had blown him out of the door of the store into the yard. The third explosion took place on the ground floor.

King & Witt Warehouse

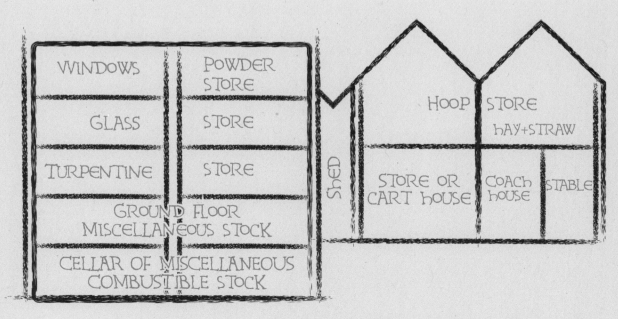

YARD LEADING FROM GATEWAY

Brewer was lucky in managing to get out of the building before it started to collapse but Gosney, along with 21 other men, was not. The inquest into their deaths took place before the coroner, George Barnard Corfe, and a 'highly respectable jury' in a room at the Rose & Crown Inn on French Street. The inquest took several days due to the difficulty in identifying the dead. The jury had to be taken to the Fountain Inn where the bodies were being stored. They found corpses greatly distorted, many had burnt skin and missing limbs. Some were so badly injured that they could only be identified by possessions on their persons. William Terry, the local police sergeant, managed to identify James Gosney who was twenty-eight and said to be powerfully built.

Such was the effect of the tragedy on the town that two plaques were commissioned and placed on the outside of Holy Rood Church to commemorate the heroism of the men who lost their lives. They became known as 'The 22 Disinterested Men'. The plaques can still be seen today. As to the cause of the fire, it was suspected that a spent rocket or squib case had caused it, as fireworks had been set off in the ditches on the evening of the tragedy. Following the disaster Joseph Stebbing established the Southampton Honorary Fire Brigade at Winchester Terrace.

The prison and the gaoler's house adjoining the tower
A View of Southampton Rev. Richard Hume Lancaster 1817 © Tate, London

In the census of 1841 one John Gosney is listed as the turnkey for the Common Gaol and House of Correction, in all likelihood the brother of the unfortunate James. John was registered along with his wife Louisa, both were aged thirty.

Brewer was working at God's House prison from at least 1837. He was from Truro in Cornwall, so probably had been recruited after the prison reforms of 1835 when the Town Sergeants were relieved of their duties as gaolers. By the 1841 census, Brewer was described at the Governor of the Town Gaol and his wife Catherine the Matron, both were aged forty. Also living at the prison were their two children John Brewer junior aged ten and Francis only three. By the 1851 census Brewer's family dynamic had changed dramatically, Catherine, and John junior were gone, with Catherine dying in November 1850. His son, Frank William aged twelve was still living with him. Brewer's niece Anne Oakley, a girl of just 18, was recorded in the position of acting Matron. Brewer was supported by Mathew Wild as turnkey and Hannah Chambers a house servant. John Brewer became the governor of the new prison 1855. He died on 25th April in 1881, styled a gentleman late of Freemantle Road. He left his worldly goods to Jane Cooper Brown, spinster, and Matron of the gaol.

GROWTH IN PRISON NUMBERS

The number of prisoners in God's House Tower continued to grow. A report of 1818 stated the gaol could contain twelve prisoners in the Common Gaol, and ten each in the Bridewell and Debtors' but that on occasion there had been twenty-four prisoners in the Common Gaol, twenty-five in the Bridewell and eighteen in the Debtors'. There were some efforts to re-configure the prison to make improvements, and by 1823 the Bridewell was said to be considerably improved. The main issue with the site was its proximity to the waterside which meant it was constantly damp. The men's day room though small was equipped with a fireplace, benches and a table and was frequently white-washed. There was only one class of male prisoner so all, debtors and felons, were kept together, their two sleeping rooms were now above stairs where previously they had slept in a dungeon. This latter was now used as a refractory cell for unmanageable prisoners. It had walls that were seven foot thick although a vent hole had been cut through the walls no doubt needed as the town drain (the former ditches) ran underneath the floor. On the second story of the tower a small chapel had been added where male and female prisoners could worship together, albeit seated in separate rooms which opened onto each other.

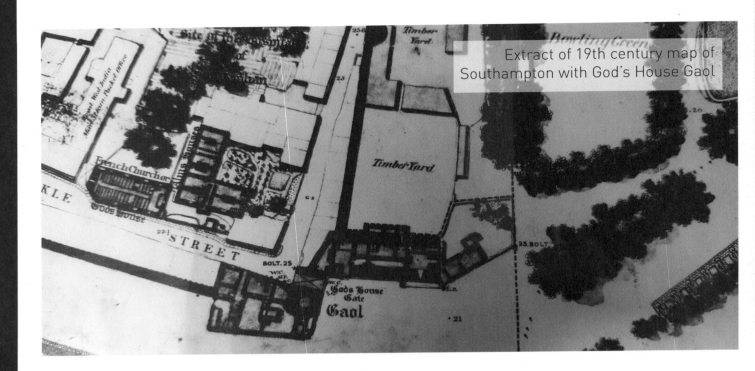

The female day room included a small laundry or washing room, there were two sleeping rooms and the windows were glazed and furnished with shade screens. Both sexes used the enclosed exercise yard, at separate times, under the watchful eye of the keeper who could observe them through a glazed aperture in the door of his house. The females were kept employed by doing needlework and washing. In this year the governor, a married man, had no turnkey to support him, only his wife who attended the female prisoners and a wardsman an orderly prisoner who was given the task of attending on the male prisoners. At the time of the visit there were only seven men and not a single woman in the prison. The inspector noted that irons were not used and the prison was well supplied with water, and the Bridewell was 'wholly unexpected evinces a spirit of improvement highly praiseworthy'. The same could not be said for the Common Gaol or the prison drains which were in a bad state. The Common Gaol had a ground floor with two rooms for the men one a day room and one a sleeping room and was so damp a fire had to be kept throughout the year. Upstairs a further two rooms consisted of a second sleeping room for the men and the other for women. The prisoners were taken to attend chapel in the Bridewell 'across the street' via a covered passage over the gateway. To stop the men and women conversing together it was planned that in future all women should be kept in the Bridewell. This inspection suggests that there was no longer a separate debtor's prison and that the tower was now the Bridewell with the Common Gaol taking over the area previously the Felons' prison and House of Correction.

By 1834 the prisoner numbers had grown again and over the year 520 male offenders and 65 female had been committed. Crimes included one murder, five attempted murders, eight manslaughters, two of sodomy, two attempted sexual assaults, five rapes of girls under ten, two attempted rapes, one rape of a girl aged between ten and twelve, seventeen assaults and ten assaults on policemen. Twenty prisoners were condemned to death, eleven transported for life, thirteen were transported for fourteen years and fifty-six transported for seven years. Twenty-four prisoners were imprisoned for six months, thirty-one for a year, five for two years and one for over one year. Not Guilty verdicts were given in 126 cases, no bills found for forty others and no prosecutions taken for nineteen. With regard to the condemned, only two were executed with the rest being transported. It was estimated that there was one offender per proportion of 536 people in the general population. The population of the town, at this time, was around 20,000 people.

Original prison door

By 1835 the prison inspectors were reporting that the debtors' gaol was scanty and ill provided with accommodation. The House of Correction was where all prisoners who were to do hard labour were sent, and it contained the female prisoners even though there were insufficient means of separation. There was a Matron appointed to this gaol. In the felons' prison there were in addition to the convicted felons all those committed for trial, and there was no Matron for this gaol. The inspector also felt the 'evil is somewhat aggravated by the number of smugglers who are brought into the port'. In 1836 the prison was finally was given official rules for its governance.

"THE EVIL IS SOMEWHAT AGGRAVATED BY THE NUMBER OF SMUGGLERS WHO ARE BROUGHT INTO THE PORT"

DPM5/2/11/19

TOWN AND COUNTY OF THE TOWN OF SOUTHAMPTON.

A

CALENDAR OF THE PRISONERS,

IN THE

Gaol at Southampton,

FOR TRIAL

AT THE GENERAL QUARTER SESSIONS,

TO BE

HOLDEN AT THE TOWN HALL,

ON MONDAY, THE 26th DAY of JUNE, 1837,

BEFORE

RICHARD MISSING, Esq., DEPUTY RECORDER.

SOUTHAMPTON:
PRINTED BY J. COUPLAND, 169, HIGH-STREET.

RULES OF THE PRISON

Common Gaol

1. That the several persons who shall be committed to the Common Gaol sentenced to hard labour shall be employed (unless prevented by ill health) every day during their confinement (except Sundays Christmas day and Good Friday) for so many hours as the day light in the different season of the year will admit not exceeding twelve hours being allowed out to rest half an hour at Breakfast an hour at Dinner and half an hour at Supper and that the intervals shall be noticed by the ringing of a bell.

2. That the Gaoler shall adapt the various employments which shall be directed by the Justices at their Quarter Sessions to each Person in such manner as shall be best suited to his or her strength or ability regard being had to age and sex.

3. That the males and females shall be employed and shall also eat and be lodged in separate Apartments and shall have no intercourse or communication with each other.

4. That the Gaoler and such other Persons (If any) as shall be employed by the Justices to assist the Gaoler shall be very watchful and attentive in seeing that the Persons so committed are constantly employed during the hours of work and if any Person shall be found negligent in performing what is required to be done by such Person to the best of his or her power or ability or shall wilfully waste spoil or damage the goods committed to his or her care the Gaoler shall punish every such Person in manner hereinafter directed.

5. That if any Person so committed shall refuse to obey the (lawful and reasonable) orders given by the Gaoler or shall be guilty of profane cursing or swearing or of any indecent behaviour an expression or of any assault Quarrel or abusive words to or with any other Person he or she shall be punished for the same in the manner hereinafter directed.

6. That the Gaoler shall have power to punish the several offenders for the offences hereinbefore described by closer confinement and shall enter in a book to be kept by him for the inspection of the Justices at the Quarter Sessions and the visiting Justice or Justices the name of every Person who shall be so punished by him expressing the offence and the duration of the Punishment inflicted reporting the same to the Visiting Justices.

7. That every Prisoner be allowed two pounds of bread daily and half a pound of meat on Sundays and Thursdays to be made into soup But Persons under the care of the Physician Surgeon or Apothecary shall be sustained with such food and liquor as he shall direct.

8. That one bushel of coals per week be allowed for every dayroom when occupied during the Winter six months.

9. That no friends be allowed to go into the Prison to see any Prisoners without an order in writing from the Mayor of visiting Justice or Magistrate.

10. That no tobacco be allowed to be brought into the Gaols nor any wine but that Friends may be allowed to bring food under the inspection of the Gaoler to Prisoners before Trial. That no convicted Prisoner be allowed to receive provisions or presents of any descriptions.

11. That the washing repairs of clothing and bedding and cleaning the Prison be performed solely by the Prisoners when practicable.

12. That the Gaoler do appoint one Prisoner to act as Monitor whose duty it shall be to keep good order and enforce the observance of such regulations as may be from time to time established.

13. That the Prisoners be examined by the Gaoler as to their personal cleanliness every Morning within one hour after the wards are unlocked.

14. That the Gaoler shall not sell or obtain any advantage from the sale of any article to the Prisoners.

15. That the female Prisoners be superintended by the Matron and that when they shall be visited by the Gaoler he shall be accompanied by the Matron or some other Female.

16. That no Prisoner be placed in irons unless he shall attempt or shew a Disposition to break out of the Prison or shall be refractory or disorderly.

17. That no Prisoner be permitted to receive anything except it has been strictly examined by the Gaoler.

18. That the male Prisoners do sleep in separate rooms, if possible, otherwise three in each room.

19. That no spirituous liquor shall be permitted to be brought into the Prison and that no smoking or games of any description be allowed.

20. That Divine Service be performed by the Chaplain every Sunday and on one other day in every week and that every Prisoner do attend as well as the Gaoler and Matron.

21. That the Gaoler do keep a book in which he shall enter the name of every Prisoner committed to his custody with the age and description of such Prisoner the offences for which they are committed the days of their committal and discharge and the sentence passed on each Prisoner tried.

Ridding
Clerk of the Peace

Whitehall, November 1836
The foregoing Rules, Orders and Regulations for the Government of the Common Gaol in the Town and County of the Town of Southampton having been submitted to me I hereby certify that they are proper to be enforced as temporary and provisional

Overleaf is the first modern National Census -
In 1841 the first modern national census took place, recording the population of the United Kingdom on the night of 6th June 1841. It listed all members of the household along with their ages and professions. The occupants of the God's House gaol were recorded as well as the families of the Keepers who also gave the prison as their address. A property had been constructed adjoining the east side of the main tower, which can be seen in contemporary paintings and is likely to be where the governor lived.

HOLY ROOD PARISH CENSUS RETURN 1841

NAME	AGE in years	GENDER
John Brewer	40	M
Catherine Brewer	40	F
John Brewer Jnr	10	M
Francis Brewer	3	M
James Gosney	30	M
Louisa Gosney	30	F
Kenneth Madus	45	M
Isaac William Cane	20	M
Charles Head	20	M
William Smith	20	M
William Attwood	20	M
George Gayton	35	M
Henry S......dale	35	M
James Kendall	20	M
George Manning	45	M
James Thomas	25	M
Henry Reynolds	20	M
Thomas Carr	20	M
Robert Corbin	35	M
Benjamin Collins	20	M
Daniel Slattery	30	M
Charles Page	15	M
John Callen	20	M

PROFESSION	Not originally from Southampton	Not British
Governor	X	
Matron	X	
Turnkey		
Turnkey's wife		
Servant	X	
Clerk	X	
Labourer		
Plasterer		
Labourer		
Porter	X	
Gent		
Scavenger		
Publican		
Linen Draper	X	
Shœ-maker	X	
Agricultural Labourer		
Stone Mason	X	
Blacksmith	X	
Fireman		Irish
Labourer		
Plasterer		

NAME	AGE in years	GENDER
George Tod	20	M
John Crump	25	M
Thomas Roberts	25	M
William Whitlock	30	M
Francis Kendall	15	M
Alfred Watts	25	M
William Adams	20	M
John Noyce	20	M
William West	20	M
John Rose	35	M
Ann Rose	40	F
Elizabeth Oliver	20	F
Ann Bush	30	F
Harriot Munday	20	F
Martha James	20	F

DEBTORS' WARD

NAME	AGE in years	GENDER
Martin Spearing	43	M
Sarah Spearing	38	F
James Spearing	3 months	M
Elizabeth Russell	75	F
Ann Ninim	15	F
John Terry Brooks	20	M
Robert Hunt	25	M

PROFESSION	Not originally from Southampton	Not British
Post Boy		
Hawker	X	
Weaver	X	
Shœ-maker		
Scavenger		
Excavator	X	
Blacksmith	X	
Labourer		
Sawyer		
News Vendor		
Upholsterer	X	
Prostitute	X	
Washerwoman		
Prostitute	X	
Servant	X	
Keeper		
Independent means	X	
Servant	X	
Builder's Clerk	Debtor	
Stage Coachman	Debtor	

François
Raison 1817

F.H.

FREDERICK HEAD 1828 1826

The prison report for the same year of 1841 gives some insight into the daily lives of the people who found themselves in God's House Tower prison. The inspector recorded that on the day of his visit there were twenty-three prisoners, six men who were awaiting trial, four who were previously convicted and ten who had been convicted at the recent sessions. Of women there were only three convicted felons and none awaiting trial. One of the prisoners in the felons' gaol had spent time in irons and six had been put in solitary confinement. In the House of Correction one prisoner had been put in irons and twenty-four had spent time in solitary confinement. The main reason for punishments was talking. The rule was that silence was enforced on convicted prisoners, but not on those who were still awaiting trial.

The inspector reported that there had been no improvements made to the gaol since his previous visit except that a portion of wall had been taken down to ascertain the reason for the bad smell in one of the female cells. It was discovered to be from an old privy that had not been properly closed. The changes made to remove the stench resulted in the creation of enough space to build a new cell for female prisoners. At the time of the visit five men and one woman were sleeping in single cells and none were sleeping two in a bed! There was a shortage of bedding in the gaol. There were forty-nine sets of bedding available but in the first six months of 1840 there had been fifty-six prisoners in the gaol.

One woman awaiting trial was sleeping in the cell of a convicted woman, but this was because the poor woman was having fits and needed someone to stay with her. The Matron responsible for the female prisoners, Catherine Brewer, received a salary of £20 a year. The Matron reported nothing of offence to herself in the conduct of the women under her supervision, although they did object to having their hair cut, which happened after conviction. The female prisoners were allowed 'lady visitors' who were usually from the 'Dissenters' community. These were people of the Methodist or Quaker community, and not members of the Church of England. Dissenters were very strong in Southampton and included many leading politicians. The lady visitors, usually one sometimes two, would come once a week and were allowed to see the prisoners in the presence of the Matron. They were permitted to teach the women to read and sometimes even to write and the Matron said that in the previous five years three prisoners had been entirely taught to read. The visitors gave books to the prisoners at the time of their discharge and tried to procure situations for any female servant that had been confined.

The one male prisoner in solitary confinement was reported as being in good health despite the solitary cells not having any light. There were no books available for prisoners and no schoolmaster to educate them, despite many being illiterate. Of fifteen prisoners sent for trial in 1837 only two were judged to be able to read and write well and five were completely illiterate. Previously it had been allowed for a literate prisoner to teach others – generally the prisoners in the debtors' prison were educated and able to read and write – but since the recent Prison Act this was not possible.

The prisoners took little exercise, but did attend chapel. The salary of the chaplain in 1834 was £50 with the average number of prisoners attending divine service being between six and eight. At that time the post was held by the curate of the Jesus Chapel in Peartree. In 1841 a new chaplain had been recently appointed. He was master of the King Edward VI Grammar School a post he combined with being vicar of St Michael's Church. This would have been Thomas Lawes Shapcott. During his headmastership the school had sunk to its lowest level as regards prosperity and reputation and his improvements to the church, the addition of internal balconies, had to be removed as they resulted in the building being in danger of collapse. His duties as prison chaplain included taking a daily morning service at 9.30am and a full service on Sundays followed by another Sunday service at 3.30pm. No singing was allowed. The sacrament had not been administered to any prisoner in the last five years, save to one young man who had died in the prison. This would have been a young man of twenty-four who had died in June. He had been in good health on his arrival in prison but after nine months of being locked up he contracted a fever and died. The Matron and another prisoner also caught the fever from the unfortunate un-named victim but made a recovery. The chaplain reported that he knew of 'two or three instances of discharged prisoners who became respectable members of society, but not amongst those who have left since he has been there'.

There were no patients in the infirmary at the time of the visit and the only prisoner receiving any treatment was an old Frenchman who was suffering from a rupture, who had been bought a truss. There had been a case of scarlet fever earlier in the year which subsequently spread to the Keeper and two of his children. The Keeper's bedroom adjoined the room used as an infirmary. There were no lunatics imprisoned at the time of the visit. Although no female prisoners were ill, all had been put onto extra diets because they were so generally malnourished and the inspector reported that they were all suffering from debility, which would mean muscle weakness and weight loss resulting in having no energy and being exhausted. The surgeon appointed to look after all the town gaols received £25 per annum and was expected to attend the vagrants.

On discharge prisoners reported to the Justice who would give them a certificate to take to the local Inspector of Police. This entitled them to 8d or 1s, and if the prisoner was destitute they were also given a day's food.

In 1844, there was a small peak in the numbers of debtors who found themselves in gaol, and they come from a range of different professions, a list of these was published in the London Gazette. The list of names included John Allcot, of Nelson Street and previously a steward of the Royal Mail now unemployed, George Smith, a mason living at Hanover Buildings, George Cull, a retailer of beer and previously of the Star Hotel, William Snook, a farmer and dealer in manure living in Millbrook and John Pembroke of Bitterne, a hoop maker. It was a challenging time for the economy in 1844 when the Act of Parliament known as the Peel Banking Act was passed as a result of recurring financial crises.

The situation had been so bad that help had had to be sought from France in order to maintain the convertibility of bank notes. In 1839, £2 million was borrowed from the Bank of France, through Baring Brothers. The 1844 Act established the Bank of England as the country's central bank. The Bank became the centre for issuing notes, limiting the issue of provincial issues. It was in the same year that Karl Marx wrote his 'Economic and Philosophic Manuscripts' which outlined his thoughts on private property, communism and money.

THE END OF THE PRISON

God's House Tower was never purpose-built as a prison and in the early days the number of prisoners it catered for was relatively small, but by the dawn of the Victorian Era, the population of the prison, like the population of the town, had soared. In 1843, 231 prisoners were committed to the Bridewell. In 1848, 342 people had been committed, in 1853 it was 495.

The inspector of prisons in 1850, W J Williams, recorded that the gaols of Southampton, Banbury, Windsor and Hastings were in a 'most discreditable condition' but he reported plans were afoot for the building of a new prison in Southampton. He noted that there were fifty-four people in the prison, twenty-seven men and two women who had been tried and found guilty and twenty-two men and three women awaiting trial. The men had been found guilty of crimes from embezzlement, to assaulting a police officer, 'exposing his person', vagrancy, using short weights and throwing items over the prison wall. The two women were inside for a felony and an assault. Sentences ran from four months to two years.

The number of juveniles in prison had decreased dramatically. The gaoler put that down to the Juveniles Offenders Act which replaced imprisonment with corporal punishment. Previously he could have had eighteen young boys in custody, but currently there were only four. He was pleased to report that the magistrate and the surgeon were always present when corporal punishment was being given. Despite the fall in the number of juveniles the inspector still thought the prison was excessively crowded.

The prison was configured to take fourteen male prisoners and eight women in relative comfort, but if forced to share, the prison could take fifty eight men and thirty women. The highest number on any one day was forty-six men and ten women, and the daily average was thirty-four men and six women. So crowded was the prison that the chaplain reported that attempts at religious moral instruction were in vain. The surgeon said that the principal ailment suffered by prisoners was venereal disease. One thirty-year old prisoner suffered from Haemoptysis, the coughing up of blood from the lungs. He was given a pardon because of his illness.

There had been attempts to escape from the prison, but only one had been successful, a smuggler who was on remand. The debtors' gaol shocked the inspector who described it as being in a discreditable condition with 'filthy productions' scrawled over the walls, drawings of ships, and inscriptions in prose and verse. He could not understand why gaolers had not cleaned them off. He also felt the 6d allowed to debtors for their food should be discontinued and that they should eat the same prison food as the rest of the inmates.

However the inspector reported some improvements. The prisoners were supplied with clothing and had clean linen weekly. The official prison diet tables had been adopted and cooking provisions removed from the day rooms. All was now under the supervision of a prison officer. There were fewer debtors, only one was there when the inspector visited, so two rooms had been taken over from the debtors' gaol and an additional officer appointed. The Bridewell had been expanded into two other Corporation buildings, Solent Cottage and Platform House, adjacent to the west of the original gatehouse.

"A PALLIATIVE FOR THE EXISTING EVILS"

These improvements were only a 'palliative for the existing evils' which could only be removed, the inspector reported, by the creation of a new prison. In the meantime he recommended prisoners serving more than three months be sent to Winchester prison to complete their sentence.

"SO LOATHSOME AND INCONVENIENT A DEN FOR THE CONFINEMENT OF PRISONERS"

The Corporation's plans for a new prison were held up by lack of funds, they considered borrowing £14,000 to build the new gaol after prompting from local magistrates. Delays caused the editor of the Hampshire Independent, Timothy Falvey, to declare in March 1850 that God's House prison was "so loathsome and inconvenient a den for the confinement of prisoners" in the country. The prison was eventually closed in 1855 following a new prison being established in Ascupart Street at a cost of £23,000, on the plan of the model prison at Pentonville.

Timothy Falvey

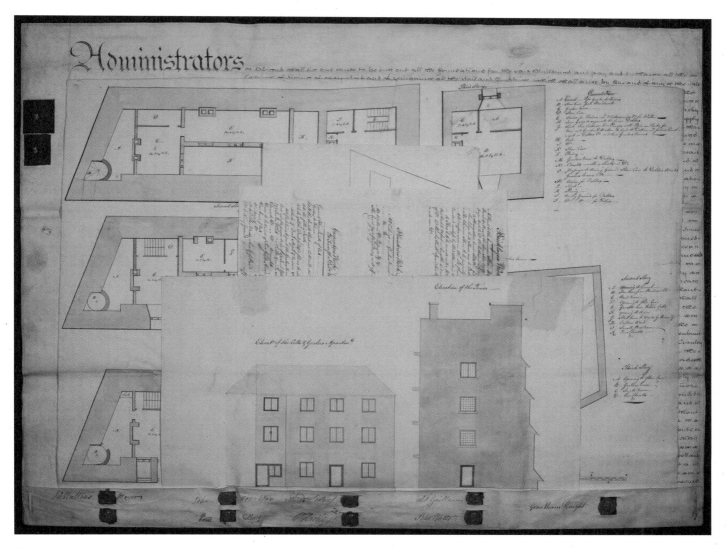

Prison plan and elevation

CENSUS 1851 GAOL & HOUSE OF CORRECTION

NAME	RELATION	CONDITION
John Brewer	Head	Widower
Frank William Brewer	Son	
Ann Oakley	Niece	Single
Mathew Wild	Servant	Single
Hannah Chambers	Servant	Married
Alfred Garnett	Prisoner	Single
Isaac Thorn	Prisoner	Married
Henry Blandford	Prisoner	Single
John Weaton	Prisoner	Married
Henry Quinten	Prisoner	Single
William Hopkins	Prisoner	Single
George Campbell	Prisoner	Single
Stephen Powers	Prisoner	Single
Frederick Weston	Prisoner	Single
James Hide	Prisoner	Single
Alfred Collins	Prisoner	Single
William Hartlett	Prisoner	Married
Thomas Henry Sherry	Prisoner	
William Barrymore	Prisoner	Single
Thomas Lewis	Prisoner	Single
John Bileharde	Prisoner	Single

AGE	GENDER	OCCUPATION	WHERE BORN
50	M	Governor of Gaol & House of Correction	Truro, Cornwall
12	M	Scholar	Southampton
18	F	Acting Matron	Southampton
23	F	Turnkey	Lyndhurst
26	F	House Servant	Newbury, Berks
29	M	Shœmaker	Maldon, Essex
32	M	Master Carrier	Eling
23	M	Waterman	Southampton
58	M	Cabinet Maker	Southampton
21	M	French Polisher	Southampton
37	M	Common Labourer	Shaftesbury
19	M	Common Labourer	Southampton
16	M	Common Thief	Somerset
16	M	Common Labourer	Southampton
17	M	Drapers Porter	Shirley
26	M	Horse Keeper	Southampton
45	M	Shœmaker	Bristol
14	M	Common Thief	Southampton
27	M	Mariner	London
16	M	Pick Pocket	Crewkerne
22	M	Common Thief	Hereford

NAME	RELATION	CONDITION
George Dunn	Prisoner	Married
John Herley	Prisoner	Single
Charles James	Prisoner	Single
Robert Turner	Prisoner	Single
William Henry Brice	Prisoner	Married
William Eggs	Prisoner	Married
Thomas Tully	Prisoner	Married
Thomas Midlane	Prisoner	Married
Isaac Osman	Prisoner	Married
Edward White	Prisoner	Single
Thomas Role	Prisoner	Single
Angus McCleade	Prisoner	Single
Henry Hill	Prisoner	Married
John Groves	Prisoner	
William Groves	Prisoner	
Samuel Newman	Prisoner	Single
John Turner	Prisoner	Single
James Hill	Prisoner	Single
James Steele	Prisoner	Single
Henry Martin	Prisoner	Single

AGE	GENDER	OCCUPATION	WHERE BORN
30	M	Common Labourer	Somerset
19	M	Mariner	Dublin
19	M	Coach Painter	Southampton
19	M	Mariner	New Orleans
34	M	Waiter at an Inn	London
24	M	Railway Porter	Southampton
51	M	Mariner	Sussex
56	M	Mariner	Isle of Wight
24	M	Mariner	Southampton
58	M	Beggar	Sussex
24	M	Bricklayer Labourer	Fareham
20	M	Mariner	Isle of Skye
25	M	Carpenter	Bristol
15	M	Scholar of Ragged School	Southampton
12	M	Scholar of Ragged School	Southampton
19	M	Reputed Thief	Southampton
23	M	Common Labourer	Greenwich
26	M	Common Labourer	Wiltshire
16	M	Reputed Thief	Southampton
17	M	Reputed Thief	London

CENSUS 1851 GAOL & HOUSE OF CORRECTION Contd.

NAME	RELATION	CONDITION
James Edwards	Prisoner	Married
George Budden	Prisoner	Single
Herbert Gardiner	Prisoner	Single
George Wareham	Prisoner	Widower
Thomas Spelt	Prisoner	Single
Joseph Turner	Prisoner	Married
John Reeves	Prisoner	Single
Robert De Gage	Prisoner	Single
Charles Jellis	Prisoner	Single
John James	Prisoner	Married
George Young	Prisoner	Married
Jane Gillet	Prisoner	Single
Mary Ann Mears	Prisoner	Widow
Amelia Chalk	Prisoner	Single
Mary Minton	Prisoner	Widow
Cicila Wallis	Prisoner	Married
Mary Ann Maloney	Prisoner	Married
Margaret Benge	Prisoner	Single
Ellen Moriarty	Prisoner	Single
Sarah England	Prisoner	Widow
Louisa Whitehorn	Prisoner	Single

AGE	GENDER	OCCUPATION	WHERE BORN
37	M	Dock Labourer	Millbrook
19	M	Common Labourer	Wareham
21	M	Bricklayer	Kent
45	M	Carpenter	Hampshire
27	M	Butcher	Southampton
45	M	Butler	York
39	M	Shœmaker	Guernsey
19	M	Boat Builder	London
20	M	Huckster	Southampton
22	M	Artificial Flower Maker	Kent
28	M	Stable Man	Southampton
20	F	Prostitute	Tunbridge
38	F	Prostitute	Southampton
21	F	Prostitute	Fordingbridge
45	F	Fortune Teller	Hatfield
28	F	Blacksmith's Wife	Ireland
27	F	Prostitute	Botley
21	F	Prostitute	Southampton
32	F	Prostitute	Jersey
44	M	Labourer	Portsmouth
25	F	House Servant	Lyndhurst

In that same year a new book of Rules was issued on 26th July which clearly defined the role and duties of the Governor, Matron, Subordinate Officers, Chaplain and Medical Officers. The Governor had 82 rules to follow and had to keep and be able to produce his journal, the prison register with the names, description and offences of the prisoners, a general daily account, a provision book with receipts and distribution, a stock book with receipts and distribution, an account of fines and penalties, a prisoners' property book, a prisoners' misconduct book, a visitors' book and a catalogue of books in use by the prisoners. In contrast the Matron only had to keep a journal.

22

MATRON.

Matron.

al Duties 83. THE matron shall reside in the prison and be under the direction of the governor. She shall have the care and superintendence of the whole female department. With respect to her general conduct, she shall conform to the rules laid down for that of the governor, as far as they can be applied to the treatment and care of female prisoners.

Inspect Fe- ison, &c. 84. She shall be present at the distribution of meals to the female prisoners, and daily visit every part of the prison appropriated to females, inspect the bedding, clothing, and food of the female prisoners, and see every female prisoner at least once in every twenty-four hours. In the event of her omitting any of these duties, she shall insert the omission, and the cause thereof, in her journal.

rt. 85. She shall make a daily report to the governor, at some stated time fixed by him, of the general condition and conduct of her department; of the names of female officers and prisoners absent from chapel, and the cause thereof; of the names of female prisoners in the infirmary, or under medical treatment in their own cells or wards, and of such as are under punishment; and she shall report without delay the names of such as require to see the medical officer.

ivine 86. She shall attend Divine Service with the prisoners, unless absent by leave, or prevented by some duty; inserting the omission and cause thereof in her

23

without the written permission of a visiting justice: whenever she absents herself she shall give notice to the governor previous to her leaving the prison and on her return.

88. She shall keep a journal for recording occurrences of importance within her department, reports made by her to the governor, and punishment of female prisoners.

89. She shall, unless unavoidably prevented, attend the governor whenever he visits the females' prison, and when so prevented, she shall be responsible that some other female officer attends him; and she shall take care that no male officer or visitor enters the females' prison, unless accompanied by herself or by some other female officer.

90. She, or some other female officer shall search every female prisoner on admission; and the sam course shall be pursued by her with reference to femal prisoners on admission as that prescribed for th governor with reference to male prisoners. All mone or other effects brought into the prison by any fema prisoner, or from time to time sent in for her use an benefit, shall be transferred to the governor.

91. She, or in her absence, some other female offic shall, whenever she thinks it necessary, or when rected by the governor, search any female visitor prisoners; the search to be in the presence of fema only, and not in the presence of any prisoner.

92. She shall give to every female prisoner who read, within twenty-four hours after her admissio

Another innovation was a certificate that the families of prisoners could apply for via the local churchwardens which confirmed that they were indigent due to the incarceration of the family breadwinner, and they could therefore apply for financial support. However the rule book warned 'but it has been greatly abused by persons obtaining the allowance, who have ample means of support them themselves whilst in prison'.

PAINTINGS:

The Tower:

Inspiration to Artists

THE GOTHIC & THE PICTURESQUE

In the eighteenth century the landscape outside of the prison was changing again. Whilst prisoners were being moved from the Bargate to the new gaol at God's House Tower, the town of Southampton was re-inventing itself has a seaside Bathing Resort, and thanks to the discovery of a chalybeate spring with health-giving properties, a Spa. For a century, visitors flooded into the town to take advantage of the new vogue for sea bathing, as well as the other facilities that were being developed. Assembly Rooms, Lending Libraries, and Coffee Houses were created. The town fathers also decided to landscape a seaside walk from God's House Tower, heading towards the River Itchen. This new promenade was known as The Beach. Visitors, including the novelist Jane Austen, would pass by the medieval tower, presumably unaware of the misery taking place inside, to take the air, admire the views, or take a boat ride.

View of the Beach Promenade

Many visitors were attracted to view the many fine houses that were built around the outskirts of the town. Some were owned or rented by admirals and senior naval officers, who had made money from taking prizes during the Revolutionary and Napoleonic Wars. Families made fabulously wealthy by working for the East India Company were also attracted to Southampton, for the benefit of their health, by its proximity to London and because it had a functioning port. They were the nouveau

Previous page: detail from Thomas Gray Hart painting *The Old Jail*

riche and desired to purchase art to line the walls of their properties. This led to opportunities for travelling artists such as Heriot, Pritchard, Sargent, Shayer, Spilsbury, Young and the Pether family.

The Old Jail, Thomas Gray Hart 1775
Southampton Cultural Services, Maritime & Local Collection

These artists were not in the first rank, like Constable and Turner who also painted views of Southampton, but they were very competent landscape artists. They responded to two artistic trends that were popular in the eighteenth and early nineteenth centuries: the picturesque and the gothic. The picturesque style of art was created by the clergyman-artist William Gilpin, when landscapes were created by showing their natural state. Paintings should be beautiful, but still show texture, wildness and the roughness of nature. Accuracy however was not required. The gothic movement was an architectural revival of styles that drew on the medieval age. This saw houses being embellished with castellations, or even in the case of the Marquis of Lansdowne the building of an actual gothic castle right in the centre of Southampton. One of the leaders of the gothic movement was Horace Walpole who built Strawberry Hill House, a Gothic villa as his home in Twickenham. Walpole had visited Southampton and travelled to the ruins of Netley Abbey looking for inspiration, not just for design but to feed his imagination as a writer of gothic

Southampton Water
Joseph Mallard William Turner 1827
©Turner Bequest, Tate, London

novels. The medieval structure of God's House Tower appealed not only to followers of the romantic and picturesque but also the Gothic, and inspired several painters as well as lithographers who produced prints suitable for holiday mementos. One family of painters who captured God's House Tower on canvas were the Pethers. Abraham Pether and his sons Henry and Sebastian were jobbing landscape painters. Abraham was known for his specialism of painting moonlit scenes, a skill he passed onto his sons. The family would paint the same scenes by night and by day, doubling the potential for a sale. The possibility of an abundance of purchasers in the town may have contributed to the family's move here around 1805, or it may have been because of the ill-health of Abraham. Pether senior died in 1812 and was buried at All Saints Church. He was a good enough artist to exhibit regularly at the Royal Academy and has thirty-two paintings attributed to him, including *God's House Tower by Moonlight.* His son Henry was still a young boy when he lost his father. As an adult he spent most of his working life in London, and ironically found himself in a debtor's prison in that city. As well as being a painter he produced ornamental bricks, some of which were used to decorate buildings in Southampton. He also painted moonlight scenes including *Z* and *'Town Quay by Moonlight'*, both of which are in the collection of Southampton City Art Gallery. He made a number of engravings of the town which were printed by his brother-in-law, the lithographer Thomas Skelton. Skelton was a producer of guides to the town for the benefit of the visitors to the Spa, so every purchaser of his publications could own a Pether work.

Moonlight Scene by Sebastian Pether
Southampton Cultural Services, Maritime & Local Collection

Details from *Moonlight Scene* by Sebastian Pether
Southampton Cultural Services, Maritime & Local Collection
Overleaf: *Southampton Town Quay at Sunset* by Henry Pether
Southampton Cultural Services, Maritime & Local Collection

Sebastian was not so prolific but did paint a view of Southampton from Itchen Ferry in 1819, a scene which would have appealed to the East India Company families like the Lewins and Lances whose homes had the same view. Unfortunately Sebastian could not make enough money from his art to support his large family, perhaps because, by then, Southampton's popularity as a Spa was beginning to wane.

"A STINKING CANAL, WHERE SMALL VESSELS MIGHT GLIDE"

THE CANAL

The paintings from the eighteenth and nineteenth centuries clearly show a canal tunnel running under God's House Tower. Canal building fever had swept the country in the eighteenth century, and even though Southampton had two rivers, it joined in the frenzy. A proposal was made for a canal to run from Southampton to Salisbury and Andover. The first phase was to start at God's House Tower and re-use the old ditches, then to extend them to run through Houndwell fields where the canal would then turn left along the then shoreline of the Western Bay. Local resident and poet laureate, Henry Pye, even composed a poem about the canal:

> O Millbrook! Shall my devious feet no more
> Pace the smooth margins of thy pebbly shore?
> Now, through the stagnant pool, by banks confined,
> Rolls the slow barge, dragg'd by inglorious hind

Pye was not convinced of the need for the canal

> Though it seems to amusing
> Southampton's wise sons found their river so large,
> Though 'twould carry a ship, 'twould not carry a barge,
> So they wisely determined to cut by its side
> A stinking canal, where small vessels might glide:
> Like the man, who, contriving a hole in the wall,
> To admit his two cats, – the one large, t'other small,'
> When a great hole was cut for the first to go through,
> Would a little one have for the little cat too.

Pye was not the most revered poet even though he was made poet laureate in an age of great poets: Byron, Keats, Shelley, and Wordsworth. His contemporaries said of him:

we are afraid that, with all our reverence for Mr Pye as a man of ancient family, unimpeachable character and high position, we must admit that as a poet, his Muse's chief attributes are Mediocrity and Morality

Lord Byron said of him a man eminently respectable in everything but his poetry. But in one thing Pye was correct, the canal was unnecessary and the enterprise failed. Traces of the canal tunnel can still be seen low down at the base of God's House Tower.

Mouth of the Old Canal
William Shayer
Southampton Cultural Services, Maritime & Local Collection

In developing the exhibition for God's House Tower, it was important to include artists as part of the process and the writer and director Deborah Gearing was commissioned to produce a sound installation. Deborah's previous work has been performed everywhere from a domestic garage to the National Theatre and she has also worked with community groups, including three years with the ex-offenders' group Over the Wall. Deborah's audio pieces can be heard in the prison exhibition where they reflect on three prisoners' stories. In deciding on which stories to develop, Deborah wanted to reflect human stories when people experience intense conflict. Deborah spent many hours doing archival research in 2016-17. Looking in particular for women's stories, trying to find relevant original material was a challenge.

Deborah spent time in God's House Tower to help get a sense of what prisoners might have been taking in, and how the duration of time feels when the walls are all you see. Her work for the exhibition is folk poetry – looking at the lives of real people in time past, 'feeling the texture of where the present time connects with theirs, making sense of journeys that repeat and drawing attention to injustice and unfairness'. The work is straightforward and made to be read aloud as well as on the page, mirroring the connection with the past when stories were orally transmitted. The piece that Deborah has contributed for this book is one of a series of poems which she created for God's House Tower.

The poem is about the prisoner Mary Rowsell, who was very important to Deborah as she was the first female prisoner that she came across in her research. Mary Rowsell was imprisoned in God's House prison in 1787 charged with the murder of her illegitimate child. The bones of the case were recorded in the Hampshire Chronicle on Saturday June 16th 1787, which reported that Mary had been removed in a chair from her home to the gaol to await trial and the next assizes for the wilful murder of her bastard child.

The Assizes were scheduled for July 14th before Mr Justice Buller. In the event Judge Grose heard the case, by special commission on 28th July, where he learnt that the child had died by suffocation in a carpet. The Judge obviously felt there was a flaw in the indictment and took evidence from Mr Mears, who was the surgeon attached to the prison. He directed the jury to find Mary not guilty.

Mary Rowsell
1787
I shut the door to my room when I felt it coming, tried so hard to be quiet.
Wanted so much to be invisible. I fought
the waves until I couldn't and then - drowned.

I fell out of the world and into darkness and when I woke
- she had pushed her way out of me.
Held her rag of a body in my hands.
I rubbed her little feet.
I took her mouth to my breast, Here, for you, drink, you
got to drink.
But she didn't take any drink. She didn't want me.
There was no cry.
She weren't fond enough to stay.
She was - all broke. Drowned in blood. Neck broke - like
a little flower, with its blue head snapped at the stem. Her
neck was broke. She hanged herself in me.
And now I shall hang for her.

I didn't name her. A name's for a livin', breathin' thing. And she was - empty.
A little scrap of'
The sacrifices of God are a broken spirit: a broken and a
contrite heart, O God, thou wilt not despise.
I am out of words.
Their talk' I can't speak for myself, there is one who must
speak for me.
But who knows the truth but me?

Now I am weighed down with unwanted milk, with blood;
I burn. Shame drags my feet. I can't eat. The turnkey's
wife spits on my bread. I don't want their bread.
Why should I eat?

Make me to hear joy and gladness; that the bones which thou
hast broken may rejoice.
The stain is on me.
They see a baby in a carpet and they make up a story, call me
wicked, wilful. Murderess.
Something to give them satisfaction, something to talk about,
sing about. They think they got a story to tell. There ent
none. I did not know her, my bastard child and no one
knows me. I got no protector.

Have mercy upon me O God, according to thy loving
kindness; according unto the multitude of thy tender mercies
blot out my transgressions.

Tomorrow the judge comes. In two days it will all
be done with me.
I'll be invisible.
But I was here.

The insertions within the poem are from Psalm 51 which was known as the 'Neckverse' because the ability to repeat the verse could allow a prisoner to escape from hanging. This had come down from the Middle Ages when there were two parallel law systems in the land, the civil court and ecclesiastical court. The latter was for trying the clergy and was generally considered a more lenient place to be tried. Originally a man had to be tonsured and able to read and write Latin as a proof of clergy but this had been diluted over the centuries and by the eighteenth century anyone who could repeat the psalm in English could claim a right to leniency. Which was important in a period when around 220 offences could result in the death penalty. In the Journal of Council Minutes of 1731 the Corporation debated whether the accused Mary Browne could be tried for a 'clergyate' offence or a misdemeanour. Mary Browne had been committed to the House of Correction for stealing money from Mrs Mary Freeman and the Town Clerk was ordered to attend on Mr Crop to get his opinion on how to proceed with the trial. In 1773 it was ordered that Edward Giddins was definitely not to be given the benefit of clergy for his crime of robbery and burglary and instead was 'extended Royal Mercy' and transported to America for seven years.

Gradually over the nineteenth century the number of capital offences was reduced to just five: espionage, murder, piracy, treason, and arson in a naval dockyard.

Gaol & Bridewell, G H Shepherd 1839, engraved by J Shury & Son
Southampton Cultural Services, Maritime & Local Collection

TOWER TO LET:

Mortuary and Warehouse, Museum, GHT Arts & Heritage Venue

TOWER TO LET - Mortuary and Warehouse, Museum,
GHT Arts & Heritage Venue.

MORTUARY & WAREHOUSE

After the 1850 prison inspector's scathing report on the cramped conditions at God's House prison, plans were developed for a new prison on Ascupart Street. Within five years the God's House Tower prison closed and its inmates were moved to the new gaol. Around the tower the landscape was changing yet again. In 1840 the mudflats were drained and a new dock was developed to the east of the old Town Quay. The London and South Western Railway had opened a railway link between the port and London in 1839. The railways and the docks brought new workers to the town and the population increased, and The Queens College Oxford, who owned most of the land outside of the eastern walls, began to sell of parcels of land for development in the 1840s and 1850s. Laishley, the radical politician and Wesleyan Methodist, purchased a whole tract of college land adjacent to the Railway Terminus and began to build houses around the areas now known as Oxford Street and Bernard Street. The old Porter's Mead was laid out as Queen's Park. God's House Tower was retreating from the sea, as the old shoreline moved further away and a road was constructed to the south of the tower.

God's House Tower with Timeball

Because of its proximity to the dockyard it was decided to erect a time signal on top of God's House Tower which enabled ships in the docks to all have their clocks telling the same time. The time signal was linked directly to Greenwich. The time signal was in the form of a mast which had a ball on top. This was released every day at midday so that clocks and watches could be synchronised. *The Southampton Observer and Winchester News* carried the following article in 1888:

THE TIME-BALL ON THE OLD GAOL

This, the latest addition to the many facilities offered by the port to commerce, which has been erected by the Southampton Harbour Board on the Old Gaol at the Platform, is now in perfect working order, and in direct communication with Greenwich Observatory, whence the current was first transmitted on Monday. From its elevated position, the ball, which is a large, but light structure, can be distinctly seen from the ships in the Docks and Southampton Water, and they are thus enabled to set their chronometers to the correct Greenwich time prior to leaving the port – a matter of some considerable consequence. The current of electricity is timed to reach Southampton at one o'clock each day, excepting Sundays and Bank Holidays, and the ball is raised, preparatory for its arrival, at about 12.55. The arrangement for raising the ball is as perfect as it is simple, and the clockwork for the same has been supplied by Mr. J. Blount Thomas, J.P., of the High-Street. The clock is wound once per week, and so set that at three or four minutes before one it gives motive power to another movement, which opens a valve and lets water from a cistern into a bucket, which is in communication, by means of a pulley, with the time-ball on the roof. As soon as the bucket is filled – about three minutes to one – it is released and slides down between the wooden framework which confines it; by its weight drawing the time-ball to the top of the pole, where it is held by a "catch" ready for the arrival of the electric current. The electricity from Greenwich knocks a wooden hammer, and this in turn sets another portion of the machinery in motion, which releases the ball and allows it to slide down to the roof, in its descent bringing up the bucket, which has, in the meantime, been automatically emptied, ready for the repetition of the operation the following day. Thus, it will be seen, that the labour of winding up the ball, and the possibility of its being some time or other forgotten, is altogether done away with, the clockwork being sure and regular in its action. We are informed that this is the only public time-ball owned by any town in the country, though there are time-guns and time-balls which are worked by private individuals, companies, &c., at different ports in the kingdom.

*The accuracy observed at St. Martins-le-Grand, in connection with the transmission of electric currents for this **purpose**, is as remarkable as it is reliable, one wire being set apart for this mercantile work 15 minutes before the time required, and in that case the electric fluid is also discharged automatically. It is to be hoped that this effort of the Harbour Board to provide a much wanted requirement by the shipping visiting the port, coupled with the extensive additions being made to the facilities already afforded by the Docks, will shortly have an apparent and desirable effect upon the commercial prosperity of Southampton. The time-ball is now in operation, and is dropped by a current direct from Greenwich Observatory at one o'clock each day (Sundays and Bank Holidays excepted). When the Harbour Board came to the determination of erecting a time-ball they called to their aid a well-known electrical engineer, who sent in an estimate of £350, the ball to fall nine feet only, and to be wound up daily by hand labour. On abandoning the South-Western Hotel site, on account of the weakness of the tower, the only other available was South Castle, but owing to the lowness of the building special arrangements had to be made – either an addition to the tower, or an unusually long drop. The former was not to be thought of; the latter, experts said, was impossible, as there must be a fall of at least thirty feet, whereas nine feet was the maximum. This has, however, been accomplished. The ball rises thirty feet on a stout iron mast, and is easily visible against the sky from the whole of Southampton Water, and drops out of sight behind the parapet wall. The machinery is entirely automatic, and requires attention but once a week, when the controlling Clock is wound up. There are four pieces of machinery. The ball is lifted by a large copper bucket, which, when filled at the proper time by about 1½cwt. of water, runs down 30 feet, lifting the ball as it descends. Arrived at the bottom it empties itself and the ball then stands locked, waiting the current from Greenwich, by which it is unlocked and falls. The Clock at a certain time sets in motion a train of wheels, which open a valve in a cistern, and fills the bucket. When filled it remains, until at 12.55 another train of wheels is set in motion, which releases the bucket. The current from Greenwich sets in action a third train of wheels, by which the bucket is hoisted and the ball falls. To check the fall of so heavy a body there is an arrangement by which the weights are picked up by the bucket line, so that at the end of the fall the ball comes gently on the roof. The whole work has been designed by Mr. J. Blount Thomas, and carried out by Mr. C. Franklin. The total cost is not more than half the original estimate for a non-automatic machine with a fall of nine feet only.*

In 1904 the time signal was moved to the roof of South Western House, on the opposite side of Queen's Park.

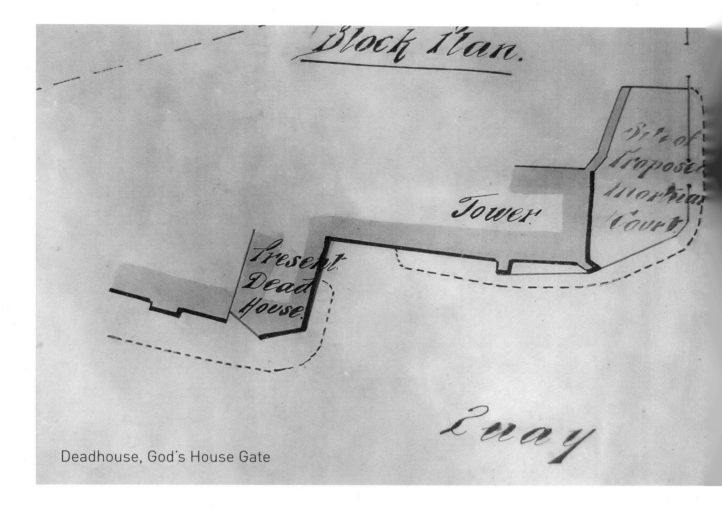

Deadhouse, God's House Gate

The building transformed into its next life in 1876 when it was taken over by the Southampton Harbour Board who wished to use it as a storage warehouse. The port had grown with the development of additional docks and storage accommodation was at a premium. A note at the time the Board took over the building reported that it had been used as a temporary mortuary after the prisoners left, and it was asked if the ground floor of the tower could still facilitate this use. The room being used is identified on a later plan as 'The Dead House' and was in the room above the gate, now the Crawford Room. As part of the conversion many of the original parts of the building from its time as a gun battery and prison were removed, and giant doors were inserted into the Town Quay frontage to facilitate the movement of stores in and out of the building. Another door was added in the south east face of the gateway flank. The frontages to the south and east of the building were restored to preserve original features.

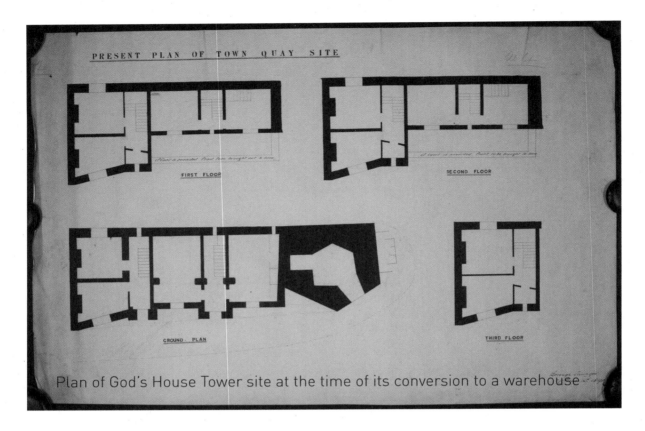

PRESENT PLAN OF TOWN QUAY SITE

FIRST FLOOR

SECOND FLOOR

GROUND PLAN

THIRD FLOOR

Plan of God's House Tower site at the time of its conversion to a warehouse

The sheds and houses which had been added to the east of the tower during its time as a prison were cleared away and in 1876 the area was graced with a statue of Prince Albert. Queen Victoria's consort had died unexpectedly in December 1861 and the country was plunged into mourning. The Queen never recovered from the loss of her husband and wore black for the rest of her long life. Buildings were re-named in his honour and many memorials were made to his memory. Alderman Sir Frederick Perkins commissioned the statue of the Prince. It was made by John Marriott Blashfield at the terracotta works originally set up by Eleanor Coade in Lambeth in 1769. The Coade works had also supplied the statue of King George III which can still be seen on the south side of the Bargate. Coade stone looked like marble, but it was actually an artificial stone and had a greater resistance to damage from frost and heat. The recipe for its manufacture was not fully understood until the 1990s. The ceramic stone was tough and hard wearing and was easier to carve and model, and detail on the statue of King George III is as clear as the day it was made. Mrs Coade was unusual, a female industrialist, born in Exeter in 1733, she had moved to London by the 1760s selling linen. She went into the business of making artificial stone in 1769 initially with Daniel Pincot but he was soon replaced by John Bacon the sculptor. It was Bacon's designs which turned Coade stone into the height of fashion and saw it embellishing many a stately home and public building. It was used by all the leading architects of the day including Robert Adam and John Nash.

After Mrs Coade's death in 1821 the firm went into a decline and it closed in 1840. As the original recipe for Coade stone was lost it is likely that the statue of Prince Albert was not made of proper Coade stone. The statue did not have a good start having originally been carved in 1865 to be erected outside the Royal Albert Infirmary in Bishop's Waltham. The Infirmary however was never used and although the statue was unveiled in its niche in the front of the building Perkins decided to reclaim it and find a new site. It had cost him £300. It was moved to the side of God's House Tower to the vacant spot where once had stood a house formerly the home of the prison governor. The statue did not wear well, further evidence that it was not made of authentic Coade stone, so when Prince Albert's grandson Kaiser Wilhelm of Germany visited Southampton in 1912 it was thought prudent to move the statue into storage. It was never moved back and the story goes that it was destroyed by the Royal Engineers during the First World War in 1915, presumably because Prince Albert was German.

Prince Albert's statue, God's House Tower

In 1891 there was a plan to convert the whole building, with a new extension to the east, into the main town mortuary, and detailed plans survive showing viewing halls, which would have three slabs for male bodies and three for female bodies. There were waiting rooms, and three caretaker's rooms as well as a room for 'conveyance'. In the new building was to be the Coroner's Court, Coroner's room, Jury room, Post-Mortem room, waiting rooms and another mortuary. Despite the detailed plans the conversion did not happen and a further lease was granted to the Harbour Board. The Harbour Board's rent for the old gaol property was £8 per annum and £20 for Platform House. After the Harbour Board gave up the building it was let to a succession of businesses up until the 1930s, and the large door built by the Harbour

ELEVATION OF PROPOSED MORTUARY

THE MUSEUM OF ARCHAEOLOGY:

In 1957, approval was granted to start the development of a new Museum of Archaeology. The restoration of the building was carried out by the Borough Architect in consultation with the Ancient Monuments Branch of the, then, Ministry of Works. Its time as a warehouse had left the main gallery as just a shell. Original staircases had long gone so a new upper floor and mezzanine had to be inserted. The ground floor was largely used for services and the upper floor included an office for the museum manager. The museum opened four years later in 1961. The museum was split into three galleries showcasing archaeological finds from the Saxon, Medieval and Roman eras.

Tudor ceramics

The room above the gatehouse was named in honour of O.G.S Crawford, a distinguished archaeologist who worked in Hampshire and was particularly renowned for pioneering photographic aerial archaeology. During the First World War he served in the Royal Flying Corps where he was involved in ground and aerial reconnaissance along the Western Front. Crawford had specialised in the study of prehistoric Britain and spent most of his career at the archaeological office of the Ordnance Survey which was located in Southampton. He toured Britain on behalf of the Ordnance Survey plotting the location of archaeological sites. He used RAF photographs to identify the extent of the Stonehenge Avenue which he excavated in 1923 and raised money to secure the site for the National Trust. This work led him to conduct aerial surveys of many counties in Southern England. During the Second World War he worked with the National Buildings Record photographically documenting Southampton, an incredible archive made more important because of the devastation of the Blitz on the town. The new museum displayed some of his photographs of archaeological sites in Wessex. Today his collection of images is in the care of the University of Southampton.

O.G.S Crawford

The new museum meant that the town's archaeological collections could be displayed and stored at God's House Tower, including some material originally assembled in the old Hartley Institute (the forerunner of Southampton University). The collection also included stone artefacts derived from the collection of the town's first honorary curator, Mr R E Nicholas. The oldest items that were displayed were a series of Palaeolithic hand axes which had come from gravel beds around Southampton. There were also teeth and bones of animals which were from the same Ice Age and inter-glacial periods. The Mesolithic period was represented by a collection of finds recovered from the submerged prehistoric forest below Southampton Water, found when the docks were constructed. There were also polished flint and stone axes from the Neolithic period, when farming was first introduced to Britain. The time of Roman Britain was illustrated by two milestones inscribed with the name of the usurper Tericus (AD 267-273) and an altar dedicated to the goddess Ancasta.

Roman milestone

There were also fine red-glazed Samian wares which had been imported from France, as well as local pottery from the New Forest. The finds came from the Roman settlement of Clausentum, on the Bitterne peninsula on the east side of the River Itchen, which was excavated in the 1950s. After the Romans left a new settlement grew up on the opposite bank of the river, a middle Saxon town called Hamwic or Hamtun, situated in the area around the church of St Mary. The museum displayed artefacts from this period, including a bone comb excavated in 1949. The medieval period was represented by the town's important collection of pottery. The museum opened in 1961, over the next 50 years its archaeology collection received designated status, which recognised it to be of national significance. The museum went on to show-case the important finds from the extensive excavation programme in the middle Saxon settlement of Hamwic, culminating in the display of the spectacular grave goods from the cemetery unearthed beneath the new St. Mary's football stadium.

The medieval displays featured the important finds made in the 60s and 70s by Dr Colin Platt, illustrating the cosmopolitan lives of the wealthy merchants who lived and worked in the medieval town. The collection of imported luxury goods, glass and ceramics was internationally renowned. However, with the opening of the Sea City Museum in 2011, the archaeology museum was closed and the artefacts moved into storage until some could be redisplayed in Sea City Museum and Tudor House. Since the closure of the Museum of Archaeology, God's House Tower stood empty until 2019.

GOD'S HOUSE TOWER ARTS & HERITAGE VENUE

'a space' arts was formed in the year 2000 as an arts charity focusing on public art, artist development and the creation of exhibition spaces within the city. Their interest in the juxtaposition of contemporary art and heritage buildings can be dated back to 2004 when the first 'Art Vaults' project was staged. This saw 12 medieval vaults hosting commissions for artists who were asked to transform and interpret the spaces. The success of the project has seen the medieval town being used for similar events under the banner 'Art Vaults Live'.

The organisation was originally based in Victorian Northam Road, before moving in 2006 to the medieval Bargate where a gallery space was created, and enabled the building to be open for the following seven years. The next move in 2011 brought the organisation to Tower House, the building adjacent to God's House Tower. Tower House, along with The Arches and the Northam Road Gallery offer work and exhibition spaces to artists and hundreds have been supported since the millenium. A full list of artists, exhibitions and projects can be accessed at www.aspacearts. org.uk. 'a space's' local public art projects can be seen at the former Ford factory site in Eastleigh and the former Fruit Market in Southampton. The latter providing an artistic interpretation of part of the eastern walls of the medieval town. In 2018 'a space' became an Arts Council of England National Portfolio Organisation for their significant work in the development and support of contemporary arts.

East Walls Public Art
Old Fruit Market site
from a design by
Dan Rawlings

In 2012 'a space' had embarked on its most ambitious project to date, the acquisition and refurbishment of the scheduled monument of God's House Tower to create a new Arts and Heritage Venue. Before any building work can be undertaken on an historic site there first needs to be an archaeological survey to explore any new discoveries that the building work might uncover and to protect important structures for future generations. As there had been many and various uses of the building over the centuries and alterations carried out without the protections that are in place today, archaeology has been lost and it was possible that there was little more to find. The key area to investigate what was that to the north of God's House Tower, the site of the new extension needed for the new café bar. The dig carried out under the watchful eye of Andy Russel, ancient monuments officer and archaeologist for Southampton City Council, did make an exciting discovery: the original toilet block dating from the time when God's House Tower was a gaol. It revealed limestone toilet seats resting on an arched brick drain, built between two buttresses and divided into three compartments. The configuration was later altered into two unequal compartments and demolished in the late nineteenth century. Stone seats were preferred in the construction of latrines as they were harder to damage or remove to facilitate an escape bid.

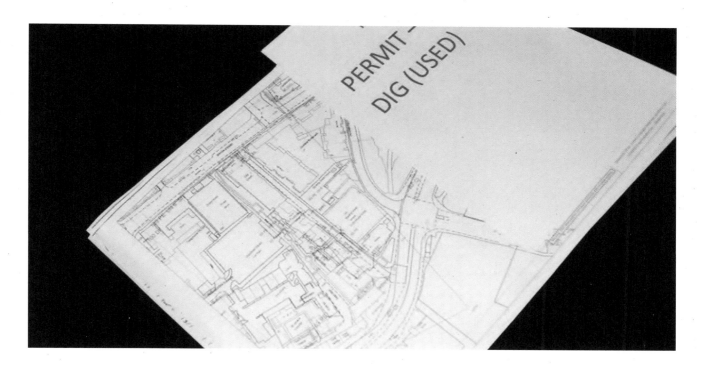

English Heritage, also, had to give their permission for any planned structural changes to the building. The majority of the work has been the taking out of old services which had made large parts of the building un-useable. The 1960s dividing walls have been replaced with glass walls so that God's House Tower can be viewed from all angles. Some of the alterations undertaken in the twentieth century represent a significant part of the building's history, so it was important that the mezzanine floor and the 1960s stairway be both retained and presented as architectural features in their own right.

God's House Tower collections gallery - 2019

One of the major changes to the fabric of the building had taken place when it was in the ownership of the Harbour Board. This was the construction of the large warehouse door, which had been filled in when the Archaeological Museum was built. The decision was taken and approved to re-open this doorway to make it the new main entrance to the venue. This process also provided the opportunity to explore the original construction of the doorway.

Surveyors from the Southampton Archaeology Society were invited to undertake a graffiti survey of the site. As much of the original interior stone surfaces had been lost, including any plastering or lime-wash, it was unlikely that much medieval graffiti would have survived. In the event two pieces were found, one that appears to be a shield on a piece of reused Portland marble in the alcove at the bottom of the stairs to the original entrance to the museum. The other was a weathered ship graffito on the south-east window embrasure in the tower, with some of the masts, sails and rigging still visible. Most of the other graffiti consisted of modern initials on the walls and newel post of the stairway to the roof, and pencil lines and calculations left by modern workmen on the tower walls. The date 1778 was found on the first floor landing but the style of the carving suggests it was made more recently than this date suggests.

A modern mason's date with the date 1959 was left over the back door, and the date 1953 and initials STC were found on the exterior north wall. A full record of the survey is maintained by the Hampshire Field Club and Archaeological Society see www.hantsfieldclub.org.uk.

Mason's date

A centre piece of the new exhibition is a scale model of Southampton in 1620, the year the Pilgrim Fathers sailed from the town on the way to the New World. The model was the creation of one of the founder members of the Southampton Tourist Guides Association, Ken Hellyar. Ken was passionate about the heritage of Southampton and engaging the public in its history, and he was also a very skilled artisan. In creating the scale model of the town there were a number of sources that Ken could draw upon: John Speed's map of 1611; Sheila Thomson's plan of the town created for the 350th anniversary celebrations of the Mayflower story; surviving medieval terriers which give a huge amount of detail on each town property and the existing defensive works. Incredibly Ken created the model in the living room of his house. The model was previously displayed in the Bargate, when it was a museum, and then moved to the Archaeology Museum. It has now been lovingly restored by the maker Kate Harrison to take centre stage as an introduction to the story of medieval Southampton.

GHT Director Dan Crow and Kate Harrison with the model of Southampton

Cleaning of Ken Hellyar model of Southampton

The build programme was only a year and great care had to be taken each step of the way and the building work itself uncovered new finds and archaeology left by those who had previously worked in the building from old cigarette packs, the remains of a shoe and dates left by those who had conserved, preserved and added to the building over the centuries. The God's House Tower Arts & Heritage Venue opened in October 2019 with two gallery spaces, one for contemporary art and one for loans from historic collections and a permanent exhibition on the history of the tower. The roof has been given a new viewing platform and provides incredible views across the old town and Southampton Water.

Cigarette packet

Shoe

POSTSCRIPT

God's House Tower gives a superb view over Southampton Water. It was built as a tall tower so that watchers could see if enemy ships were appearing on the horizon, like the fleet of French ships that threatened the town in 1542. But it also witnessed the sailing of some of the most iconic ships in the long history of Southampton. A time line for the ships is part of the roof top exhibition.

1420 THE GRACE DIEU

When Henry V was planning his invasion of France, he wanted to ensure that the English Channel was secure, to protect his lines of communication. To that end he started to build ships for a fledging Royal Navy rather than rely on the short-term borrowing of merchant vessels. The *Grace Dieu* was Henry V's flagship. Twice the size of the *Mary Rose*, it was the largest ship in Europe and built and launched in Southampton. It was the fourth of Henry V's warships and the most expensive. There would not be a bigger ship built in England for a further 200 years – she was comparable in size to Nelson's *Victory*.

The *Grace Dieu* was constructed in a specially built dock at Southampton near Town Quay surrounded by a hedge of spines and stakes to safeguard the timbers and other materials from pilfering. Work began in 1416 with workmen coming from as far away as Devon and Cornwall. The *Grace Dieu's* construction was under the direction of local resident William Soper and funded directly by the king. William Soper was one of Southampton's wealthiest burgesses, twice mayor of Southampton, Member of Parliament and verderer of the New Forest. He began his association with the king's navy in 1414 and was created clerk to the king's ships whilst the building of the *Grace Dieu* was in progress, then appointed keeper and governor of the ships from 1423 until 1442.

The work on the *Grace Dieu* continued under Soper's supervision until December 1416 when Robert Berde was appointed clerk of the works for her construction which was led by a team of shipwrights under master shipwright John Hoggekyn. In July 1418, the Bishop of Bangor was sent down from London to consecrate the ship and received £5 for his expenses. Ships at that time were given religious-inspired names. The ship was launched in 1418, William Payne was appointed as her master in December 1418 and the ship was commissioned in 1420.

It was said that from the crow's nest you could see nine nautical miles. As she was such a prestigious ship she would have had cabins and a galley on board. Humphrey, Duke of Gloucester, regarded her as 'the fairest (vessel) that ever man saw'. The Treaty of Troyes which saw Henry V made Regent of France meant however that ships like *Grace Dieu* were no longer needed. The *Grace Dieu* only made one voyage in 1420 and was subsequently laid up on the River Hamble serving as a political reminder to foreign visitors of England's power over the seas. The commander of the Florentine merchant fleet, Luca di Masa degli Albizzi, said of the ship 'I never saw so large and so splendid a construction'. Whilst mothballed at Hamble the ship was struck by lightning and burnt to the waterline.

1588 THE ANGEL

In 1588 the whole country was in great peril of invasion from the European superpower that was sixteenth-century Spain. Philip II of Spain launched a great Armada with the plan to seize the Isle of Wight and then launch an invasion of England via Southampton. Towns around England were asked to supply ships to form part of the English Fleet. Southampton supplied just one ship *The Angel* a merchant ship owned by Richard Goddard, a former mayor of Southampton. It was commanded, like most of the English ships, by a former privateer, Lawrence Prowse. As one of the smallest ships in the fleet, it was one of eight vessels used as fireships against the Spanish fleet when it was at anchor in Calais. At that time a strategy of using fireships to attack and create disarray had been successfully developed by an Italian engineer named Federigo Giambelli, who was then living in London and working for the English. It was decided at a council of war led by Lord Howard of Effingham on board the *Ark Royal*, early Sunday morning on 7th August, that a fireship attack should be employed against the Armada. It was decided that eight privately owned ships would be sacrificed for the war effort. The ships were coated with pitch and tar, and their guns filled with double shot to explode when the fire took hold. Skeleton crews were given a share of a bounty of £100 to sail the ships towards the Spanish Armada. The English did not have enough spare gunpowder to pack the fireships, but the Spanish did not know that. The Spanish thought the ships were floating bombs and took the decision to cut their anchors to enable them to sail quickly away. As the English Fleet blocked the way south the Spanish had to sail north around the coast of Scotland and Ireland to find their way home. Goddard received £450 compensation for the loss of *The Angel*. Lawrence Prowse eventually became mayor of Southampton.

1620 THE MAYFLOWER AND THE SPEEDWELL

A group of dissident religious non-conformists gathered in Southampton in August 1620 to start a journey to the New World where they planned to set up a new colony. They had two ships: the *Mayflower* and the *Speedwell*. The *Speedwell* however proved to be unseaworthy for such a long voyage so the group, which became known as the Pilgrim Fathers, had to put in unexpectedly to Plymouth. They abandoned the smaller ship and made the rest of the journey on the *Mayflower*. There is a possibility that one or both were originally built in Southampton. The *Speedwell* particularly, could have been built by Esau Whittiffe who worked from the West Quay. What is known is that the ship was about 60 tons. It was in service for many years before being used to transport the Pilgrim Fathers from their settlement in Holland, back to England to rendezvous with the *Mayflower* in Southampton. The Separatists, as they were known at the time, had been disappointed with King James I when he came to the throne in 1603. Coming from Calvinist Scotland they thought he would bring Puritan reforms to the Church of England. The king however saw this as an attack on his power, saying "No bishop, no king!" This led the Separatists to first emigrate from England to Holland before deciding that the better course would be to establish their own colony along with their own beliefs in the New World.

It took two weeks to load the ships with provisions and stores from the markets in Southampton. During that time they were joined by John Alden, a local cooper, who went on to become one of the Founding Fathers of their new colony. After losing the *Speedwell* and some of their number deciding not to continue, 103 people eventually made the voyage to America.

1820 PRINCE OF COBURG

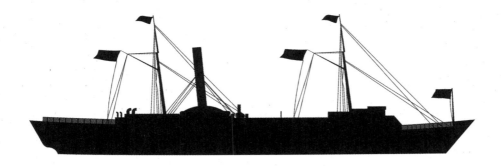

In 1820 Southampton was still promoting itself as a Spa and Bathing Resort but in that year the paddle steamer ship the *Prince of Coburg* made its first trip to the Isle of Wight. This was the time of a revolution in ship design, with bigger ships which did not have to rely on sail and ships which would carry more passengers and would soon embark on longer voyages across the Atlantic. Southampton saw an opportunity to return to its primary purpose as an international seaport.

It was Captain James Hoskins Knight of Cowes master and part-owner of several sailing passage vessels, including the mail packets, who proposed the introduction of steam vessels from Southampton to Cowes. Ship owners George Ward and William Fitzhugh, also of Cowes, took up the Captain's proposal, establishing the Isle of Wight Royal Steam Packet Company, the first steamer service between Cowes and Southampton. The *Prince of Cobourg*, commanded by the Captain, was the first paddle steamer to operate the route. She was named after the husband of the heir apparent Princess Charlotte Augusta, daughter of the Prince Regent, who had married the previous year. The steamer was built in Gainsborough, Lincolnshire in 1817 and arrived in the Solent one week before going into service on 24th July

1820. Her passage time was approximately 1½ hours. The steamer did have some 'teething problems' including the loss of one of the cabins which gave way and fell over the side and sank.

After six years on passage, the *Prince of Cobourg* was finally taken out of service in October 1826. However, she continued to serve as a workshop at Woolston after her engines had been removed. Her end or 'breaking up' appears to have gone unrecorded.

1884 THE MIGNONETTE

Local sailors were prized yachtsmen and yacht racing became very popular amongst the elite. In 1884 an Australian lawyer, Henry Want, bought a yacht which he wanted transported to Australia to race on that continent. *The Mignonette* set sail on 19th May with a crew of four: Thomas Dudley master, Edwin Stephens mate, Ned Brooks able seaman and Richard Parker ordinary seaman or cabin boy.

On 5th July the yacht foundered in bad weather. The crew survived the sinking in a small dinghy, but without much food and no fresh water. They managed to survive for fifteen days by eating a turtle they had captured. When that sustenance ran out, they were without water for nearly four days. They decided to resort to the custom of the sea, that is, by drawing lots where one is sacrificed to save the others. Richard Parker was already delirious having tried to drink sea water, so it was decided that the cabin boy from Itchen Ferry be cannibalised. A few days later on 29th July the three remaining crew were picked up and returned to England. They gave statements as to what had happened on the voyage and to Richard Parker but much to their surprise, found themselves on trial for murder. A trial that made legal history and is still studied today. Brooks, who took no active part in the killing, turned Queen's evidence. Dudley and Stevens were sentenced to death by hanging but, thanks to public support, including from Richard Parker's brother Daniel, this was commuted to transportation to Australia.

This case established the precedent in law which still stands today that 'the doctrine of justifiable homicide has no foundation in English law except in the case of unavoidable self-defence'. A memorial stone for Richard Parker was erected in Peartree churchyard on his unmarked parents' grave by John Haskins, a London engineer. This can now be seen inside the church, a new memorial replacing it in the churchyard.

1899 THE STELLA

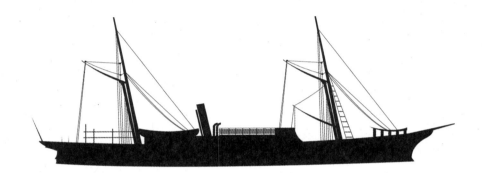

In 1899 the *Stella* was a passenger ship going to the Channel Isles, when it struck rocks and foundered. The stewardess Mary Anne Rogers gave her lifebelt to a passenger and was drowned herself as a result. The London and South Western Railway Company, owner of the *Stella*, were in competition with the Great Western Railway who had its own Channel Islands service operating out of Weymouth. Both companies' ships were making a crossing on 30th March with the aim of docking at St Peter's Port at 5.30 pm. Unfortunately there was only one berth available. The *Stella* got caught in fog, and when the fog cleared went full steam ahead at 18 knots. The ship hit the Casquet rocks, despite the lighthouse blasting out warnings. The bottom was ripped out of the hull and the ship went down in eight minutes. There was no panic, the men lined up on deck and quietly watched as women and children got onto lifeboats. The Reverend Clutterbuck fell to his knees and led a group in prayer. Senior Stewardess Mary Anne Rogers after helping her ladies from their cabins, distributed lifebelts to the women and children and guided them into the lifeboats. She gave up her own lifebelt to a young girl who had lost her mother in the confusion and refused (even when urged) to get into a lifeboat herself for fear of capsizing it. Declaring that she, 'could not save her own life at the cost of fellow creatures'. She then waved the lifeboat farewell saying 'goodbye, goodbye' and bidding the survivors to be of good cheer. She then raised her hands to heaven and said, 'Lord have me' as she sank beneath the waves. Her body was never found.

Eighty-six passengers died, along with 19 crew. Following the disaster, the two steamship companies agreed to run services on alternate days so that there would be no more competition for the berth.

Mary Anne Rogers is the only woman commemorated by a memorial in Southampton, a drinking fountain that is not even called by her name but is known as the *Stella* Memorial. The memorial, situated on Cuckoo Lane, was paid for by public subscription. It was designed by Herbert Bryans, and is a drinking fountain surrounded by columns with a metal plaque telling story which was written by Frances Power Cobbe. It was unveiled in 1901. In 1973 the wreck of *Stella* was discovered by two Channel Islander divers south of the Casquets.

1912 TITANIC

In April 1912 the *Titanic* departed on her fateful maiden voyage, which would become Southampton's greatest maritime disaster. During her stay in Southampton, a significant amount of work had to be done to make her interiors ready, including painting, securing racks, electrics and other fittings before arranging furniture, stores, provisions and hiring crew for her maiden voyage to New York. On the first day, a local photographer, Mr H Symes, was allowed on board *Titanic* to take photographs which he turned into postcards for purchase. Although *Titanic* had a full complement of her Deck Department amongst others, Firemen, Trimmers, Stewards, and Galley the other 'black gang' workers had to be selected from a potential crew who called Southampton home. There were many unemployed in the town due to the coal strike of 1912 which had left 17,000 out of work. Ships, with no coal to fire their boilers, had lain idle since 12th January creating 'Log Jams' of ships moored alongside each in the port for lack of berth space. Any coal that was to be had was taken from other White Star ships currently laid up and extra coal was brought back on the Olympic from New York. There were 724 crew members aboard the *Titanic* the majority coming from the Southampton area, 549 died in the sinking and only 175 returned home. Areas of Southampton were devastated by this disaster and it was reported that nearly every household in Northam lost a family member in the sinking. The story of the *Titanic* and its impact on the town is the major exhibit of the Sea City Museum.

1937 SS HABANA

On 23rd May 1937 The *SS Habana*, a 10,800 ton transatlantic steamer, arrived in Southampton. The quay was still adorned with bunting from the coronation of George VI which had taken place ten days earlier. But no ship's siren was sounded in case it frightened the passengers: 4000 child refugees from the Spanish civil war.

The *Habana* had sailed from Santurce docks close to Bilbao in the Basque region of Spain two days earlier. It had capacity for 800 passengers, but on this day carried over 4,000 (3,886 children; 96 teachers; 118 helpers; 16 priests; and 2 doctors). The children were crammed into the boat and slept where they could, even in the lifeboats. Following the previous month's destruction of Guernica, around 20,000 children were being evacuated from northern Spain to seven countries to save them from bombardments and famine. This was the first mass evacuation of child refugees to Britain. Nicknamed Los Niños (the little ones), they are normally referred to as "Basque refugees" although they also included non-Basques. Commanded by Captain Ricardo Fernandez, the *Habana* had already made one such run to France; its second was to Southampton. The UK government had refused to be responsible for the children saying this would violate its non-intervention policy. The transport, care and accommodation of the children was provided and funded entirely by voluntary means. From Southampton docks, the children travelled by bus to North Stoneham Camp near Eastleigh until more permanent accommodation could be found. Local farmer Mr G H Brown of Swaythling Lane Farm had provided three of his fields for the camp. Getting the camp ready in less than two weeks was a remarkable effort by the whole community; volunteers had worked around the clock to prepare it (originally for only 2,000 children) and nearly 500 tents were erected. A large house at Moorhill, West End was used as the children's infirmary and for some adult accommodation. By mid-September 1937 all children had been dispersed around Britain and the camp was closed. The children progressively returned to Spain, but in 1948 there were still 280 in Britain who settled in Britain permanently.

Built by J Thornycroft and Co. Ltd. of Woolston, on 8th April 1936 the *Gracie Fields* was launched by her namesake, Lancastrian singer Gracie Fields, who had to be reminded to release the lever controlling the traditional bottle of champagne to christen her bow. Gracie sang 'Sing as we Go' at the launch and the crowd responded with another popular song of Ms Fields', 'Sally'. It was unusual for a ship to be named after a celebrity rather than royalty or nobility. In 1939 *PS Gracie Fields* was requisitioned for minesweeping and became *HMS Gracie Fields*. Despite the twin trails of turbulence from her paddles there is no evidence that she was ever targeted by submarines. In 1940 as the Nazi army swept through Belgium and France, Allied troops were trapped in Normandy – it was estimated up to 400,000 troops were there. After some hesitation by the War Office about the practicalities of carrying out such a massive rescue mission, Operation Dynamo was launched and 1003 'little boats' sailed to the Normandy coast and Dunkirk to assist in uplifting troops from the beaches to the battleships and larger vessels for evacuation. Twenty-three of the vessels were paddle steamers. Between 26th May and 3rd June, 338,266 troops were evacuated. On 28th May *Gracie Fields* evacuated 280 troops successfully; returning the following day she had another 750 on board when she came under fire from enemy aircraft and took a direct hit. Her rudder stuck and she was unable to make headway. HMS Pangbourne rescued the evacuees and some of the crew with the assistance of other boats – *HMS Pangbourne* was herself holed above and below the waterline on both sides. On 30th May *HMS Gracie Fields* was sinking whilst under tow, the remaining crew were taken off and the tow slipped and she sank. *HMS Gracie Fields* was one of six paddle steamers sunk at Dunkirk. The heroism and dedication of her crew were praised by Isle of Wight based author J.B. Priestley in a broadcast made 5th June 1940;

I tell you we were proud of The Gracie Fields, she was the glittering queen of our local line and instead of taking an hour over her voyage, she used to do it – churning like mad – in forty-five minutes. And now, never again will we board her at Cowes to go down into her dining room for a fine breakfast of bacon and eggs. She has paddled and churned away forever. But now look, this little paddle steamer, like all her spirited brave and battered sisters, is immortal. She'll go sailing proudly down the years in the epic of Dunkirk and our great grandchildren, when they learn how we began this war by snatching glory out of defeat and then swept on to Victory, may also learn how the little holiday steamers made an excursion to Hell and came back glorious.

1982 THE CANBERRA

In the years before the Second World War, Southampton became associated with glamorous cruise liners, like the Cunard 'Queens'. Many a famous film star was photographed arriving in Southampton on the deck of the *Queen Mary* and later the *Queen Elizabeth*. Many shipping lines were based in Southampton including The Peninsular & Oriental Steam Navigation Company, more usually known as P&O.

In 1982 the *Canberra*, a P&O liner which served as a troop ship in the Falklands War, returned to Southampton. She followed a long tradition of passenger liners pressed into military service at time of war. The *Canberra* was built to be a liner on the London to Australia route. Her design was distinctive with a double funnel at the rear. It was too big for the company's home port of Tilbury so she was based in Southampton. She was the mainstay for the £10 passage emigrants to Australia in the 1960s before the advent of jumbo jets. She then converted from a two-class liner to a one-class cruise ship on the New York run. In 1982 she was requisitioned as a troop ship during the Falklands War, and was used to land the ground force on the Islands. The *Canberra* had been in the thick of the action and was known as 'The Great White Whale'. After the war she returned to cruising duties but as the liners got larger the *Canberra* could not compete, despite being very popular with her passengers. In 1997 she made her last voyage, before sailing to Pakistan to be broken up. Southampton is undergoing another renaissance as a cruise port destination, now for superliners like the *Queen Victoria* and German ships like the *Aida*.

GOD'S HOUSE TOWER

TIMELINE ▶

LOCAL ◀

▶ NATIONAL

TIMELINE SOUTHAMPTON

TIMELINE NATIONAL

1066
The Norman Conquest

The Normans start to build the stone walls of Southampton after the 1066 Conquest

1153
Treaty of Winchester, King Stephen promised Henry Plantagenet the stronghold of Southampton

1154
Accession of Henry II

1170
Murder of Thomas a Becket

1174
Henry II lands at Southampton on the way to do penance at Canterbury after the murder of Thomas a Becket

1189
God's House Hospital and alms houses are built in the south east corner of the town

1202
King John gives Southampton a grant to fortify the town

1215
Magna Carta

1233
Franciscan Friars settle in the town

1290
Grant of Spring in Hill Lane to the Friary

1290
The Jews expelled from England

1299
The Platform quay constructed outside God's House gate

1326
Grant of new toll 1d in the pound to complete town wall and quay

TIMELINE SOUTHAMPTON

TIMELINE NATIONAL

1338
French raid on Southampton at the start of the 100 years war. The town starts to build the seaward defences

1338
Start of the 100 years war

1346
The Battle of Crecy

1348
The Black Death enters England via Southampton, nearly half the population die

1356
The Battle of Poitiers

1381
Peasants' Revolt

1415
The Southampton Plot against Henry V discovered, some believe the plotters were held in God's House Tower

1415
The Battle of Agincourt

c1417
Construction of the God's House gun battery

1475
The gun Thomas with Beard fired at an enemy French ship. The gun broke and had to be repaired

1485
Battle of Bosworth

1500
Salt Marsh Riot against the enclosure of common land outside God's House gate

1522
Visit of the Emperor Charles V

1535
The Reformation, Henry VIII proclaims himself head of the Church of England

1538
Friary dissolved

1542
The gunner Herman Schmidt killed when his gun burst while defending the town against six French ships

1547
Edward VI visits Southampton for his health

1554
Philip of Spain lands at Southampton with 140 ships, on his way to marry Queen Mary Tudor

1556
3 pirates executed on the waterside gallows outside God's House gate as 'a terror and example to others'

1558
Accession of Elizabeth I

1572
Huguenot refugees settle in Southampton and use St.Julien's chapel as the 'French Church'

1572
St Bartholomew's Day massacre of French Protestants in Paris

1575
Robert Knaplocke leased the right to fish in the town ditch outside God's House

1588
Robert Goddard's merchant ship *The Angel* used as a fireship by Francis Drake

1588
The English Fleet battle the Spanish Armada off the Isle of Wight

TIMELINE SOUTHAMPTON

TIMELINE NATIONAL

1603
Outbreak of Plague
in Southampton

1603
Accession of James I

1620
The Mayflower Pilgrims
depart from Southampton
on their way to America

1625
Charles I stayed at 17
High St and signed Treaty of
Southampton with the Dutch

1642
Start of the
English Civil War

1649
Charles I executed

1660
The restoration of Charles II

1665
Plague in Southampton

1666
Great Plague in Southampton

1702
Accession of Queen Anne

1707
Gate house became the town
Bridewell, or House
of Correction

1731
George Rowcliffe, shipwright,
leased the tower for £7 a year

1746
Mineral Springs
discovered and
Southampton
becomes a Spa Town

1746
Battle of Cullodden

1761

The town sells the old iron guns and cannonballs from God's House Tower

1769

The Beach, a tree lined walk, built on the old causeway from the Platform to the Cross House

1769

James Cook lands in New Zealand

1776

Start of the American War of Independence

1783

James Lawrence, God's House prisoner, transported to America for 7 years

1783

The last prisoners transported to America, as the colony is lost in the War of Independence

1786

God's House Tower adapted to be the Debtors prison

1786

1786 Edward Jenner introduces vaccine against smallpox

1787

First Convict Fleet sails to Australia

1793

War against France

1795

Plans to build a canal between Southampton and Salisbury, partly using the ditch under God's House

1798

Income Tax introduced

1800

Act of Union

1805

Battle of Trafalgar

TIMELINE SOUTHAMPTON

TIMELINE NATIONAL

1806
Jane Austen and family move to Southampton

1807
The salt marsh outside the gate freezes and is used for skating by Frank Austen, brother of Jane

1810
Prince of Wales becomes Prince Regent

1812
War with America

1815
The Battle of Waterloo

1820
The stench of the canal was reported as being injurious to the prisoners

1826
Prisoners, the twelve year old Frederick Head and twenty year old George Jenninge Ball, transported to Australia

1832
Cholera epidemic

1833
Princess Victoria opens the Royal Pier

1834
Poor law creates workhouses

1836
Formation of the Southampton Dock Company

1837
James Gosney the yardman of the Bridewell killed helping to put out the fire in the King & Witt warehouse on the High Street

1837
Accession of Queen Victoria

162

1841
The canal is filled in after a woman drowned in the stagnant ditch

1854
Crimean War, Florence Nightingale pioneers modern nursing

1855
Prisoners transferred to a new prison in Ascupart Street

1860s
God's House Tower used as a temporary town mortuary

1864
Contagious Diseases Acts

1874
God's House used as a warehouse by the Southampton Harbour Board

1877
Statue of Prince Albert erected to the east of the tower

1888
Electrical time-ball installed on the roof linked to the Greenwich Observatory

1899
Sinking of the Stella

1901
Death of Queen Victoria

1902
First council houses built in Britain

1912
Titanic sinks on her maiden voyage from Southampton
Tudor House Museum opens

1914
Start of World War I
Southampton designated No 1 Military Embarkation Port

1914
Start of World War I

TIMELINE SOUTHAMPTON

TIMELINE NATIONAL

1918
End of World War I

1920
Boundaries of Southampton
extended to include Bassett,
Bitterne, Itchen and Swaythling

1927
Work starts of the
'New' Western Docks

1939
Start of World War II

1940
Southampton heavily
bombed in the Blitz

1944
American troops march past
God's House during the
D Day campaign

1945
End of World War II

1961
God's House Tower becomes
the Museum of Archaeology

1964
Southampton
becomes a City

2019
God's House Tower
Arts & Heritage Venue opens

Select Bibliography

Primary Sources

D/PM/5/2/6 Warrants & Pardons

D/PM/5/2/10 Indictments

D/PM/5/2/6/1 Prisoner delivery

D/PM/5/2/6/5 Transportation of prisoners

D/PM/5/2/5/7 Pardon of Elizabeth Harding

D/PM5/2/6/8 Pardon of Elizabeth Harding

D/PM/5/2/6/9 Warrant Elizabeth Shepphard

D/PM/5/2/6/10 Warrant Richard Sturgess

D/PM/5/2/11/1 Frederick Head, George Jennings Ball

D/PM/5/2/11/7 John Kingsmill & John Hills

D/PM/5/2/11/19 Calendar of Prisoners

D/PM/5/2/20/3 Thomas Michell, James Lawrence, David Williams, John Iago

D/PM/5/2/20/5 William Shawyer verdict

D/PM/5/2/20/6 William Shawyer, Charles Stuart

D/PM/5/2/20/9 Mary Rowsell

D/PM/5/2/20/10 Lewis Edwards, William Thomas

D/PM5/2/20/11 Jacob Duell

D/PM/5/2/20/12 Lewis Edwards, Tilliam Thomas, William Griffiths, Christian Lisle

D/PM/5/2/20/7 John La Lacheur, William Greenaway

D/PM/5/3/41 Rules of the Gaol 1837

D/PM/5/3/4/2-3 Rules of the House of Correction

D/PM/5/3/25-6 List of boys in the Bridewell

D/PM/5/3/7/16 Gaol Contract 1786

D/PM Box 44/76 Draft Power of Attorney John Geagan

D/PM Box 45/3/60 Cornelius Rose smuggler

D/PM 45/3/165 Harriet Mansbridge

D/PM Box 45/3/196 Francois Raison

D/PM Box 45/3/198 William Macdonald, Charles Barret

D/PM Box 51/5/1-3 Sarah Robinson

D/PM Box 51/13/1-6 Maria Knight, Hannah Frey, Fanny Whitehorn,

Abigail Sullivan, Charlotte Mist

D/PM Box 52/ 27 Mortgage documents JJ Truss

D/PM Box 58/1/69 Lease Grove

D/PM Box 70/1/1-2 Plans of the former prison

D/PM Box 77/17 Correspondence of John Geagan

D/PM Box 78/28/1-2 Royal Assurance

D/PM Box 83-4 Bail bonds

D/PM Box 84/10/11 Calendar of Prisoners

D/PM Box 84/11/3 Deserters

D/PM Box 88/5/4 Letter S G Willington

D/PM Box 89/22/6 Examination of Antoine Legaldie

D/PM Box 90/4/9 Warrant Eliza Harding

D/PM Box 91/5/1 Forbidding licencing of prisons

D/PM Box 93/11/62 Advertisement re Henry Ball murder suspect

D/S 19/1/1 The Atherley Papers Vol II, Reveries in Confinement by George Byles

SC2/1/9 Journal of Council Minutes 1670-1734

SC2/6/5-6 Book of Instruments

SC3/1/1 Burgess Roll

SC4/3/1031 Lease of Truss property

SC4/3/1033 Lease of Truss property

SC4/3/2076-7 Leases to Debtors' prison to Harbour Board

SC4/3/2099 Lease of Platform House to the Harbour Board

SC4/3/2285 Lease to the Harbour Board

SC4/3/2304 Lease of Debtors' prison to the Harbour Board

SC6/1/1-119 Stall & Art Lists

SC9/4/190 Petition of Debtors

SC9/4/536 John Andrews

SC9/4/557 John Richardson and William Lucas

SC9/4/573-4 Mary Wright

SC9/4/580 Bill for fettering

SC9/4/607-8, 626-7, 629-30 Thomas Cooper the younger

SC9/4/660-61, 666-670 William & Joseph Stow

SC9/4/670-1 Bond Thomas Dormer

SC9/4/684 Warrant to Convey Anne Marshall

SC9/4/721 Samuel Laws

SC9/4/741 Edward Giddins

SC9/4/793 Prison visits of Rev Mear

SC9/4/788 Warrant Joseph Cole

SC9/4/799 William Dymott keeper of the Common Gaol

SC9/4/801 Repairs to gaol

SC9/4/802 Joseph Payne keeper of Bridewell bill for gaol

SC9/4/806 J J Truss bill for gaol supplies

SC9/4/820 William Dymott salary

SC9/4/850-1 Warrant Robert Hill

SC10/1/1 Poor Book 1552-3

SC 13/2/2-10 Musters 1556, 1567, 1573, 1577, 1583

SC15/17a Waterworks Assessment

SRO All Saints Church Parish Register

SRO Holy Rood Church Parish Register

SRO St Mary Church Parish Register

SOU1754 Archaeology Report

Holy Rood Census Return 1841 Southampton Central Library Local Collections

HRO 5 M62/19 979 Will of John Brewer

HRO Winchester B1604

Hampshire Medieval Graffiti Project: Graffiti survey summary for

God's House Tower, Southampton

Primary printed sources

Account of Gaols, Houses of Correction & Penitentiaries 1818, Parliamentary Papers 1819 XVII 371

Fifth Report of the Committee of the Society for the Improvement of Prison Discipline, London 1823

Inspection of Prisons of Great Britain III, Southern & West District, Parliamentary Papers 1836, XXXV, 269

Inspection of Prisons Reports 1810, 1834, 1835, 1836, 1837, 1841, 1849, 1850

A Letter on The Nature and Effects of The Tread Wheel as an instrument of Prison Labour and Punishment addressed to The Right Hon Robert Peel MP by One of His Constituents, and a Magistrate of the County of Surrey, London 1824

R C Anderson (ed) The Book of Examination 1601-2 (Southampton Record Society) 1926

L A Burgess (ed) The Southampton Terrier of 1454 (Southampton Records Series) 1976

C Butler The Southampton Book of Fines 3 Vols 1488-1594 (Southampton Records Series) 2007, 2009, 2010

B Chichen Transcriptions of the Southampton Stewards Books 1513, 1521, 1539, 1555, 1557, 1561, 1562, 1563, 1566 Hartley Library

H W Gidden (ed) The Book of Remembrance of Southampton 3 vols (Southampton Record Society) 1927, 1929, 1930

H W Gidden ed The Stewards. Books of Southampton 1428-34 2 vols (Southampton Record Society) 1935

F J C & D M Hearnshaw (eds) Southampton Court Leet Records (Southampton Record Society) 1906, 1907

J W Horrocks (ed) The Assembly Books of Southampton 1602-1618 3 vols (Southampton Record Society) 1917, 1920, 1925

A L Merson (ed) Third Book of Remembrance of Southampton 1514-1602 3 vols (Southampton Records Series) 1968

T Olding (ed) The Common Court and Piepowder Courts of Southampton 1566-7, 1571, 1726-6 (Southampton Records Series) 2018

E Roberts & K Parker (eds) Southampton Probate Inventories 1447-1574 2 vols (Southampton Records Series) 1992

J Stovold (ed) Minute Book of the Pavement Commissioners for Southampton 1770-1789 (Southampton Records Series) 1990

Secondary Sources

J S Davies A History of Southampton (Southampton) 1883

S McConville A History of Prison Administration (London) 2015

R A Pelham The Old Mills of Southampton (Southampton Papers No 3) 1963

C Platt Medieval Southampton: The Port and Trading Community A.D. 1000-1600 (London) 1973

C F Russell A History of Edward VI School Southampton (Cambridge) 1940

J S Sharpe Crime in Early Modern England 1550-1750 (London) 1984

L Stratmann The Secret Poisoner: A Century of Murder Yale (University Press) 2016

A Temple Patterson A History of Southampton 1700-1914 vol I Oligarchy in Decline 1700-1835 (Southampton Records Series) 1966 vol II The Beginnings of Modern Southampton 1836-67 (Southampton Records Series) 1971

Online

Rictor Norton, "The First Public Debate about Homosexuality in England: The Case of Captain Jones, 1772", The Gay Subculture in Georgian England, 19 December 2004, updated 10 May 2014

www.tudorrevels.co.uk

www.convictrecords.com.au

www.prisonhistory.org

Acknowledgements -

We would like to thank Jo Smith and her team at Southampton City Council Archives for providing access to original documents associated with God's House Tower and reproduced in this book.